The California Campaigns
of the U.S.–Mexican War,
1846–1848

The California Campaigns of the U.S.–Mexican War, 1846–1848

Hunt Janin *and*
Ursula Carlson

McFarland & Company, Inc., Publishers
Jefferson, North Carolina

Hunt Janin and Ursula Carlson have cowritten two other books for McFarland: *Mercenaries in Medieval and Renaissance Europe* (2013) and *Trails of Historic New Mexico* (2010). In addition Hunt Janin is the author or coauthor of eight other books for McFarland: *Rising Sea Levels* (and Scott A. Mandia, 2012), *The University in Medieval Life* (2008), *Islamic Law* (and André Kahlmeyer, 2007), *The Pursuit of Learning in the Islamic World, 610–2003* (2005; softcover 2006), *Medieval Justice* (2004; softcover 2009), *Four Paths to Jerusalem* (2002; softcover 2006), *Claiming the American Wilderness* (2006), *Fort Bridger, Wyoming* (2001; softcover 2006), *The India-China Opium Trade in the Nineteenth Century* (1999; softcover 2014)

LIBRARY OF CONGRESS CATALOGUING-IN-PUBLICATION DATA

Janin, Hunt, 1940–
 The California campaigns of the U.S.–Mexican War, 1846–1848 / Hunt Janin and Ursula Carlson.
  p.   cm.
 Includes bibliographical references and index.

 ISBN 978-0-7864-9420-0 (softcover : acid free paper) ∞
 ISBN 978-1-4766-2093-0 (ebook)

 1. Mexican War, 1846–1848—Campaigns—California.
 2. California—History—1846–1850. I. Carlson, Ursula, 1943– II. Title.

 E405.2.J36 2015
 973.6'24—dc23   2015012263

BRITISH LIBRARY CATALOGUING DATA ARE AVAILABLE

© 2015 Hunt Janin and Ursula Carlson. All rights reserved

No part of this book may be reproduced or transmitted in any form or by any means, electronic or mechanical, including photocopying or recording, or by any information storage and retrieval system, without permission in writing from the publisher.

On the cover: *The Battle of San Pascual*, artist Col. Charles Waterhouse, USMCR (deceased), part of the Marines in the Conquest of Southern California collection (courtesy Command Museum, MCRD, San Diego)

Printed in the United States of America

McFarland & Company, Inc., Publishers
 Box 611, Jefferson, North Carolina 28640
  www.mcfarlandpub.com

Table of Contents

Preface	1
Introduction: Causes and Conduct of the U.S.–Mexican War	8
1 • Peoples of California	25
2 • Foreigners in Alta California	47
3 • The Mexican Army in Alta California	57
4 • Preludes to War	62
5 • A Secret Mission to California	73
6 • The *Californios* Expel an American Expedition	77
7 • Frémont Prepares for War	85
8 • The Bear Flag Revolt	91
9 • The "Battle of Monterey" and the End of the Bear Flag Revolt	99
10 • The California Battalion	105
11 • Naval and Amphibious Operations I: From the Establishment of the American Blockade to the Capture of La Paz	111
12 • Naval and Amphibious Operations II: From the Capture of La Paz to the Return of the Sloop-of-War *Cyane* to Norfolk, Virginia	122
13 • The *Californio* Uprising and Its Aftermath	132
14 • The Army of the West and the Mormon Battalion	139
15 • The Battle of San Pascual	145

Table of Contents

16 • The Treaty of Cahuenga	149
17 • The Earliest Days of the Gold Rush	152
18 • Frémont Is Court-Martialed	159
19 • The Treaty of Guadalupe Hidalgo	163
20 • From Military to Civilian Rule	167
21 • Significance of the Pacific Campaigns of the U.S.–Mexican War	174
Chronology	181
Chapter Notes	189
Bibliography	202
Index	211

The combination of forces employed in the conquest of California and New Mexico were of various organization [sic], both military and naval, and were launched forth, by sea and land, at different periods. The points of their distinct embodiment were almost as many thousands of miles apart as their destined points of concentration on the soil of Mexico. It will therefore be impossible in the circumscribed limits of this work, to follow each detachment on their separate marches, voyages, and exploits.

—James Madison Cutts
*The Conquest of California and New Mexico,
by the Forces of the United States,
in the years 1846 & 1847*
(published in 1847)

Preface

This book is a far-ranging introductory survey of the California campaigns of U.S.–Mexican War of 1846–1848—a war which, taken as a whole, remains controversial even today. It focuses not only on military and naval operations *per se*, but also on the cultures and social classes before, during, and after the war. Perhaps most importantly, it introduces some of the contemporary men and women who were directly or indirectly caught up in the war, especially the *Californios*.

"*Californios*" is a term used in historic and regional Spanish to designate any Spanish-speaking Roman Catholic of non–Indian descent who was born in Alta California between 1769 and 1848.[1] The province of Alta, or Upper, California was formed in 1804 out of the northern part of the former province of *Las Californias*. It included the modern states, or parts thereof, of California, Nevada, Arizona, Utah, western Colorado, and southwestern Wyoming. Baja, or Lower, California, is the long, narrow peninsula extending south from Alta California.

Although the war lasted only two years, it had a long prologue and a longer afterlife. To help keep the complicated chronological record of the California campaigns straight, the chapters in this book focus chiefly on the *highlights* of these campaigns. The first paragraph of most chapters is usually a short summary printed in italics. For further clarity, the dates mentioned in this book include the year as well as the month and the day. Chapters vary in length.

Some specialized operations related to the California campaigns were more complicated than others: they began earlier and went on longer. American naval and amphibious operations along the Pacific coast, for example, began as early as 1821 and continued for several

Preface

weeks after the end of the war because of the delay in receiving news of the war's end. These operations are almost never treated in depth by modern books on the war, but they receive full coverage in this work. Due to their complexity, however, they are not discussed here in the same step-by-step chronological order used for other chapters, but are condensed and studied in their entirety in two chapters (chapters 11 and 12) of about equal length.

Wars do not occur in an ideological vacuum. In this case, although some prominent Americans of the era rejected the simplistic but very popular notion of Manifest Destiny, this conviction was inherent in the genesis and conduct of the war. It was the belief that the American people were somehow "destined"—divinely or otherwise—to expand all the way from the Atlantic to the Pacific. American control of California by the United States was to be the keystone in the arch of Manifest Destiny.

One of the most prominent Americans not enamored of Manifest Destiny was Ulysses S. Grant, initially of U.S. Civil War fame and later the 18th president of the United States. He was only a junior officer during the U.S.–Mexican War, but it made a life-long impression on him. He later wrote of the 1845 annexation of Texas, which was a precursor to the war itself:

> I was bitterly opposed to the measure, and to this day regard the war which resulted as one of the most unjust ever waged by a stronger against a weaker nation. It was an instance of a republic following the bad example of European monarchies, in not considering justice in their desire to acquire additional territory.[2]

The issue of slavery, which was also deeply implicit in the war, inflamed New England in the 1840s and 1850s. Grant was convinced that the U.S.–Mexican War was one of the root causes of the American Civil War. He stated that "the occupation, separation and annexation [of Texas] were ... a conspiracy to acquire territory out of which slave states might be formed for the American Union."[3]

The results of the war are still evident today. Having lost the war, Mexico was forced to surrender to the United States more than half a million square miles of its territory, i.e., the lands which now constitute California, Utah, Nevada, and parts of Arizona, New Mexico, Wyoming, and Colorado. The war also left a lasting—and continuing—residue of bitterness in the minds of many Mexicans, who felt that their honor had been trampled under foot by their aggressive, more powerful, self-centered, and racist northern neighbor.

The U.S.–Mexican War featured both land and sea campaigns in and along the Pacific Coast, but these have not received a great deal of detailed attention when compared to other theaters of the war. There is one notable exception: Neal Harlow's exhaustively thorough 499-page book (with 68 pages of endnotes), entitled *California Conquered: The Annexation of a Mexican Province, 1846–1850*. This work, first begun in the 1930s, was published in part in 1950 and finally appeared in its present form in 1982.

The California campaigns have been treated only very briefly, if at all, in many other books. To take one example, Philip Katcher's short but useful *Men-at-Arms* monograph on the uniforms, equipment, and organization of the U.S.–Mexican War has been reprinted thirteen times since it was first published in 1976, but it still contains only one brief paragraph on these campaigns.[4]

The bottom line here is, as Richard W. Amero, an award-winning historian of the war, put it succinctly in 1984, "most historians of the Mexican-American War (1846–1848) spend *hours* describing the invasion of Mexico and *minutes* summarizing events in Alta California."[5]

Two closely related components of the Pacific campaigns were the deployments of U.S. Navy ships and of amphibious Marine Corps forces. Some nautical definitions may be helpful now:

- In 19th century nautical terminology, a ship was a large vessel with three masts, with tops and yards on each. To keep matters as simple as possible, however, in this book "ship" is often used in general terms to mean any vessel that could carry sizeable numbers of men and supplies for a considerable distance.
- The prefix "USS" stands for "United States ship," as in "the USS *Portsmouth*."
- The Pacific Squadron was a unit of the U.S. Navy and will be discussed in several places in this book.
- A ship's boat could be any one of a number of relatively light small craft carried aboard a ship, powered by oars or sails,

and used to transport personnel and goods between ship and shore.

Although very few historians have written at any length about naval operations in the Pacific theater of the Mexican-American War, there are at least two useful monographs (see the bibliography): K. Jack Bauer's book *Surfboats and Horse Marines*, published by the United States Naval Institute in 1969, and Gabrielle M. Neufeld Santelli's "Marines in the Mexican War," published as an Occasional Paper in 1991 by the History and Museums Division of the Marine Corps.

Despite the great controversy the war generated at the time, it has since then been overshadowed by the American Civil War for so long that today many readers will know very little, if anything at all, about it. Indeed, it has even been labeled by one scholar as "America's Forgotten War."[6]

This is especially true of the "conquest of California," as contemporaries put it. The use of this phrase in a public document dates at least from 1847, when Carey & Hart, a Philadelphia publisher, printed a book by James Madison Cutts entitled *The Conquest of California and New Mexico, by the Forces of the United States, in the Years 1846 & 1847*. In his Introduction, Cutts modestly explained why he wrote this historically useful book:

> The purpose here is to sketch the geographical and historical outlines with equal impartiality and with such fidelity as the records now admit of; so that the Public may have before them an unpretending, yet useful *compendium*. At least, such is the Author's only design, and this he hopes to accomplish satisfactorily, the more so that he makes no literary pretensions.[7]

It is clear today that the "conquest of California" differs fundamentally in scale and in character from clashes in other theaters of the U.S.–Mexican War. It takes place on a more intimate and geographically more constricted stage. It does not have many dramatic death-or-glory scenes, being characterized instead by a series of small-scale, low-level incidents. Nevertheless, as the U.S. Navy chaplain and *alcalde* (mayor) of Monterey Walter Colton (1797–1851) would remark (he is such an excellent contemporary source that he will be quoted frequently in this book simply as "Colton"),

Preface

The war here is not on a great scale, but it impinges, at certain points with terrific energy. It is not always the magnitude of the field and of the interests at issue, which most severely test the resources of the general. This California war has to be carried on by means which requires consummate tact, coolness, and courage.

It is an idle dream to suppose the Californians will not fight; give them faithful and competent leaders, and they evince a dashing bravery which lifts them immeasurably above contempt. He who presumes on their timidity will learn his error when it may be too late.[8]

A total of 17,435 Americans died during the U.S.–Mexican War, about two-thirds (11,550) from illness or other non-combat causes.[9] There are no firm figures on total Mexican losses, but about 25,000 Mexicans are thought to have been killed or wounded in the war.[10] Remarkably, however, there were very few American or Mexican casualties during the California campaigns themselves. Many towns in the Californias immediately surrendered without a shot being fired by either side. The modest amount of fighting that did occur involved only small groups of *Californios* who were opposed to the American invasion, and equally small groups of American soldiers, Marines, militiamen, and sailors who supported it.

There was in fact only one "real" battle in the California campaigns—the bloody battle of San Pascual on 6 December 1846. Historical accounts vary slightly but it appears that in that fight, out of a total of 153 Americans involved, only 18 were killed and 13 were wounded; on the other side, out of 75 *Californios*, none was killed, 12 were wounded, and one was captured. In fact, much of the "action" in the California campaigns simply boils down to verbal, political, and military posturing.

These were skills practiced by Mexican and American leaders alike but in which the Mexicans often had the upper hand. For example, upon learning of the Bear Flag Revolt in northern California, which will be discussed later, Pío Pico (1801–1894), the last Mexican governor of California, exhorted his fellow citizens—from the safety of his own home base in southern California—with these ringing words:

Fly, Mexicans, in all haste in pursuit of the treacherous foe; follow him to the farthest wilderness; punish his audacity; and in case we fail, let us form a cemetery where posterity may remember to the glory of Mexican history the heroism of her sons, as is remembered the glory won by the death of that little band of citizens posted at the Pass of Thermopylae under General Leonidas.[11]

In this book, the Introduction outlines, very briefly and as an essential first step, the causes and conduct of the war considered as a whole. The text itself is buttressed by extensive quotations from contemporary sources. In the opinion of the authors, these quotations are of great importance because they give not only local color but also invaluable "I-was-there" personal insights into the war. The text provides background information on the region and, in chapters of varying lengths, then looks at the two now-nearly-forgotten Pacific Coast campaigns of the war, namely, the California campaigns ashore and the operations of the U.S. Navy's Pacific Squadron at sea and on land.

One of the goals of this book is to introduce the reader to a wide range of contemporary men and women. Biographical sketches, often by using flashbacks to elucidate the past and flash-forwards to see what the future will hold for them, appear when or shortly after a person's name is mentioned for the first time.

A great deal of biographical material is available on the men of this era, but much less on the women. When in the early 1870s the celebrated historian, compiler, and editor Hubert Howe Bancroft (1832–1918),[12] who will be quoted here frequently, sent out his interviewers to collect oral histories from the remaining pre-statehood gentry of California, the interviewers usually wanted to meet with the men of a household. If the men were not available, however, the interviewers would then talk with the women instead. The long-delayed but eventual result of their labors was a remarkable 2006 study *Testimonios: Early California Through the Eyes of Women, 1851–1848*, by Rose Marie Beebe and Robert M. Senkewicz.

In a few cases, modern punctuation has been substituted within 19th century quotations to improve readability, but this never affects the meaning of the quotations themselves. Lengthy quotations have often been subdivided or lightly edited for ease of reading. Endnotes have been used very generously here, both for attribution and to elaborate on little-known points which are relevant but which might otherwise detract from the flow of the text. The selected chronology will help keep dates, personalities, and events in their proper order.

Preface

It now remains for the authors of this book to extend their sincere thanks for the advice and encouragement so kindly provided by Professor Richard Griswold del Castillo of San Diego State University; by Ken Sullivan, Director of Library and Instructional Technology at Western Nevada College in Carson City, Nevada; by Pat Regains, Business and Government Librarian at the University of Nevada in Reno; and by Professor Linda Arnold of Virginia Tech. However, any oversights or errors in this book are of course the authors' own responsibility alone.

Introduction
Causes and Conduct of the U.S.–Mexican War

In the United States, this conflict is variously known as the U.S.–Mexican War, the Mexican-American War, the Mexican War, the Invasion of Mexico, the U.S. Intervention, or the U.S. War Against Mexico. In Mexico, names for the conflict include *La Interevención Norteamericana* (The North American Intervention), *La Guerra de Defensa* (The Defensive War), *La Invasión Estadounidense* (The United States Invasion), and *La Guerra del '47* (The War of '47).

These sharply differing names reflect the fact that the United States saw the war as an inevitable conflict between different national perceptions. From the American point of view, the United States was clearly in the right. Mexico, on the other hand, was convinced that it had been attacked unjustly and without provocation. For better or for worse, Mexico's acute sense of honor ruled out the possibility of any surrender of its "national heritage," i.e., of Mexican territory, to the United States. The upshot was that Mexico felt that it had no choice but to go to war against its hostile and far more powerful northern neighbor.

Some Mexican army officers did in fact realize that, given the many weaknesses of Mexico and the many strengths of the United States, Mexico was virtually certain to be defeated in such a conflict. However, these men were not recruited for their analytical abilities and were not expected to engage in deep geopolitical thinking. Most of them had joined the army purely for social and political reasons. When war broke out, there were as many as 24,000 officers, many of them on half-pay and therefore not on active duty, plus some 20,000 illiterate, poorly-trained, badly-treated, and ill-armed enlisted men.

Nor did Mexico have any small-arms factories of its own. It had to equip its troops with obsolescent, discarded European firearms, almost all of them flintlock muskets, which were not very reliable.[1] A few words on firearms and artillery may be useful here:

- In flintlock firearms, a piece of flint flies forward when the trigger is pressed and, upon striking an angled piece of steel, sends a shower of sparks which ignite the priming powder in the priming pan. This burns fiercely and ignites the main gunpowder charge in the barrel. If the priming powder does not ignite the main charge, however, the result is a "flash in the pan" and in this case the weapon will not fire.
- The bore (i.e., the inside) of a barrel of a musket is smooth, not rifled. A musket is much easier and faster to load than a rifle, but much less accurate because the lead ball, i.e., the bullet, is not forced to spin in flight and thus to stabilize itself.
- In percussion firearms, when the trigger is pulled a small explosive device known as a "cap" is struck by the falling hammer and ignites the charge of gunpowder in the barrel of the weapon. A percussion firearm is inherently more reliable and more accurate than a flintlock.
- The cannons of the American artillery arm had a longer range than Mexican artillery pieces and fired deadlier projectiles. The Mexican guns used such inferior gunpowder that their cannonballs traveled slowly enough for American troops to see them in the air and dodge them. Thanks to rigorous training and frequent practice, American artillerymen could set up, fire, and move their cannons much more quickly than the Mexicans could handle theirs. Indeed, American gunners were so fast that their artillery units became known as the "flying artillery." The net result was that, as the military writer John S.D. Eisenhower put it, "in the artillery arm, at least, the American army was the peer of any army in the world."[2]

Introduction

In contrast to the inferior weapons in the hands of Mexican troops, the U.S. Army's Model 1841 percussion rifle was the most reliable and accurate firearm of its time. Shipments of this new rifle reached New Orleans in time to supply a regiment of volunteers who would subsequently be known as the "Mississippi Rifles."

The profound weaknesses of the Mexican army, its poorly-trained and poorly-equipped troops, and its concomitant feeble fire power were exacerbated by the lack of a separate and competent navy. From 1821 until 1939, the navy coexisted, together with the Mexican army, in the Ministry of War, but apparently did not engage in any major actions. It was ineffective and in fact played no role whatsoever in the California campaigns.

As the writer David Nevin (1927–2011) put it in *The Mexican War* (1978), which is arguably the best short treatment of the war and probably the best-illustrated book on it,

> Independent from Spain for barely two decades, Mexico had already lost Texas. With that territory about to join the Union, Mexicans sensed that their expansionist neighbors to the north hungered for New Mexico and California as well. Mexican newspapers cried out for a preventive war, predicting that American conquerors would wipe out the Catholic religion and turn Mexicans into slaves.
>
> But Mexico was ill-prepared for war. Her generals fought each other for the presidency: her army bulged with untrained officers commanding underfed, underequipped Indian conscripts. Yet war fever forced one president out of office when he attempted to negotiate with Washington.[3]

A contemporary American army officer had a very low opinion of his Mexican counterparts, dismissing them simply as "young men of corrupt morals, dissipated habits, and with little courage or enterprise ... they never LEAD their men."[4]

In much the same vein, the British minister (a senior diplomatic official) in Washington, D.C., wrote home in April 1846: "The officers ... are, as a Corps, the worst perhaps to be found in any part of the world. They are totally ignorant of their duty."[5]

Nevertheless, Mexico's senior politicians and military leaders were not stupid. They realized full well that any surrender of Mexican territory to the United States—that is, before Mexico was actually defeated in combat by the Americans—would be a political death sentence for them. Thus, in order to hang onto power themselves and to continue to enjoy the many rewards of office, they felt they had no choice but to keep their country intact. They realized that their country was facing grave dangers from an expansionist United States, but they did little to deal with this threat.

In October 1837, for example, Andrés Castillero, a Mexican army officer, was sent to Alta California to prepare for the arrival of a military force which the Mexican government planned to send there to prevent California from being conquered by the Americans, as Texas had been. However, a change of the Mexican government at the end of 1845 abruptly ended this idea, so the force was never sent and California remained virtually defenseless.

Castillero was a good observer and wanted to do his job well. He worked hard to unite the opposing political factions of the Californias, i.e., of Alta and Baja California. Toward this end, he wrote to the minister of war in Mexico City, putting forward an accurate, unvarnished assessment of the situation in the Californias and strongly urging the minister to strengthen the Mexican military presence in both of them.[6]

Castillero himself was keenly aware of the increasing influence of foreigners, especially Americans, on the Pacific coast and knew how easy it was for them to evade Mexican customs regulations, which, though rarely enforced, were designed to be the main financial prop of the regional government. On 21 October 1837, Castillero wrote to the minister in Mexico City:

> New California [Alta California], due to its topographic situation, carries on the exchange of its products along the coast very easily. All its towns and missions are established very near to the best ports, so that national and foreign vessels are like "moving stores" that remain more than a year, selling their merchandise and collecting the payment of hides and tallow to carry them to Lima and North America.
>
> The national vessels that trade on these coasts, and also the schooner *California*, should in my opinion be armed for war, for the safety of those ports and the waters of the Department. The Frontier of Lower California should have a stronger force, increasing the number in the company up to one hundred men in order to aid the Government of the Department and to prevent the raids of the savages [Indians] in the southern part.
>
> It seems to me convenient that, so long as the Government does not place a respectable force in the Department, for the safety of California,

Introduction

in the advanced posts of which I have spoken—Altar [a small city in northwestern Sonora] and [those] on the Frontier of Lower California—should be kept reinforced.

It is necessary to place a garrison in [Baja California] at Cabo San Lucas [Cape San Lucas, at the southernmost tip of the Baja California peninsula]; all vessels that sail from the ports of Guaymas, Mazatlán, and San Blas must pass near it, and if the Americans, due to the ambitious aims which they manifest, should seize this point and should fortify it and keep two warships cruising these waters, they would hold a small Gibraltar which would deprive us of the trade of the South Sea [the Pacific Ocean], and they could attack our coasts; furthermore, there are fifty or sixty American whaling ships which alternately go there annually on the pretext of refreshing their stores and carry on a scandalous contraband.

The national schooner *Correo Mercado* should be in the port of La Paz at the orders of the General Commandant so that the coast may be looked after and so that it may carry the money to pay for the troops from Mazatlán by a paymaster.[7]

There is no evidence, however, that the minister of war paid the slightest attention to Castillero's good advice. Thus, for better or for worse, many patriotic Mexicans felt that a resort to arms was the only honorable option open to them if they wished to maintain their pride, defend their rights, and preserve their country's territorial integrity. Nevertheless, it has long been evident that, as the American historian Barbara Tuchman might have put it, going to war in 1846 against the United States was truly "an act of folly" on Mexico's part. By this phrase, Tuchman meant an act which was *contrary to the self-interest* of the government sponsoring it and which was certain to fail.

Many of Mexico's contemporary leaders used popular resentment against American aggression—a resentment which they themselves had strongly encouraged—as a stepping-stone in their pursuit of political power. Once in power, however, these same men then found themselves captives of their own propaganda and therefore could not easily oppose their government's venture into a doomed war with the United States.[8] In short, although they had fueled Mexican resentment against the Americans, they did nothing in practical terms to strengthen their country militarily.

Some educated Mexicans did entertain doubts about their country's prospects in any war with the United States. In 1844, President

John Tyler had appointed Wilson Shannon as his envoy to Mexico. Writing about the strong feelings in Mexico against the American annexation of Texas, Shannon noted that

> many intelligent Mexicans privately entertain and express opinions favorable to the amicable arrangements of the difficulties.... But there are few who have the boldness to express these opinions publicly, or who [would] be willing to stem the current popular prejudice by undertaking to carry them out.[9]

Moreover, in 1845 the Mexican minister of foreign relations, Manuel de la Peña y Peña, sent to all the states of Mexico his pessimistic analysis of the current situation and of Mexico's prospects in a war with the United States. He pointed out the extraordinary economic and military advantages enjoyed by the United States and tried to rally domestic support within Mexico for a negotiated settlement with the Americans.[10] The minister even requested a vote in Mexico on whether or not Mexico should engage in such a war.

Before that vote could take place, however, General Mariano Paredes staged a coup and overthrew the federal government in Mexico City. His lack of interest in California itself can be seen from the fact that, earlier, funds had been sent to him to finance an expeditionary force to bring the then-rebellious province of California back into line. Rather than using them for this purpose, however, he had used them instead to pay for the troops which, as part of his rebellion, had marched on Mexico City.[11]

Although Paredes himself was a professional soldier, he did not pay any attention to the fact that the United States had recently upgraded its entire arsenal and now had the ability to overwhelm militarily both the Mexican army and the fledgling Mexican naval force. What Paredes hoped to do was to wage a limited but successful war against the United States in order to increase Mexico's bargaining power. He also hoped to win indemnification over Texas and to encourage intervention by European powers to keep the United States at bay. He singularly failed in all these efforts, however, and American forces consistently defeated the Mexican army in May 1846. Paredes himself was soon overthrown by General Antonio López de Santa Anna.

On the American side of the border, on 13 May 1846 a joint resolution by both houses of the U.S. Congress had asserted that a state

Introduction

of war between the United States and Mexico existed "by an act of the Republic of Mexico." President Polk had signed a proclamation of war that same day.[12] This vital bit of news would not officially reach the American forces campaigning in California until 17 August 1846. On 25 May 1846, however, California governor Pío Pico informed the Mexican Ministry of Foreign Relations in Los Angeles that war was now in the offing. He wrote:

> The uncertainty in which we find ourselves in this Department concerning the true state existing in the political affairs between our Government and the Republic of the United States of the North, the excessive introduction of armed adventurers from the Nation, leaves us no doubt of the war we shall have with the North Americans.
>
> The critical situation in which we find ourselves constrains me more and more to politely arouse His Excellency the President through Your Excellency's mediation so that he may take care of us efficaciously, providing us with the necessary resources for an honorable resistance, that may serve as a warning to the depraved plans of that piratical Nation.
>
> The Departmental Treasury is exhausted and there is no hope whatever of pecuniary aid.
>
> May it please Your Excellency to make the contents of this note known to His Excellency the President, to whom equally with Your Excellency I offer my obedience and esteem.
>
> God and Liberty, Los Angeles, May 25, 1846.
>
> Pío Pico[13]

The Ministry of Foreign Relations never replied to the governor's urgent plea for help or money.

In fairness to the Ministry, however, it must be noted that President Polk, for his part, also seriously misjudged the likely course of the war. For example, when he delivered his war message to Congress, he did not think that the conflict would last any appreciable length of time because Mexico was so much weaker than the United States. It was thus very likely, he believed, that Mexico would quickly sue for peace during the first weeks—or at least during the first months—of the war.

To his great surprise, however, successive Mexican governments were quite unfazed by the unbroken series of military setbacks they experienced and simply refused to surrender. Their reason was not sheer bravado but probably the realization that, having already lost the war as a practical matter, they now had nothing more to lose. In their view, refusing to surrender might force the Americans to offer them significant concessions to end the war sooner rather than later. The net result was that President Polk found himself casting around for a way to end the war quickly.[14]

The Causes of the War

If there was one fundamental cause for the war, it was that a very weak, disorganized Mexico was physically too close to a very strong, unified, expansionist United States. As General Porfirio Díaz, president of Mexico from 1877 to 1911, would later put it with a memorable turn of phrase: "¡Pobre México! Tan legos de Dios, y tan cerca de los Estados Unidos"[15] ("Poor Mexico! So far from God, and so close to the United States").

In less sweeping terms, however, it was Mexico's loss of Texas, which was annexed by the U.S. in 1845, that probably made war inevitable. In 1835, Texas (then part of Mexico) had risen in revolt. After some initial military setbacks, the Texas rebels won the battle of San Jacinto in 1836 and captured Mexican general Antonio López de Santa Anna. They had forced him to recognize Texas as an independent country, but Mexico refused to accept Santa Anna's agreement with the Texans, arguing, correctly, that it had been made under duress. Mexico continued to insist that Texas was simply a rebellious province. Tensions remained very high along the border, and in 1845 the United States began the unilateral process of annexing Texas and making it part of the United States.

At the same time, President Polk and many other American leaders also wanted to buy—or, if necessary, simply to seize by force—Mexico's northwestern territories, especially California, which would be a real prize for the United States. As U.S. President Franklin Delano Roosevelt would write in 1939 in his Introduction to a book on *Naval Sketches of the War in California*, by Captain Dudley W. Knox, U.S.N.: "Incapable of united resistance from within and devoid of any protecting power from without, the vast territory of California lay an easy prize to any strong power that might wish to seize it."[16]

Some key scenes in the history of California, particularly of the early Spanish involvement there, may therefore be of interest here:

Introduction

The name "California" comes from a Spanish novel, *Las Sergas de Esplandián* (*The Labors of the Very Brave Knight Esplandián*), which was published in Seville in 1510 by the Spanish author Garcí Rodriguez Ordóñez de Montalvo. This novel was well known to the Spanish and Spanish-backed explorers of the New World. In the novel, Montalvo assured his readers:

> Know ye that on the right hand of the Indies [the West Indies] there is an island called California [early explorers thought that Baja California was an island], very near the Terrestrial Paradise and inhabited by black women without a single man among them and living in the manner of the Amazons. They are robust of body, strong and passionate in heart, and of great valor. Their island is one of the most rugged in the world with bold rocks and craigs. Their arms are all of gold, as is the harnesses of the wild beasts which, after taming, they ride. In all the island there is no other metal.[17]

As part of Spain's campaign to learn more about this fabulous land, in 1539 the Spanish navigator Francisco de Ulloa sailed about three-quarters of the way up the western coast of Baja California, but he did not get as far north as Alta California.[18] The first European to visit Alta California was the Portuguese (or Spanish) explorer and adventurer Juan Rodriguez Cabrillo, who was sent out by the viceroy of New Spain. In 1542 he sailed northwest from Navidad, Mexico, to explore the coasts of the Californias.

Las Californias—a Spanish phrase meaning "the Province of the Californias" or, more simply, "the Californias"—was the name given by the Spaniards to the northwestern territory of New Spain. This region included the present-day Mexican states of Baja California and Baja California Sur, and the U.S. state of California. Cabrillo had planned to sail from the Californias to China, but he ran into such heavy weather and mountainous seas off the northern coast of California that he was forced to turn back towards Mexico. He died on Santa Catalina Island in 1543 when a leg injury he suffered there led to gangrene. His second-in-command brought the ship safely back to Mexico that same year.

The Spanish had failed in earlier attempts to find a safe port on the California coast suitable for their treasure-laden Manila galleons, i.e., the large, multi-decked sailing ships used by European states from the 16th to 18th centuries. Due to the strong currents of the Pacific Ocean, the best way for such awkward, unseaworthy ships to get from the Philippines to the Spanish colonies in America which were fronting the Pacific Ocean was first to reach America well north of the Baja peninsula, and then turn south.

The Spanish tried again in 1595, when Captain Sebastián Rodrigo Cermeño, commander of the galleon *San Augustín*, was ordered to survey the California-Oregon coast south to Mexico during his voyage from the Philippines. He successfully made landfall off the California-Oregon border, duly turned south, and headed down the coast. At Drake's Bay, north of present-day San Francisco, he formally took possession of this land for Spain—not knowing that the English explorer Sir Francis Drake had already landed there sixteen years earlier and had claimed it for England.

Drake's Bay, however, is not a secure anchorage because it offers no protection from storms. A gale came up suddenly while the *San Augustín* was anchored there, and the big ship was soon driven ashore and broken up by powerful waves. Its valuable cargo of beeswax, silk, and porcelain was lost. However, much of the porcelain cargo (now reduced to colorful little pieces) was later salvaged by the local Coast Miwok Indians, who turned some of the 800 porcelain shards into useful beads, pendants, and scrapers. These artifacts provide physical evidence of one of the earliest European-Indian contacts in the New World.

Another intrepid Spanish explorer was Sebastián Vizcaíno, who in 1602 led a four-ship expedition north from Acapulco, Mexico, looking for a safe harbor along the California coast. He charted the coast with precision (indeed, his charts were so good that they were used for nearly 200 years), describing San Diego Bay and Monterey Bay as having the potential to become very useful Spanish ports. In 1603, a report that Vizcaíno sent to King Felipe III of Spain also describes the local Indians in very positive terms. He wrote:

> The area is populated by people whom I consider to be meek, gentle, quiet, and quite amenable to conversion to Catholicism and to becoming subjects of Your Majesty.... I traveled more than 800 leagues along the coast and kept a record of all the people I encountered. The coast is populated by an endless number of Indians, who said there were large

Introduction

settlements in the interior ....They are very knowledgeable about silver and gold and said that these metals can be found in the interior.[19]

A Spanish expedition of 1769, designed in part to counter any possible British, Russian, or French thoughts of setting up their own colonies in California, was led by Gaspar de Portolá. It included the formidable Franciscan friar Junípero Serra (1713–1784), who was a driving force in the Spanish conquest and colonization of California. Portolá's expedition initially overshot Monterey, its goal, but during the search for Monterey, San Francisco Bay was sighted by Spanish soldiers exploring ashore. Spain's occupation of Alta California began in 1769 with the founding, by Serra, of Mission San Diego de Alcalá at what is now San Diego. Later expeditions, e.g., by Juan Bautista de Anza in 1771–1776, would further solidify Spain's hold on the region.

By 1824, the Spanish had established a chain of 21 missions along much of the coastal area of California. These were designed with two ends in mind: first, to make sure that Spain would have unchallenged political and economic supremacy in the region, and second, as Spanish missionaries might well have put it, to save the souls of the *bárbaros infiéles* ("barbarous infidels"), i.e., the Indians. The missions, which past and present critics have long denounced as being little more than forced-labor camps, would ultimately employ 142 priests and would baptize 87,787 Indians. Some of the few but essential supplies needed by the missions were provided by sea from the Spanish naval base at San Blas on the Pacific coast of mainland Mexico.

In 1804, Spain divided the Province of California into Baja California and Alta California. Baja California was a long, narrow, arid, mountainous peninsula totaling about 55,000 square miles, where most of the small population lived along the coasts. A classic and truly outstanding book on Baja California is Walter Nordhoff's *The Journey of the Flame*, first published in 1933. It is a fictional account of the travels of an Irish-Mexican boy who in 1810 accompanies the Spanish viceroy of Baja California and his wife and son on a long and very perilous overland journey from the southern tip of Baja to Monterey in Alta California.

Alta California was huge but very lightly populated. Some contemporary maps show its borders as including all or parts of present-day California, Arizona, Nevada, Utah, New Mexico, western Colorado, and southwestern Wyoming. In point of fact, its eastern boundaries were never officially defined. In 1828 the border was variously said to have been either the Colorado River or the Sierra Nevada mountains ("Sierra Nevada" means "snowy range" in Spanish). Other schools of thought held that Alta California was bordered on the east by the Spanish settlements in Arizona and New Mexico or, more explicitly, that its eastern boundaries were the Arkansas River, the Red River, and the Sabine River.

Its non–Indian population was tiny but its total area was perhaps more than 445,000 square miles. Mexican immigration to Alta California, however, was almost non-existent. In an ill-considered plan to reverse this trend, between 1825 and 1830 the Mexican government even shipped 150 convicts there. Moreover, many of the soldiers posted to the province's presidios (i.e., frontier military garrisons, including any civilian settlements built close to them) had been rounded up from Mexican jails. Since these men were rarely paid, they were forced to steal from the local citizens, thus exacerbating the negative feelings between the rulers and the ruled.[20]

Alta California was so far from the more "civilized" parts of Mexico, however, that officials in Mexico City must have done their utmost to avoid being assigned to remote Monterey. Today, Monterey is some 2,151 miles northwest of Mexico City; this distance is by car via modern highways. Nineteenth century journeys by horseback, mules, or crude wagons and carts jolting along poorly-marked and badly-maintained rocky trails would have been much longer.

The energetic Americans, who were more farsighted and more aggressive than the Spanish and the Mexicans, had long cast covetous eyes on California. As early as 1819, for example, when John Quincy Adams was secretary of state he had argued that the whole of the North American continent was the proper dominion of the United States.[21] In 1822, Joel R. Poinsett, an envoy sent to Mexico by President Monroe, had proposed a new boundary between the United States and Mexico which would have turned over Texas, New Mexico, and California, along with other northern Mexican territories, to the United States.[22] During the Andrew Jackson Administration, in 1835 Secretary of State Forsyth wrote to the American chargé d'affaires in Mexico:

Introduction

> It having been represented to the president that the port of St Francisco, on the western coast of the United Mexican States would be a most desirable place of resort for our numerous vessels engaged in the whaling business in the Pacific, far preferable to any to which they now have access, he has directed that an addition should be made to your instructions relative to the negotiations for Texas. The main object is to secure within our [national] limits the whole bay of St Francisco. If you can induce the Mexican government to agree to any line which will effect this, you are authorized to offer the sum of [$5 million].[23]

Nothing came of Forsyth's instructions, but many Americans of the day nevertheless believed that possessing California would offer them four important benefits:

(1) It would expand the continental United States from sea to sea, all the way from the Atlantic to the Pacific. This would be essential if a transcontinental railroad under American control was ever to link the two coasts.

(2) It would provide American harbors for whalers and for merchant ships trading with Asia, especially with China. Whaling was already big business. For example, a Congressman from New Bedford, Massachusetts, a center of the American whaling trade, reported that by the end of 1844 the American whaling fleet in the Pacific consisted of 650 ships which had cost $20 million to build and which employed 17,000 men.[24] The China trade, for its part, seemed to offer unlimited potential rewards.

(3) American possession of California would also deter any other nations, notably the British but to a lesser extent possibly the Russians and French as well, from toying with the idea of planting their own colonies there.

(4) Last but not least, California would be a remarkably fine place to live. As mentioned earlier, Colton was a chaplain for the U.S. Navy and in 1846 became the *alcalde* of Monterey during the U.S.–Mexican War. (An *alcalde* was the traditional magistrate, e.g., the mayor, who combined both judicial and administrative functions.) Colton's invaluable book, *Three Years in California*, written in 1850, is one of the best contemporary accounts of life there before the Gold Rush.

Colton was favorably impressed by many aspects of *Californio* culture. He wrote:

> There are no people I have ever been among who enjoy life so thoroughly as the Californians. Their habits are simple; their wants are few; nature rolls almost everything spontaneously into their lap. Their cattle, horses, and sheep roam at large—not a blade of grass is cut, and none is required. The harvest waves wherever the plough and harrow has been; and the grain which the wind scatters this year, serves as seed for the next. The slight labor required is more of a diversion than a toil; and even this is shared by the Indian. They attach no value to money, except as it administers to their pleasures.
>
> There is hardly a shanty among them which does not contain more true contentment, more genuine gladness of the heart, than you will meet in the most princely palace. Their hospitality knows no bounds; they are always glad to see you, come when you may; take a pleasure in entertaining you while you remain; and only regret that your business calls you away.... If I must be cast in sickness or destitution on the care of the stranger, let it be in California; but let it be before American avarice has hardened the heart and made it a god of gold.[25]

Colton was quite struck not only by the fine climate and boundless natural resources of California but also by the mini-population explosion taking place among its Mexican inhabitants. This certainly exceeded what must have been the relatively high death rate among the children of a society that could provide very little if any medical care. For example, José María Amador (1794–1883), a *Californio* soldier, mission administrator, rancher, and gold miner who will be quoted at some length in the final chapter of this book, was married three times and had 22 children.[26]

Colton wrote of this population growth:

> The fecundity of the Californians is remarkable, and must be attributed to the climate. It is no uncommon sight to find from fourteen to eighteen children at the same table, with their mother at their head. There is a lady of some note in Monterey, who is the mother of twenty-two living children. The youngest is at the breast, and must soon, it is said, relinquish its place to a new-comer, who will, in all probability, be allowed only the same brevity of bliss.[27]

Wonderful as the *Californios* were in Colton's eyes, he was much less impressed by the foreigners living in Alta California. Writing in Monterey on 30 July 1846, he noted in his journal:

> Today I entered on the duties of my office as alcalde of Monterey: my jurisdiction extends over an immense extent of territory, and over the

most heterogeneous population. Almost every nation has, in some emigrant, a representative of its peculiar habits, virtues, and vices.

Here is the reckless Californian, the half-wild Indian, the roving trapper of the West, the lawless Mexican, the licentious Spaniard, the scolding Englishman, the absconding Frenchman, the luckless Irishman, the plodding German, the adventurous Russian, and the discontented Mormon.

All have come here with the expectation of finding but little work and less law. Through this discordant mass I am to maintain order, punish crime, and redress injuries.[28]

Looking beyond these colorful individuals, it must be remembered here that it was the disputed southwestern border between the United States and Mexico that would prove to be the flashpoint for the U.S.–Mexican War. Citing the 1836 Treaties of Velasco (two documents signed by the Republic of Texas and by Mexico after Mexico's defeat at the decisive battle of San Jacinto), the United States claimed that the border was the Rio Grande River. Mexico, on the other hand, rejected these treaties as having been made under duress and claimed that all the land as far north as the Nueces River, which lies about 150 miles north of the Rio Grande, was in fact Mexican territory.

Matters came to a head in this contested area in 1846, when President Polk ordered a U.S. army unit under Brigadier Zachary Taylor to occupy the disputed border area. As a result of this order, on 25 April 1846 a 70-man squad of American cavalrymen under the command of Captain Seth Thornton was on patrol in the disputed territory when his unit was attacked by a 2,000-man Mexican cavalry force. Sixteen Americans were killed in the melee. President Polk therefore asked Congress to declare war because he claimed that, in what came to be known as the Thornton Affair, "after reiterated menaces, Mexico has now passed the boundary of the United States, has invaded our territory and shed American blood upon the American soil. She has proclaimed that hostilities have commenced and that the two nations are now at war."[29]

The Conduct of the War

The two nations soon declared war on one another: the U.S. on 13 May 1846 and Mexico on 7 July 1846. The major campaigns of the war have been studied at such length by past and modern historians that nothing radically new can be added now. A very brief overview of this modest but kaleidoscopic war, however, may be of use to readers who are not familiar with it.

The war consisted of four major closely-linked campaigns by American forces, fought both on land and at sea. These campaigns can be summarized as follows[30]:

- The campaign in northern Mexico

On 8 May 1846, the 2,400-man army of Brigadier General Zachary Taylor was en route to relieve Fort Texas (near Brownsville, Texas) when it met and routed Mexican general Mariano Arista's 3,400-man force. Taylor then moved south into Mexico and captured the fortress-city of Monterrey. At the battle of Buena Vista in February 1847 his 4,000 men won a stunning victory over 20,000 Mexican soldiers.

- The war in New Mexico and California

When war was declared on 13 May 1846, President Polk ordered Brigadier General Stephen W. Kearny (1794–1848; his name is pronounced "KAR-nee"), and his army of the West to capture Santa Fe and California, which they did. In this process, Kearny was helped by a battalion of Mormons, who spent 15 arduous weeks blazing a trail to the Pacific for the wagons carrying supplies for his troops. The Pacific campaigns themselves will be discussed at length in later chapters.

- Naval and Marine Corps operations

By establishing and maintaining control of the sea, the U.S. Navy enabled American forces to seize and to hold Mexican territory temporarily.[31] By blockading Mexico's major ports, the Navy strangled Mexico's maritime trade. It also carried troops to and participated in the attack on Veracruz, which surrendered to American forces on 28 March 1847. The battle of Veracruz was the first large-scale amphibious assault ever conducted by American forces.

In the Pacific theater of the war, eight of the ships of the Pacific Squadron had Marines stationed aboard them. These ships, the USS *Congress, Cyane, Dale, Independence, Levant, Portsmouth, Savannah,* and *Warren*, will be mentioned in later pages. Eighteen ships of the Gulf Squadron also carried Marines, but these vessels will not be discussed in this book because they were not involved in the operations highlighted here.[32]

- The march to Mexico City and the Treaty of Guadalupe Hidalgo

General Winfield Scott attacked Mexico City itself on 13 September 1847 and conquered it. The Treaty of Guadalupe Hidalgo on 2 February 1848 officially ended the war between the United States and Mexico.

• 1 •

Peoples of California

The four most significant groups in California were the Indians, the missionaries and their converts, the ranchers, and the foreigners. Knowing something about each of these groups will lead to a better understanding of the Pacific campaigns of the war. The first three groups will be discussed in this chapter. The roles of the foreigners will be discussed at greater length in the next chapter.

The Indians

The greatest authority on the California Indians was American anthropologist Alfred L. Kroeber (1876–1960). His studies on their arts of life, their societies, and their religions and ranges of knowledge underpin many of the following comments.[1]

It is important for modern readers to understand that the California Indians played a now-unsung but nevertheless crucial role in California's early history. The Indians who lived in the Coast Range, in the Sierra Nevada mountains, or in the lower San Joaquin and Sacramento river valleys generally remained outside the effective reach of first the Spanish and then the Mexican authorities. Many of the other Indians, however, were gradually swept up into the mission system. The net result was that by about 1800 they provided the labor for all of the 21 Spanish missions, and would later do the same for all of the Mexican ranches and for many of the early enterprises run by Americans and other foreigners. Their jobs typically involved herding cattle, slaughtering them as needed,[2] processing tallow in huge iron pots, harvesting crops, tending gardens, and providing household services.

The California Campaigns of the U.S.–Mexican War, 1846–1848

Salvador Vallejo (1813–1876), the younger brother of General Mariano Guadalupe Vallejo, explained their duties in more detail:

> Our friendly Indians [the Indians may have been "friendly" toward their Mexican employers—indeed, this would have been a mandatory requirement for keeping their jobs—but they were not *free*; i.e., they could not voluntarily leave their place of work and live elsewhere] ... tilled our soil, pastured our cattle, sheared our sheep, cut our timber, built our houses, paddled our boats, made tiles for our houses, ground our grain, killed our cattle, dressed their hides for market, and made our unburnt bricks; while the Indian women made excellent servants, took care of our children and made every one of our meals.[3]

With few exceptions, most of the California Indians sat on the sidelines during the U.S.-Mexican War. This is in sharp contrast with other regions, where the Comanches, Kiowas, Navajos, and several different tribes of Apaches increased their own attacks in northern Mexico—to the extent that the Mexicans there were left militarily unprepared and quite unable to resist American forces.[4] Nevertheless, it is still important to understand how the California Indians fared before their initial contact with foreigners—and what happened to them later on.

The California Indians are believed to have reached California about 13,000 to 15,000 years ago. Before their first contacts with Caucasian and other newcomers to California, they fared very well, within the limits imposed by their pre-literate culture. It must be noted here that "tribes" did not exist in California in the same sense as this word is more correctly used to describe the well-organized political and social systems of other North American Indian groups. Instead, it is better to use the anthropological shorthand of "tribelet" to describe the social and economic systems of the California Indians.

Tribelets were small, independent groups, each consisting of 50 to 500 individuals who shared a common language and who lived in a central village, perhaps with a cluster of several smaller villages nearby. By the time of contact, these Indians had organized themselves into about 500 tribelets, which spoke over 300 dialects of about 100 distinct languages. This surprisingly large number of dialects and languages was due to the great ecological diversity and size of California. Some 275,000 Indians were living in California when the Spanish first arrived there.[5]

1 • Peoples of California

The California climate was very mild in most regions and it was easy enough for Indian families to find enough to eat simply by hunting and gathering: the hard work and social cooperation needed for efficient agricultural production was entirely unnecessary. Acorns were plentiful in many areas and could be gathered and stored easily. With little effort, and in a pleasant, communal, sedentary way of working which encouraged friendly gossip, Indian women could, simply by leaching and boiling acorn meal, turn an endless supply of acorns into a simple but nourishing mush or bread. This staple was easily augmented by fish, shellfish, deer, rabbits, insects, seeds, and plants as seasonally available.

The California Indians' way of life was exceptionally simple: in fact, it struck most 19th century observers as being exceptionally "primitive." Men either wore nothing at all, or a skin folded about their hips; women wore only a short two-piece skirt. In rain, wind, or cold, both sexes could drape light leather blankets made from animal skins, or fur blankets, over their shoulders. Sea-otter fur made the best and the warmest blankets. Leather moccasins lined with grass were worn in cold weather but normally the Indians went barefoot, even over the rockiest or most cactus-studded ground. When carrying loads in baskets on their backs, women wore a basketry cap to protect their heads against the chafing of the pack strap. Men never carried loads when traveling, since they needed to keep their hands free so they could use their bows and arrows if necessary.

Housing styles varied considerably. Some tribelets made earth-covered dwellings; others used brush, bark, or planks. The earth-covered sweat house served in some respects as a clubhouse for men, who often slept there. Women were admitted only on special occasions.

California Indians used three types of boats: wooden dugouts, plank canoes, and tule (bulrush) rafts. None of these rudimentary craft, however, could be used on the open sea any distance from shore. Fish were taken by nets, weirs, poisonous plants,[6] and harpoons. Deer, rabbits, bears, and other game fell to the bow and arrow, usually at close range after a very careful, quiet, upwind stalk.

The most developed art among the California Indians was basketry. Wicker baskets were used to store and to carry goods. Remarkably, they were also used for cooking. Selected stones were heated in a fire and were then plunged into water-filled baskets, which were so tightly woven that they were waterproof. After several changes of very hot rocks, the water would boil and could then be used to cook acorns or other foods.

Cloth was unknown. Rush mats could be used in place of cloth blankets and were often sewn together; strips of rabbit fur or soft cords made of feathers or duck skin could serve as blankets, too. Pottery was crude and apparently of little importance. Rattles were variously used for dancing or for religious practices, but the only musical instrument was a very simple flute.

The Indians used two kinds of money: dentalium shells and clamshell-disk beads. Tobacco was smoked in moderation and was also mixed with shell lime and eaten. Stone axes or adzes were not known; instead, the Indians used wooden wedges or chisels made of antler to split and shape wood.

Very little is known about the roles of the chiefs in these tribelets, but a reasonable guess is that a chief's influence arose from some combination of his hereditary position, his personal wealth, and his abilities as a warrior. What seems clear is that, as was the case with many tribes in other parts of North America, the chief could never rule simply by fiat, but only by persuasion and by setting a good example.

Marriage was by purchase in most parts of California, though social customs varied enormously. In some parts of the region, a man and a woman simply lived together; their marriage was recognized as long as their union endured. In other parts, bride-purchase was the norm. A liberal payment by the groom to the bride or to her family enhanced his own status, the bride's status, and the status of any children to come from this union. In still other areas, a young man showed his matrimonial intentions simply by making presents of game to the bride's family or by performing some service for it.

A kinship taboo which forbade parents-in-law and children-in-law to look each other in the face, or to speak to or otherwise communicate with each other, was a common custom among the California Indians. A California Indian would have felt it a positive disgrace to speak brusquely to a parent-in-law, but the reasoning behind this particular taboo remains obscure.

1 • Peoples of California

Due both to the Indians' political fragmentation and to the enormous size of California, there was no organized, large-scale warfare, but only infrequent small-scale clashes. The usual motivation for fighting was to avenge an individual's death, not to eradicate an enemy tribelet, to plunder it, or to win military glory. Men captured in combat were usually killed and decapitated on the spot. Women and children were more likely to be slaughtered than enslaved. Scalps (usually including the ears, as well as skin cut from around the eyes and nose) were taken and became focal points for triumphal dances in Indian villages.

The Indians' favorite battle weapon was the bow and arrow, but spears, war clubs, and slings were used as well. Shields were made from rawhide. Primitive armor, made of elk hide or of wooden rods twined with string into waistcoat shape, could offer a fighter some protection in a skirmish. Fighting in most of California, however, was shieldless, armorless, low-level, and produced relatively few casualties.

Interviewed in 1874, Isadora Filomena, the 90-year-old widow of the Suisun chief Francisco Solano (c. 1798–c. 1851), had this to say about California Indian warfare:

> When Solano would go off to fight, he would arm his people with flint daggers, flint lances, and flint arrows. All the weapons were made poisonous with herbs.... Solano's warriors did not wear a jacket, a shirt, shoes, pants, or a hat. They were not stupid. They wore nothing on their bodies that a white man or another Indian could grab onto. They went into battle buck naked. Only on their head would they put some feathers. The Indians who carried the food would wear an ash-gray feather taken from a wild chicken. The soldiers who fought with lances and arrows would wear white duck feathers. All the chiefs would wear black feathers.
>
> In the beginning, Solano would put feathers on his head, but not after all the Indians were ordered to dress like *gente de razón*. [This Spanish phrase, which means "people of reason," i.e., the ruling Hispanic socioeconomic group, implied that the Indians were considered "people without reason."] Vallejo [the famous *Californio* military commander, politician, and rancher Mariano Guadalupe Vallejo, 1807–1890, who would become Solano's friend and who will be discussed later] gave him a fine weapon [very probably a musket—a smoothbore shoulder-fired weapon which, when carefully loaded and shot from a rest, was accurate up to about 50 yards], and the missionaries gave him a hat and some boots.[7]

Interviewed in Monterey in 1874, a *Californio* woman, Dorotea Valdez, who was a servant in the household of an upper class lady, described Solano in the following words:

> When Solano visited Monterey, I was living with Señora Prudencia Amesti. I especially noticed how tall that dark-colored savage was [Solano; his name in his native language was Sem Yeto, i.e., "Mighty Arm," and he was reputed to be 6 feet 10 inches in height, handsome, and brave], and that he was dressed like people of my race. His many followers, however, were dressed like Indians. They wore feathers around their heads, and many of them had tattoos around their wrists, arms, and legs. We did not like having them here, because their behavior was really overbearing.
>
> Solano and his Indians all rode fine horses. They all had *jáquimas* [equine headstalls], but few of them had saddles. Their hair was long and they carried bows and arrows. Their looks inspired fear in everyone. I firmly believed that they were devils from hell. Not all of the Indians had dark skin like Solano; some had white skin. However, most of them had very red faces.
>
> I heard Señora Amesti say that the arrival of these savages in Monterey was a plague sent by God to punish us for our sins. Solano did not stay very long in Monterey. Governor Alvarado and Don Pablo de la Guerra persuaded Solano to return to Sonoma.[8]

The California Indians followed a variety of religious practices but they are too detailed to describe here. Basically, however, these Indians were animists; that is, they perceived supernatural qualities as being inherent in all living beings and in all non-living things. They also believed that certain men and women, known as shamans, had the ability to act as intermediaries between the visible world and the invisible spirit world. Among the California Indians, these shamans tried to heal illness, to predict the future, and to exert control over natural events. They were thought to be able to wield enormous spiritual power.

The grizzly-bear shaman is a good example. The faithful believed that the grizzly-bear shaman could, at will, transform himself into a grizzly bear—the most powerful, most ferocious, and most dangerous of all the wild animals of California. In his supernatural bear-form, they believed, a shaman could destroy all his enemies. Some Indians held that such a shaman actually turned into a bear during his ritual performances. Others thought it was only the bearskin robe he was wearing, the religious paraphernalia he was carrying, and his skills as an actor that gave him an apparent supernatural power. In any case, grizzly-bear shamans were respected and feared. They were considered as either being invulnerable or at least as having the power to return to life if they were killed.

Virtually all the Indians of California held puberty ceremonies for adolescent girls, usually by staging long, elaborate dances and other complex ceremonies. Boys had less impressive ceremonies but were formally initiated into one of the two tribal religions, i.e., the Kuksu cult or the Tolache cult. The former involved elaborate acting and dancing ceremonies, performed in traditional regalia, to ensure good health, bountiful harvests, good weather, and successful hunts. Adherents of the Tolache cult ritually consumed datura, a very dangerous hallucinogenic substance which can cause amnesia, delirium, and even death.

These Indians did not record the passage of long intervals of time, so no one knew his or her own age or how long ago an event that happened, say, more than about six years earlier by the European calendar, had taken place. Astronomical knowledge was slight but the Milky Way was well-known and was often called the "ghosts' road."

The California Indians suffered very grievously at the hands of the Spanish, the Mexicans, and the later newcomers. The Spanish reduced to peonage[9] many of the Indians who lived near the coast, forcing them to live and work in the missions, where they usually survived mission life for only 10 to 12 years. As one Franciscan missionary lamented, "They live well free but as soon as we reduce them to a Christian and community life ... they fatten, sicken, and die."[10]

Interviewed in 1878, a former mission Indian named Julio César remembered very well the harsh treatment he had received in about 1838 at Mission San Louis Rey de Francia, which is located in what is now the city of Oceanside, California. At that time, all the missions had been fully secularized for five years and were being run by Mexican civilians, not by Roman Catholic friars. A reasonable guess, however, is that there was little, if any, difference between these two forms of mission rule.

César told an interviewer:

> When I was a boy, the way the Indians were treated was not good at all. They only gave us food, a loincloth, and a blanket which they replaced every year. They did, however, give us plenty of whippings for

any wrongdoing. We were at the mercy of the administrator, who ordered that we be whipped as many times and whenever he felt like it.

Pío Pico, as well as those who followed him, were despots. Señor Pico required us to carry our hat in our hand as long as we were within his range of vision, even if we were at a distance from him.[11]

If there was any good news in this sorry tale, it was that the Spanish and the Mexicans did accord *a positive value* to the Indians. In sharp contrast to some of the Americans and other foreigners who arrived during the 1849 Gold Rush, the Spanish and the Mexicans judged that the Indians were in fact real human beings, though of what they considered a very primitive sort.

Two important conclusions emerged from seeing the Indians in this light. The first was that, as real human beings, they had souls which needed to be saved by the missionaries. The second was that the Indians could become valuable in real-world terms as well. When properly trained, carefully supervised, and strictly disciplined, they had the potential to become very useful workers; i.e., to become economic assets for the missionaries and ranch owners of California.

As a practical matter, the California Indians' traditional ways of life would be entirely destroyed by about 1900 at the latest. These Indians had no natural immunities to European diseases and died in very large numbers when exposed to them. The measles epidemic of 1806 killed about one-quarter of the Mission Indians, i.e., the Indians living in and working for the missions in the San Francisco Bay area.[12]

The Indians were also subjected to a great deal of widespread and unpunished violence before, during, and after the Gold Rush. From 1842 to 1846, Mexican military and civilian parties routinely raided Indian villages, killed the adults, and seized the children, who were then sold to the wealthy as servants.[13] In fairness, however, it must be added that, in some cases, the Indians were guilty of aggression themselves.

For example, after the Mexican government secularized the missions in the 1830s, thereby permanently throwing many nominally–Christian Indians out of work, relations between Indians and *Californios* deteriorated significantly, particularly in the San Diego area.[14]

There, hostile Indians even forced the *Californios* to abandon their ranches on several occasions. By 1846, the Mexican population of the area had fallen sharply, leaving behind a Christian Indian population of about 2,500 and an unknown but probably sizeable number of non–Christian Indians. During the American invasion of Alta California, Indians renewed their attacks on *Californio* ranches. For example, 11 *rancheros* died in December 1846 after being taken captive during an Indian raid on the 13,310-acre land grant Rancho Pauma not far from San Diego. By June 1847, Indian attacks had risen to the point where many *Californios* were considering abandoning their ranches unless they received some military protection from the Americans.

To avoid this drastic outcome, three prominent *Californio* residents of San Diego—Miguel de Pedrorena, Santiago E. Arguello, and Juan María Marrón—convened a meeting on 27 June 1847 and put forward eight resolutions to the San Diego authorities. Of these, three are the most relevant here (punctuation as in the original):

- That the injuries and losses which the inhabitants of this district are suffering from the depredations of the Indians is so notorious that if some efficacious remedy is not immediately applied we shall be compelled to abandon our farms and property, as in fact many are now doing, rather than take upon themselves the responsibility of defending them by force of arms.
- That as a remedy of the many evils we are suffering, one of the first importance is to prevent these Indians in Villages from roaming at large through the Country in armed parties, contrary to the usage of Civilized countries, as well as the established Laws and usage of this use, till this present time.
- That the inhabitants of San Diego desire that the Committee [which was created by this meeting] should impress upon the government that, not withstanding the repeated and sensible injuries which they have received from the Indians, still they are not actuated by feelings of revenge so natural to man but are disposed to submit with pleasure to the actions of government, confident that they will receive all that assistance and protection which can be afforded them, and for which the undersigned offer their assistance.[15]

Together with the *Californios*, the Americans tried to stop Indian attacks by organizing a militia and by giving arms and ammunition to local residents. Nevertheless, the attacks continued through 1847 into 1848. In skirmishes with the Indians, the Americans even suffered one or two defeats. The last straw came in 1851, when the Christian Indians revolted against the Americans in San Diego and tried to unite all the Indians of southern California—and the *Californios* as well—into a united front to expel all the Americans from the region. Their revolt failed, however, and the Indian leaders were executed.[16]

Space does not permit any further comments on the Indians of California. Suffice it to conclude here by noting that their numbers went into free-fall, plummeting from over 200,000 in the late 19th century to approximately 15,000 at the end of the century.[17]

The Missionaries and Their Converts

The 21 Spanish missions in Alta California were religious and military outposts established by the Franciscan Order between 1769 and 1833 to spread Christianity among the Indians and to colonize parts of California in order to keep it out of foreign hands. In their 60 years of operation, the missions employed 142 priests and baptized 87,787 Indians.[18] The missions were located only in coastal regions of California or in the lower San Joaquin and Sacramento river valleys. Thus, as indicated earlier, most of the tribes living elsewhere, i.e., in the Coast Range, in the Sierra Nevada mountains, or in northern California, would always remain outside of the direct control of the Spanish or, later, of the Mexicans.

From Mexico, the missionaries introduced European livestock (cattle, sheep, horses, mules, goats, and pigs), fruits, and vegetables into California, with the long-term goal of making the missions self-supporting. They experienced some successes on this front but, taken as a whole, the mission era has long been a controversial one in California history. On the plus side, its defenders conjure up the pastoral, agriculturally-productive, and esthetically-pleasing nature of the missions. In a report published in 1846, Thomas O. Larkin (1802–1858), who was the U.S. Consul in Monterey and who will be discussed later at more length, reported,

> In the year 1825, the Missions might be considered at the height of their prosperity. At that time, they counted from 2,000 to 3,000 Indians and from 60,000 to 100,000 head of black cattle; an equal number of sheep,

and such immense herds of horses that large numbers were killed in order to avoid the destruction of pasturage.[19]

That said, however, critics of the missions have long denounced them as being little more than colonial slave labor camps ultimately governed by brute force. After having entered a mission (ostensibly of their own free will, but in practice often to get some free food), the Indians—and, later, their descendants—were strictly forbidden to leave it without permission, and were doggedly pursued and severely punished if they did so.

What is clear is that, beginning with the onset of the Mexican War of Independence in 1810, Mexican government support for the missions slowly dwindled, both because of the costs involved and, more to the point, because Mexican republicans wanted these potentially valuable mission lands for themselves and their families. As a result, missionaries and their converts had to become increasingly reliant on their own limited resources.

As the new-born Mexican republic began to find its feet, Mexican citizens increasingly called for the secularization of the missions. In 1826, José Maria de Echeandia, the first Mexican-elected governor of Alta California, issued a Proclamation of Emancipation. This decree freed from mission control the Indians living within the military districts of San Diego, Santa Barbara, and Monterey. The next year, the Mexican government passed the General Law of Expulsion, which provided that, unless otherwise excepted, all Spaniards less than 60 years old, i.e., the missionaries, were now considered to be illegal immigrants and, as such, had to leave Mexican territories.

In 1833, the Mexican Congress passed an act for the secularization of the missions. This called for the sale of mission properties to Mexican citizens. The proceeds from these sales were supposed to be used to bring new inhabitants into Baja California, but, in practice, the revenue thus raised went directly into private pockets instead. Writing in 1895, the journalist and historian Charles Fletcher Lummis described the effects of this act in the following words: "'Disestablishment'—a polite term for robbery—by Mexico ... in 1834, was the death blow of the mission system. The lands were confiscated; the buildings sold for beggarly sums, and often for beggarly purposes. The Indian converts were scattered and starved out; the noble buildings were pillaged for their tiles and adobes."[20]

Due to the confiscation of mission lands between 1834 and 1838, about 15,000 Indian converts lost not only the protection of the missionaries but all their own livestock and other moveable property as well. Later, when California became a Territory of the United States in 1848, they had no legal claim to any former mission lands. If there was any positive result of the decline of the missions, it may have been the subsequent growth of extensive ranching along the California coast in the Sacramento Valley. This very colorful era of California's history, during which the most prosperous Mexican ranchers enjoyed a patriarchal, colorful, and nearly–Arcadian existence, is discussed below.[21] (An Arcadian existence is a pleasant, simple, peaceful way of rural life.)

The Ranchers

During the last quarter of the 18th century, Spanish settlements were founded in the Las Californias Province of the Viceroyalty of New Spain, i.e., in colonial Mexico. These settlements took the form of large land grants (*ranchos* in Spanish), which were used to raise cattle and sheep. In 1784, for example, Manuel Nietos, a retired Spanish sergeant, was given one of the first, and the biggest, land concessions, namely, Rancho Los Nietos, a 167,000-acre spread in what is now Orange County and Los Angeles County. Almost all mission property and livestock were eventually taken over (through government grants) by such men. The ranches averaged nearly 19,000 acres each.

The Mexican owners of these ranches wanted very much to model their newly-won life-styles on those of the aristocratic dons of Spain, but often fell far short of this ambitious goal. (The honorific "don" was initially only used to address members of the Spanish nobility, but in 19th century California it referred to any Hispanic man of upper class status.)

Mexican California was a remote, relatively poor, and lightly-populated frontier region. Nevertheless, by studiously ignoring all the downsides of life there, many 19th century American books and illustrations chose to present it to their readers simply as a sunny, halcyon-

1 • Peoples of California

days-paradise peopled by handsome *vaqueros* (cowboys), flirtatious but virtuous women, selfless friars, and devoted Indian servants. Hubert Howe Bancroft, for example, explicitly linked pastoral California to the lotus-eaters of Greek mythology, citing Tennyson's poem by this name. The lotus was a plant with narcotic qualities and was said to cause its addicts to doze their lives away in peaceful apathy. This poem is so evocative of pre-war Mexican California that it needs to be quoted in part here.

Tennyson wrote:

> "Courage!" he said, and pointed toward the land,
> "This mounting wave will roll us shoreward soon."
> In the afternoon they came unto a land
> In which it seemed always afternoon.
> All round the coast the languid air did swoon,
> Breathing like one that hath a weary dream...
> Let us swear an oath, and keep it with an equal mind,
> In the hollow Lotus-land to live and lie reclined
> On the hills like Gods together, careless of mankind...
> Surely, surely, slumber is more sweet than toil, the shore
> Than labor in the deep mid-ocean, wind and wave and oar;
> O, rest ye, brother mariners, we will wander no more.[22]

In 1888, Bancroft described the *Californios* of the 19th century in phrases which today may strike some readers as patronizing. Nevertheless, it is still important for modern readers to understand what this famous writer had to say about the peoples he and his assistants studied so carefully, if only because so many educated Americans of the 19th century shared these views. The purpose of the following quote is not to present all aspects of this issue, but merely to present what Bancroft himself believed.

In his exceptionally detailed (808-page) study, *California Pastoral*, Bancroft assessed the *Californios* as follows:

> They were a frank, amiable, social, hospitable people.... No obligations of any kind weighed very heavily upon them. They were an emotional race; their qualities of mind and heart floated on the surface; they not only possessed feeling but they showed it.
>
> Great was their opportunity, exceedingly great at first if they had chosen to build up a large and prosperous commonwealth; and later no less marvelous, had they possessed the ability to make avail [to take advantage] of the progress and performance of others.

Nevertheless, as I have said, it would be difficult to find in any age or place a community that got more out of life, and with less trouble, with less wear and wickedness, than the people of Pastoral California.[23]

It would also be difficult to find horsemen willing to risk their lives by roping grizzly bears. As *Californios* began to establish huge ranches in Alta California, the numerous grizzly bears there sometimes killed their livestock and even posed threats to human life. To demonstrate their courage and horsemanship, *vaqueros*, working as a team, would rope a grizzly and drag it into a corral for a life-or-death battle with a wild bull placed there for that purpose. Since being close to a grizzly so terrified a horse that it became almost uncontrollable, a *vaquero* needed horsemanship of the very highest caliber to do this.

Colton describes such a grizzly bear hunt as follows:

> The king of all sports in California is the bear-hunt.... Each rider now uncoiled his lasso from its loggerhead [the place on the saddle where it was carried, coiled] and held it ready to spring from his hand, like a hooded serpent from the brake [from the canebrake, a dense thicket]. The bear ... plunged from the thicket ... and was leaping, with giant bounds ... for the dark covert of the forest beyond ... one [*vaquero*] looped him around the neck and brought him to a momentary stand. As soon as the bruin felt the lasso, he growled his defiant thunder and sprung in rage at the horse.... The horse knew as well as its rider that the safety of both depended on his keeping the lasso taught [*sic*; here Colton means "taut"].[24]

In addition to being able to participate in such exciting pursuits, the *Californios* did not have to struggle along under a heavy burden of legal baggage. On 1 June 1847, for example, U.S. Consul Larkin wrote to the New York *Herald* describing what he called the "lawless blessedness" of life there: "'Tis said that Mexico had laws in C[alifornia], but they cannot be found and the oldest residents have no remembrance of them either in theory or practice."[25]

When the war was over, however, and a careful search was made of the Mexican archives in Monterey, some Mexican laws were finally discovered. After being translated and edited, they were published by the Americans on 20 September 1849 under the title of *Translation and digest of such portions of the Mexican laws of 20 March and 23*

May 1837, as are supposed to be still in force and adapted to the present condition of California.[26]

There was another and very different point of view about life in pastoral California. In 1919, for example, the American historian and Pulitzer Prize-winner Justin Harvey Smith (1857–1930), an early specialist on the U.S.–Mexican War, offered his scathing and highly prejudiced comments on this seigneurial society. (In this context, "seigneurial" is a much more accurate term than "feudal." It comes from the French *seigneur*, i.e., "lord," and evokes the paternalistic rule of a leader or a boss—*jefe* in Spanish—over his extended family, his workers, and his lands.)

Smith wrote:

> Under Mexican rule, California, the Golden West, was anything but golden. It was poor, shiftless, and pitiful; unprotected, underdeveloped; unenlightened; unconsidered; helpless and almost hopeless. Although the province extended from the Pacific to the Rocky Mountains, only a small strip some fifty miles wide was occupied by white men, and but a small part of that fraction consisted of farms regularly [legally] owned. The famous missions, wrecked by the Mexican government, lay in ruins. In ten degrees of latitude there was but one considerable seaport, Monterey, a village of about one hundred small houses; and the only other sizeable town, Los Angeles, contained some 1500 persons, with perhaps an equal number in places depending upon it.
>
> The Californians were genial, kindly, hospitable, faithful in their married life and gracefully polite; but in the view of many, if not the majority, courage and truthfulness were either follies or luxuries, and no element of practical efficiency entered into their composition. A man got up some time before noon. [Here Smith is describing the life of a very rich and very lazy rancher; a poor rancher would have to rise before dawn.] He would not work or even walk [rich or poor, a *Californio* would never walk if he could ride]. He neither read nor thought. A monotonous diet of beef, beans, wine, brandy, and chocolate, supplemented with cigarettes and a guitar, satisfied his appetite perfectly. What he demanded next was a horse. As an infant he had begun life with a ride to be baptized, and the saddle was his real home.[27]

An equally vivid but more positive description of the pleasure-loving *Californios* comes from Colton. He wrote:

> You might as well attempt to extinguish a love of air in a life preserver as the dancing propensity in this people.... They think nothing of riding

a hundred and forty miles in a day, and breaking down three or four horses doing it.[28] [There were so many horses running wild in California that they had very little value. Riders could therefore use and discard them at will.]

In 1847, First Lieutenant William T. Sherman (later of U.S. Civil War fame) also had good things to say about the *Californios*:

> The people are very fond of riding, dancing, and shows of any kind. The young fellows took great delight in showing off their horsemanship, and would dash along, picking up a half-dollar from the ground, stop their horses in full career and turn on the space of a bullock's hide, and their skill with the lasso was certainly wonderful. At full speed they could cast their lasso about the horns of a bull, or throw it as to catch any particular foot. These fellows would work all day on horseback in driving cattle or catching wild horses for a mere nothing, but all the money offered would not have hired one of them to walk a mile. The girls are very fond of dancing, and they did dance gracefully and well. Every Sunday, regularly, we had a *baile*, or dance, and sometimes interspersed through the week.[29]

In about 1846, Alta California had a non–Indian population of appreciably less than 10,000 men, women, and children—a very small total even when compared to the lightly-settled remainder of northern Mexico.[30] The big ranches were the homes of about 800 prosperous ranchers and their families, who were known as *Californios*. Writing in 1890, Guadalupe Vallejo, the nephew of one of their most able leaders, General Mariano Guadalupe Vallejo, described their style of life in these perhaps too-glowing terms:

> No one need suppose that the Spanish pioneers of California suffered many hardships or privations, although it was a new country. They came slowly, and were well prepared to become settlers. All that was necessary for the maintenance and enjoyment of life according to the simple and healthful standards of those days was brought with them.
> They had seeds, vines, cattle, household goods and servants, and in a few years their orchards yielded abundantly and their gardens were full of vegetables. Poultry was raised by the Indians [who served as subsistence-level workers for the Hispanics], and sold very cheaply; a fat capon cost only twelve and a half cents. Beef and mutton were to be had for the killing [these domestic animals multiplied so rapidly on the free range land that they had very little value and could be used by any

1 • Peoples of California

Hispanic who needed them], and wild game was very abundant. At many of the Missions there were large flocks of tame pigeons.

In the old days every one seemed to live out-doors. There was much gaiety and social life, even though people were widely scattered. We traveled as much as possible on horseback. Only old people or invalids cared to use the slow [two-wheeled] cart, or *carreta*. Young men would ride from one dance to another for parties, and whoever found his horse tired would let him go and catch another.

In 1806 there were so many horses in the valley about San Jose that seven or eight thousand were killed [to preserve the pasturage]. Nearly as many were driven into the sea at Santa Barbara in 1807, and the same thing was done at Monterey in 1810. Horses were given to the runaway sailors, and to trappers and hunters who came over the mountains.[31]

The other side of this socio-economic coin, however, was that the poorest *Californio* ranchers lived in miserable one-room homes, where as many as 10 to 15 family members and retainers slept crowded together on a dirt floor. Colton found that

the house of the humbler Californian has often but one apartment [only one room], and is without fireplace or floor. Here a family of ten or fifteen tumble in and sleep on the ground. If they have guests, which is often the case, they turn in among the rest. The thicker they lie, of course the less covering they need.[32]

Virtually all the lowest-level manual workers on these ranches were California Indians who, as former residents of the missions, had learned to speak some Spanish and knew how to handle and ride horses with consummate skill. For their labor on the ranches, however, they received only rudimentary room, board, and clothing—but no pay.

One of the best examples of an early California rancher is Mariano Guadalupe Vallejo (1808–1890), who was also a *Californio* military commander and a politician. He was reputed to have been the richest man in California before the Gold Rush and it is worth learning something about him here.

Vallejo was an extremely intelligent man whose life spanned the colonial, Mexican, and American eras of California.[33] Born into an upper class *Californio* family in Monterey, the capital of Alta California, Vallejo was honed for leadership at an early age. His mentor was Governor Pablo Vincente de Solá. Thanks to their close relationship, Vallejo read government documents and newspapers from Mexico City and was given access to the governor's personal library.

Vallejo later worked as a clerk for William Hartnell, an English merchant, who taught him English, French, and Latin. When news of Mexico's independence from Spain reached Monterey, Vallejo, who was then the personal secretary of the new governor of California, Luis Argüello, promptly joined the army as a cadet. He was so able that he was soon appointed to the territorial legislature and then, in 1829, successfully led a group of Mexican soldiers against a rebellious band of Indians led by Chief Estanislao.

Chief Estanislao (c. 1798–1838) was notorious for leading groups of armed Indians in attacks against Mexican outposts and missions. Because he is one of the few California Indians of the time for whom there are good historical records, it is worth digressing here to say something about him. An excellent source on his life is a remarkable 220-page handwritten memoir of Mexican California life drafted in 1851 by the cattle rancher and Mexican customs official Antonio María Osio (1800–1878).

In 1843, Osio had been granted a 48,189-acre ranch in what is now western Marin County and also held other large ranches in this region. His memoir is the earliest extant narrative account of the period 1821 to 1846. It is written more in the vein of a long, informal "conversation" between author and reader than a formally-structured essay.[34] Osio was a very patriotic *Californio*. One of the most moving points of his manuscript is how bitter he became because, for many years before the war, the Mexican government had consistently ignored the *Californios*, had done nothing to protect Alta California from an American invasion, and had singularly failed to develop it economically. He wrote:

> No *hijo del país* [literally, "son of the country," i.e., a *Californio*] was recognized by the Mexican government during its different periods.
> The Mexican government declared itself California's stepfather and denied it protection as if it were a bastard child.
> The government never considered the advantages to be gained by stimulating development in different parts of this territory, which was so ready for it.[35]

1 • Peoples of California

Osio's comments on Chief Estanislao are equally important. They can be summarized as follows, while retaining, word for word, as much of their original flavor as possible. Osio reported: "In 1829, the Mexican government had prohibited its officers from punishing the local Indians for minor offenses. As a result, these Indians started to behave insolently and began to entertain subversive ideas, i.e., how to free themselves from Mexican rule."[36]

At Mission San José (located about 50 miles southeast of San Francisco), Estanislao, who was the Indian *alcalde* (head man), fled from the mission in 1829 with all the members of his tribe. He was a natural-born leader, both by mentality and by physique. He could read and write, and a Mexican who had seen him was quite impressed, reporting that "he was about six feet tall, his skin was more white than bronze, and he was very muscular like a horse. [California Indian men tended to be short, dark-skinned, and wiry.] He had a very masculine-looking face."[37]

He and his followers moved to their *ranchería* (a small Indian settlement located about 50 miles east of the mission), which was made of wood and was well-camouflaged in a large grove of willow trees densely intertwined with vines and other climbing plants. The local priest, Father Narciso Durán, complained about their escape to the commander of the San Francisco presidio, and begged him to send enough soldiers to bring the fugitives back to the mission.

The commander accordingly sent out Sergeant Don Antonio Soto and 15 men on this assignment. As Soto and his men neared the grove, the Indians shouted the vilest possible personal insults and obscenities at them. Since Soto understood the Indian language, Estanislao guessed—correctly—that these shouts would so enrage him that he would throw caution aside and would order his men to attack the *ranchería* itself.

Soto thereupon entered the grove with six of his best men, who were wearing arrow-proof leather jackets. (Known as a *cuera* from the Spanish word for "hide" or "leather," such a jacket was a heavy, knee-length, usually sleeveless and collarless, protective garment made of up to seven layers of buckskin or cowhide and bound at the edges with a strong seam. For this reason, Hispanic soldiers were known for more than two centuries as *soldados de cuera*, i.e., "leather-jacket soldiers."[38])

The Indians aimed their arrows only at the unprotected parts of the soldiers' bodies. Four of the soldiers were immediately wounded by arrows fired at their faces and heads at very close range from Indian archers hidden in the dense undergrowth. Soto himself was hit under his right eye by an arrow. In order to continue to fight and defend themselves, the wounded men had to jerk the arrows out of their bodies, leaving the sharp flint arrowheads still embedded in their flesh.

The soldiers were forced to retreat from the grove in order to seek medical help. Soto himself later died from his arrow wound, but most of the others eventually recovered. This encounter was the Indians' first victory over the soldiers, and they celebrated it with great festivities and dancing. The commander of the San Francisco presidio, however, wanted to punish the Indians very severely, so he decided to send out another and more powerful expedition against them.

An expedition led by an experienced frontier officer, Lieutenant Don José Sánchez, was accordingly assigned this task. As a preparatory step, Sánchez had a stiff leather collar specially made and had it sewn onto his own leather jacket. This was a very wise decision. When he and his men reached the grove, they tried to set it on fire but the wood was too green to burn. Nevertheless, his soldiers continued to attack the Indians hidden there. An arrow struck the collar of the jacket Sánchez was wearing: it was deflected safely but otherwise it certainly would have killed him. To avoid any Mexican casualties, Sánchez and his men were forced to retreat.

The commanders of the presidios of San Francisco and Monterey then decided to send out a very powerful expedition headed by Lieutenant Don Guadalupe Vallejo and equipped with cannons. In the next battle, the Indians opened fire with their arrows but the Mexicans returned fire with their cannons, which proved to be the decisive weapons. Even when the cannon balls themselves did not kill or wound the Indians, the great number of sharp splinters they blew off the sides of the *ranchería* certainly did.

Seeing that the *ranchería* was too vulnerable to be a safe refuge, the Indians then retreated to foxholes which were hidden in the ground and were covered by blackberry brambles. The Mexicans ordered both their troops and those of their Indian allies (who were fierce enemies of Indians in the *ranchería*) to "kill and destroy." This they did with pleasure. Some of the Indians who were considered by the Mexicans

1 • Peoples of California

to be "very evil" were hanged from the tallest trees with ropes made of vines. Estanislao himself managed to escape and, at the request of Father Durán, he was later pardoned.

To return now to Vallejo: his rise to power continued as he became commander of the presidio of San Francisco in 1833; supervised the secularization of Mission San Francisco Solano; was granted Rancho Petaluma by a new governor; and, in 1835, was named *comandante* (commander) of the highest military command in Northern California. To counter a perceived but non-existent Russian threat from Fort Ross, which is located about 70 miles northwest of San Francisco, Vallejo later began to build a presidio in Sonoma, about 35 miles north of San Francisco Bay. He had a fine two-story house constructed there (most of the buildings in California at that time had only one story), even though a contemporary observer thought that Sonoma itself was only a "most dull and ruinous" outpost.[39] In a remarkable example of Mexican-Indian military cooperation, he also formed a lasting friendship and alliance with Chief Solano, who provided Vallejo with over 1,000 Indian warriors to use in Mexican campaigns to defeat Indian rebels.

Increasingly involved in domestic and regional politics, Vallejo came to believe that Mexico's best hope for economic, social, and cultural progress lay with the United States. Thus in April 1846, when he was commandant of the Mexican garrison in Sonoma, he could ask rhetorically,

> Why then should we hesitate still to assert our independence? We have indeed taken the first step, by electing our own governor, but another remains to be taken ... [annexation by the United States]. In contemplating this consummation of our destiny, I feel nothing but pleasure, and I ask you to share it.
>
> When we join our fortunes to hers, we shall not become subjects, but fellow-citizens, possessing all the rights of the United States and choosing our own federal and local rulers. We shall have a stable government and just laws. California will grow strong and flourishing, and her people will be prosperous, happy, and free.[40]

During the 1846 Bear Flag Revolt (this was a 26-day rebellion by American settlers in California against Mexican rule and will be discussed later), Vallejo was taken prisoner by the Americans and was held without any formal charges being filed against him. Despite the harsh treatment he received in his captivity (he contracted malaria then, which reduced him to a weight of only 98 pounds), he eventually decided to cast his lot with the American victors—in hopes of improving post-war conditions for his fellow *Californios*.

Once the U.S-Mexican War was over, Vallejo persuaded wealthy *Californios* to accept American rule, but he himself fell upon hard times. A protracted legal challenge to his land title cost him a great deal of money and deprived him of almost all his land and livestock. When he finally died in 1890 at his simple ranch in Sonoma, he had been reduced to a very modest lifestyle.

Since Vallejo had been the leading member of the *Californio* community, it is not surprising that he shared their common fate after the war. The Americans treated almost all Mexicans and Mexican-Americans simply as foreigners, depriving them of any political power and forcing them down to near the bottom of the social and economic ladder. Only the California Indians were in a worse position.

• 2 •

Foreigners in Alta California

There were not many foreigners living in Alta California, but some of them would play important roles in the run-up to the U.S.–Mexican War, in the war itself, and during the transition to civilian rule after the war.

By the end of 1845, there were probably about 800 American residents in California and perhaps 500 other foreigners of various nationalities, most of them living in the Sacramento Valley or along San Francisco Bay.[1] Almost all of these individuals devoted themselves to business, unlike the *Californios,* who much preferred the freedom and romance of ranching.

A few of the foreigners went through the process of acquiring Mexican citizenship so they could become legal owners of land, but most did not trouble to do so. Some of them were cultured, disciplined, hard-working individuals, but as the American historian Justin Harvey Smith tells us in his uncharitable but probably accurate fashion,

> by far the greater number were mere squatters ... working a little, hunting or trapping more, but mainly waiting for something to turn up. They were in general a rough-looking set: the vicious, devil-may-care sailor, the gaunt, awkward, ragged immigrant, the heavily bearded, leather-coated hunter with his long hair turbaned in a colorful handkerchief; and while some had excellent brains and hearts of gold, the scale ran down to a very low point. Little work and less law was the motto of not a few ... probably almost all agreed in despising the inefficiency of the native [the *Californio*], his passion for dress and dancing, his guitar, his bland smile and his dainty politeness.[2]

One of the earliest Americans to foresee the commercial potential of the Pacific coast was the explorer, adventurer, and author John Ledyard

(1751–1789). Noticing during his extensive travels that sea otter furs from the American northwest were much appreciated by Chinese officials in Macau, who valued their luxurious warmth and who would pay very high prices for them, Ledyard lobbied in the 1780s for the establishment of sea otter fur trading companies, presumably with himself as a major figure. Such companies would trade sea otter furs for Chinese silk and porcelain, for which there was a ready market in the United States.

Ledyard failed to find backers for his plan and he must drop out of this book now. However, his idea was a very good one and was seized upon both by the Russians and the Americans. Historians at present-day Fort Ross State Park tell what happened next:

> The Russian-American Company ... hunted with no regard for the future of the sea mammals. Nor did the merchant trade ships of the north Pacific. From 1803 to 1805, over 17,000 sea otter pelts were taken in California waters. At times, American trade ships worked together with the Russian-American Company. The American merchants supplied the ships and the Company supplied the labor of the Native Alaskans. A joint venture between the Company and American Captain O'Cain resulted in the highest known catch of otter in one year—9,356 pelts were taken.
> The Company hunted all the way from Trinidad Bay in Humboldt County to Baja California. Ivan Kuskov, Ross's first manager, reported that over 2,000 pelts were taken in the first years at Ross. In the 35 years that the Russian-American company was in California, over 100,000 pelts were taken. Most of these pelts were shipped to China via these same merchant vessels. By the 1820s, the California sea otter had almost completely disappeared.[3]

One of the earliest American businessmen in Alta California was Alfred Robinson (1806–1895), who sailed to Monterey in 1829 as an employee of Bryant, Sturgis and Company, a Boston-based firm specializing in the California hide and tallow trade. In this business, hides from California cattle were stockpiled by Mexican ranchers at ports such as San Diego and Monterey. Crews from foreign ships (usually American ships) dried and cured the hides and then transported them to Boston, where they were turned into fine shoes and boots. Hides were such an important and such a lucrative trade item that they became known as "California banknotes." (The price of one dried hide on the California coast was $1.50, but when that same hide was carried by ship to Boston and was sold there, it cost about $4 to $5.00.[4]) Tallow was sent by ship to South America (often to Peru or Chile), where it was used to make soap and candles.

Robinson is remembered today for his book, *Life in California*, which he began well before the war broke out but did not publish until 1847. It is a generally sympathetic but sometimes highly critical account of *Californio* life and of its political turmoil during the Mexican Republic.[5] Robinson strongly believed that the United States should annex California. He wrote rhetorically:

> During the anarchy which existed [in Mexican California] in past years, throughout this fertile country, there were many of the native Californians who would have been thankful for the protection of either England or America; and indeed, a great many desired it, in preference to the detested administration of Mexico.
>
> Perhaps, there are many who still feel as they did then: and in this age of "Annexation" [here Robinson is referring to the annexation of Texas by the United States], why not extend the "area of freedom" by the annexation of California? Why not plant the banner of liberty there, in the fortress, at the entrance to the noble, the spacious bay of San Francisco?
>
> It requires not the far-reaching eye of the statesman, nor the wisdom of a contemplative mind, to know what would be the result. Soon its immense sheet of water would be enlivened with thousands of vessels, and steamboats would ply between the towns, which would, as a matter of course, spring up along its shores.... All this may come to pass; and indeed it must come to pass, for the march of emigration is to the West, and naught will arrest its advance but the mighty ocean.[6]

Although many *Californios* had a high regard for Robinson as a person, some thought that he had painted an inaccurate, i.e., too negative, picture of their history and culture.[7] What is clear is that he did have a very low opinion of Mexican officialdom itself, writing that

> if Mexico, in her zeal for the welfare of her territories, had been more circumspect in the choice of officers for California, she would have not experienced the humiliation that she has borne, nor incurred the expense of so many expeditions to reconquer it. Her own people have been in all cases the fomenters; and here, as has frequently been done in Mexico, they have aimed at the removal of certain governmental officials, not so much for the desire for reform, as for the division of the spoils! This is the pretended patriotism of all Mexicans who have taken

active part in revolutionizing their own country, which has been disseminated by them amongst the Californians, till, like themselves, they have become *"Patriotas de bolsa!* ("Patriots of the pocket").

The cause of such ungovernable desires may be traced to their education [there were very few schools in Alta California], and the indolent manner in which they have been reared. Thus we may trace its origin to the time when Spain held sway over the American republics [and also] to the old Spaniards, who, whilst rolling in wealth, indulged in excessive indolence. This trait of character still exists among their descendants, and you might as well expect a sloth to leave a tree, that has one inch of bark left upon its trunk, as to expect a Californian to labor, whilst a *real* [a silver Mexican coin worth 12½ American pennies] glistens in his pocket![8]

After California was annexed by the United States in 1848 and became a state in 1850, Robinson worked as a ranch investor and land manager from the 1850s through the 1880s. Earlier, in 1836, he had married 15-year-old Anna Maria, a young daughter of José de la Guerra, who was one of the largest landowners in California. (It was not uncommon on the American/Mexican frontier for older men to marry much younger women.) Anna Maria died in 1855, however, and Robinson never got over this loss. He never married again and died in San Francisco in 1895.

The most famous foreigner who was active along the California coast before the U.S.–Mexican War was the seaman-author (and later eminent lawyer and politician) Richard Henry Dana, Jr. (1815–1882). Dana came from a prosperous family and enrolled at Harvard College. During his freshman year there, however, he contracted measles, which seriously affected his vision and thus his ability to continue his studies. Since the local doctors could do nothing for him, Dana decided to take a job as a merchant seaman, in hopes that two years of hard physical labor and outdoor living, well away from his books, would improve his eyesight.

So, in sharp contrast to others of his class, rather than embarking on a fashionable tour of Europe as a pampered passenger, in 1834 in Boston he joined the crew of the brig *Pilgrim* as a "light hand," i.e., an apprentice sailor who was not strong enough or experienced enough to do all the heavy work required of an older able-bodied seaman. As a common sailor, he served "before the mast," i.e., living in the dark, damp, cramped crew's quarters in the forward part of the *Pilgrim*, a vessel only 86 feet long, rather than in the more comfortable officers' quarters further aft.

The *Pilgrim* sailed from Boston, loaded with New England's manufactured goods, such as good quality shoes, foodstuffs, and ironware. When the ship arrived on the coast of Alta California, her crew gradually sold or traded all these goods for the dried cattle hides which had been collected and stored by local ranchers.

Dana's travels along the coast of Alta California brought him to Monterey, San Pedro, San Juan Capistrano, San Diego, Santa Barbara, Santa Clara, and San Francisco during 1835–1836. His job ashore was to cure the hides of California cattle and to load them aboard ship for transport to Boston. In the process of this tedious and back-breaking labor, not only did Dana regain his sight but he also wrote a diary which is now a treasure-trove of historical information. It was published in 1840 as an outstanding book, *Two Years Before the Mast*. Reading it today gives a vivid picture of Mexican California just before the U.S.–Mexican War.

After his tour of duty in California, Dana returned to Boston in 1836 as a common sailor aboard the East Indiaman *Alert* (an East Indiaman was a large ship, often British, engaged in trade with India). He then reentered Harvard, graduating in 1837; studied law; and as a lawyer and writer he championed the downtrodden members of society, e.g., seamen and slaves. Dana died of influenza in Rome in 1882 at the age of 67.

Dana Point itself and the city of Dana Point, California, located about halfway between Los Angeles and San Diego, are now named for him. The original *Pilgrim* sank in 1856, the result of a fire at sea. However, a modern full size reproduction of the brig *Pilgrim*, built in Denmark in 1945, has been sailed around Cape Horn and is now on permanent display at the Ocean Institute in Dana Point in California.[9]

Dana had many insightful things to say about California. Like so many of his contemporaries, he did not hold the *Californios* in very high regard. On the political front, for example, he says that

> revolutions are matters of constant occurrence in California. They are got up by men who are at the foot of the ladder and in desperate circumstances, just as a political party is started by such men in our own

country. The only object, of course, is the loaves and fishes,[10] and instead of caucusing, paragraphing, libeling, feasting, promising, and lying, as with us, they take muskets and bayonets, and seizing upon the presidio and custom-house, divide the spoils, and declare a new dynasty. As for justice, they know no law but will and fear.[11]

Despite his low view of the leaders of California, Dana presciently foresaw the future of this region. He wrote:

Such are the people who inhabit a country embracing four or five hundred miles of sea-coast, with several good harbors; with fine forests in the north; the waters filled with fish, and the plains covered with thousands of herds of cattle; blessed with a climate, than which there can be no better in the world; free from all manner of diseases, whether epidemic or endemic; and with a soil in which corn yields from seventy to eighty fold. In the hands of an enterprising people, what a country this might be![12]

Many Americans would come to share Dana's views. They would also begin to look upon California not only as a potentially valuable possession but also—given what they saw as its incurable mismanagement under the Mexicans—as *a rightful possession* of the United States.

Another important foreigner in Alta California was Johann Augustus Sutter (1803–1880). "Captain John Sutter," as he preferred to be addressed, was a Swiss adventurer who became a Mexican citizen and who is best known for his close association with the California Gold Rush. Before then, however, his fabled hospitality had already attracted many newcomers to what is now the Sacramento, California, area.

Leaving his wife and five children behind in Switzerland, Sutter came to San Francisco in 1839, hoping to make his fortune. In July of that year he paid a formal call on Mexican Governor Juan Bautista Alvarado to discuss his plans to settle in California.[13] Sutter had already decided to establish himself in the interior of California, i.e., on the Sacramento River, and asked Alvarado to appoint him as an *impresario de colonización* (a "contractor of colonization") to oversee the settlement of the lands he hoped to obtain.

Alvarado, however, demurred: an *impresario* was required to settle many families, and Sutter had only his Indian workers and some Caucasian employees. Nevertheless, Alvarado liked the idea of a permanent settlement inland, so he encouraged Sutter, explaining that if Sutter became a Mexican citizen (which he could easily do simply by living in California for one year), he would then be eligible to receive a grant of land. Alvarado added that Sutter could go to the Sacramento Valley himself and choose the land that suited him best.

Alvarado then warned Sutter about the Indians in this region, some of whom had become horse thieves when the missions closed and they lost their jobs there. To help Sutter control the traffic in stolen horses, Alvarado gave him a high-sounding official title—but nothing else. Sutter was now the *Representante del Govierno en las fronteras del Norte, y Encargado de la Justica* (i.e., the "representative of the government and agent of the law on the northern frontier").

Sutter was enormously pleased to have received, simultaneously, both official permission to settle in California and a sonorous title. He interpreted them to mean that he now would be able to exercise absolute power—civil, judicial, and military—over his new domain. This turned out to be true to some extent: the Sacramento River was so far away from Mexico City that the Mexican government's writ did not run there, and Sutter's 30 well-armed frontiersmen-employees (including Germans, Swiss, Canadians, Americans, Frenchmen, and Englishmen) would be more than a match for any handful of Mexican soldiers ever sent against them.

Sutter employed the local Indians, not only as laborers but also as reliable guards. In a letter of 13 March 1847, George McKinstry, the sheriff of Sacramento, advised Captain I.G. Hall, the commander of the Army's Northern District of California, that

> the soldiers of this Garrison [Sutter's Fort] are Indians instructed in the science of war by Capt. J.A. Sutter for the past seven years and can be employed at one half the expense that white men can and are far preferable for this service. Capt. J.A. Sutter has heretofore kept up a strong Garrison at this post at his individual expense which has had the effect of keeping the Indians of both valleys [the Sacramento and San Joaquin] quiet and the settlers have been protected at his expense. But now that an enlightened nation [the United States] has raised her Flag, Capt. Sutter will throw down the walls of his Fort that have protected him against the half-civilized Californians and the savage Indians at great expense and as an American citizen [will] look to that Flag for protection.[14]

In 1840 Sutter established near what is now Sacramento a colony he called "Nueva Helvetia" (New Switzerland). It quickly became a major attraction for all the trappers, traders, and immigrants who were passing through or settling in the region. In fact, Sutter's venture was so successful that he was soon a wealthy businessman and exercised a great deal of local power. As he put it, "I was everything—patriarch, priest, father, and judge."[15]

Other commentators, however, were not so charitable. In 1866, L.S. Tichenor, one of Sutter's own friends, said of him: "A heroic figure he was not, although his romantic position in the great valley [the San Joaquin-Sacramento] made him seem so to many travelers and historians ... his fate was the ordinary one of the persistent and unteachable dreamer."[16]

As the American philosopher Josiah Royce (1855–1916) described Sutter much later, "In character, Sutter was an affable and hospitable visionary, full of hazy ideas, with a great liking for popularity, and a mania for undertaking too much."[17]

In 1841, Sutter had his eye on a property—an Indian *ranchería* which he called Hock Farm, named after the nearby Hok Nisenan Indian settlement. The grant Sutter wanted the Mexican government to give him included two widely-separated properties and it was huge— more than 60 miles in length and embracing more than 48,000 acres. Sutter finally did get the grant, but the process became so marred by imprecision, errors, and a lost map that in the future he would run into enormous problems with squatters and in the courts.

Sutter's holdings were very well-situated for a commercial enterprise because they could draw trade and immigrants from three important travel corridors which converged there. These were (1) the inland waterways of the San Francisco Bay region itself; (2) the California Trail across the Sierra Nevada mountains; and (3) the Oregon-California Trail. When John Bidwell, the exceptionally able leader of a covered wagon expedition,[18] arrived in California with his followers in 1841 along what would become the California Trail, he reported that

> Sutter received us with open arms and in a princely fashion, for he was a man of the most polite address and the most courteous manners, a man who could shine in any society. Moreover, our coming was not unexpected to him. It will be remembered that in the Sierra Nevada one of our men named Jimmy John became separated from the main party. It seems that he came on into California, and, diverging to the north,

found his way down to Sutter's settlement.... Through this man, Sutter heard that our company of thirty men were already somewhere in California. He immediately loaded two mules with provisions taken out of his private stores, and sent two men with them in search of us.[19]

After his initial success, Sutter decided to expand his business and to build an impressive fort and trading post at what is now Sacramento. Finished in 1843, Sutter's Fort, as it was known, was about 170 feet by 425 feet in size. It boasted thick adobe walls (for protection against hostile Indians) which were 15 to 18 feet high and 3 feet wide at the base. It also housed cannons, shops, houses, mills, and warehouses, all staffed by assorted blacksmiths, millers, bakers, carpenters, and blanket-makers. The Indians who worked there were paid in a special coinage which could be only used to buy items in Sutter's stores. A visitor marveled at this enterprise as a "European-style fort—thick walls, gun towers, a great gate: the most ambitious fortification in California to that time."[20]

Nevertheless, Sutter's own failures as a manager kept him on the edge of financial failure. To quote John Bidwell again,

> Nearly everybody who came to California made it a point to reach Sutter's Fort. Sutter was one of the most liberal and hospitable of men. Everybody was welcome—one man or a hundred, it was all the same.... [But] he failed to keep up with his payments. And so he soon found himself immensely—almost hopelessly—involved in debt.... Every year found him worse and worse off, but it was partly his own fault. He employed men—not because he always needed and could profitably employ them, but because in the kindness of his heart it simply became a habit to employ everybody who wanted employment.[21]

In 1845, Lansford Hastings (1819–1870), a pioneer who developed and promoted a Western trail known as the Hastings Cutoff (this was a shortcut across what is now the state of Utah) expressed his thanks to Sutter in print, writing that "Captain Sutter ... rendered everyone of [Hasting's] party every assistance in his power; and it really appeared to afford him the greatest delight to thus be enabled to render important aid to citizens of his former, adopted country."[22]

Sutter's Fort marked the high point of Sutter's career. In 1847, he and James Marshall went into partnership and built a sawmill at Coloma, on the South Fork of the American River, upstream from

Sutter's Fort. The lasting fame of this location, however, was not due to trees: on 24 January 1848, Marshall noticed some sparkling objects in the gravel bed of the stream alongside the mill. These objects turned out to be tiny pieces of pure gold, which set in motion the California Gold Rush.

Sutter later lamented:

> As soon as the secret was out, my laborers began to leave me, in small parties first, but then all left, from the clerk to the cook, and I was in great distress. What a great misfortune was this sudden gold discovery for me! It has just broken up and ruined my hard, restless, industrious labors, connected with many dangers of life, as I had many narrow escapes before I became properly established.[23]

By the end of 1849, more than 100,000 people from all over the world had flooded into California to join the Gold Rush. Without his workers, Sutter was not able, by himself, to defend his property. As a result, his sheep and cattle were stolen, his land was occupied by squatters, and he went bankrupt in 1852.

• 3 •

The Mexican Army in Alta California

Under Mexican rule, presidios were the keystones of the Mexican army's role in Alta California. There were four presidios in Alta California—at San Diego, Monterey, San Francisco, and Santa Barbara—but they were only lightly staffed and very poorly provisioned. They could manage to keep the unarmed and unorganized Mission Indians in line and they could protect the missions from depredations by "savage" (non–Mission) Indians. They singularly failed, however, to deter the aggressive, well-organized, and heavily-armed Americans.

In 1781, Governor Felipe de Neve's *Reglamento é Instruccion para los Presidios de la Península de California* (Rules and Instructions for the Presidios of the California Peninsula) went into effect and gave the governor authority over both Californias.[1] The seat of government was Monterey. Alta California itself was split into four military districts, each with a presidio whose commander exercised civil and criminal jurisdiction within its limits.

At first, there were only three presidios—at San Diego, Monterey, and San Francisco. A fourth presidio, at Santa Barbara, was added later. The geostrategic importance of each of them, together with their date and place of founding, was as follows[2]:

- San Diego: Founded in 1769 at San Diego Bay, this presidio was the closest to other parts of Mexico. The bay was big but did have a narrow entrance which afforded some protection from ocean winds.
- Monterey: Although reports by the 17th century explorer Vizcaino had greatly exaggerated the size and safety of

Monterey Bay, a presidio was nevertheless built there in 1770 and became the capital of Alta California.
- San Francisco: The narrow entrance of San Francisco Bay (the Spaniards called it the *Boca de San Francisco*, that is, the mouth of San Francisco) made it a very protected anchorage. This was the northernmost presidio and was established in 1776. It also served the symbolic purpose of reinforcing Spanish claims on the northern coastline.
- Santa Barbara: The presidio, founded in 1782 in the Santa Barbara Channel, bridged the long distance between the presidios of San Diego and Monterey. It established a nominal Spanish military presence along the narrow corridor between sea and mountains, which otherwise would have been more vulnerable to Indian attacks.

The total military force of all the presidios in Alta California was remarkably small, given the great size of the region. It consisted of only four lieutenants, four sub-lieutenants known as *alféreces*, one doctor, six sergeants, 16 corporals, and 172 privates. The privates manned the presidios, cared for the horses and cattle, and carried the mail. Each soldier was issued a broadsword, lance, musket, pistols, six horses, a colt, and a mule. At every presidio, one horse was always kept saddled and ready for immediate use, day and night.

Social class played a major role in the selection of soldiers. In addition to the common rank-and-file troopers, there were usually some cadets and "distinguished soldiers" (*soldaros distinguidos*) at each presidio. The cadets were appointed by the viceroy and came from upper class families. When they joined the army, they initially had to serve in the ranks with the common soldiers but they lived and socialized with the officers. Upon being promoted, they became officers themselves, i.e., sub-lieutenants.

A "distinguished soldier" was anyone of "distinguished birth," such as an officer's son. He had to live with the troops but was exempt from doing any menial work. After being promoted to corporal and then to sergeant, he would become a sub-lieutenant, too.

No real military effort was made to defend Alta California against any foreign invasion: the region was too remote, too poor, and too

3 • The Mexican Army in Alta California

lightly settled. The best that could be done was to have, in theory at least, batteries of eight 12-pounders (cannons firing 12-pound balls) at each of the presidios, with gunners to man them. An inspection by an engineer-officer of the fortifications at three presidios (Santa Barbara had none) in 1797, however, proved that these installations were virtually useless, due to the lack of supplies and a total disregard for routine maintenance. The net result was that the long coastline of California thus lay virtually unprotected.

In 1810, as a rough guess, there seem to have been a total of about 500 men in the Mexican army in California. The enlisted men began their military careers at the age of 16. If parents had two or more sons, they kept one on their homestead and let their other(s) enlist if they wished. When enlisted men were not on duty, they could use their free time to make a little extra money by cutting firewood, making shoes, or repairing clothing.

Discipline was very strict. Even the time-honored soldier's pastime of grumbling could lead to severe punishment. For example, in one case cited by the historian Bancroft, a group of soldiers at the presidio in Santa Barbara made it known to their captain (through their sergeant, as military discipline demanded) that they wanted to learn how much money their unit had in its army account. In reply, after first forming the company into line, the captain walked up and down the line; asked who had any complaints; and told his troopers that he knew of cases where soldiers had been shot simply for complaining about the poor quality of the bread they had been given to eat. His soldiers were so terrified by this and similar stories he told that they begged his pardon. He granted it, and nothing more was said about the men's account.[3]

This same flawed military system continued long after Mexico became independent from Spain in 1821. It appears that there were then fewer troops in California than there had been previously. In 1835, for example, there were a total of only 307 military men, including 22 officers of all ranks, two of whom were naval lieutenants. According to an 1840 report of the Mexican minister of war, there were only 30 cannons of various bores in California. Some were made of iron and others of brass, but a number of them were dismounted; i.e., they could not be fired. The last report of the San Diego company, which dates from

November 1842, listed 14 men there—but without any arms or ammunition. At that time, the tiny port of San Diego was at a very low ebb: a contemporary illustration shows only a handful of small adobe houses scattered along the curving bay.[4]

Perhaps the best commentary on the deplorable state of the *Californios'* armed forces comes from the historian Bancroft, who recounts how, in July 1846, 400 to 500 *Californios*, all mounted, gathered together to attack Los Angeles. They had had neither food nor shelter for several days and to survive they were reduced to stealing pears and apples from private orchards. During their march, even their officers went hungry. There was only a single exception to this fact: José Castro, the commanding officer.

Lightly edited for clarity, here is Bancroft's description of what happened:

> In the Soledas valley, he [José Castro] received from the Guadalupe rancho a large supply for himself—namely, cooked provisions, poultry, and pastry. He supped alone, under a tree, with his back turned to his hungry companions. When he had satisfied his appetite, he wrapped up the things, and left the bundle on the ground, covered by his saddle.
>
> About midnight, Lieutenant José Antonio Chavez crawled to the spot, and brought away the eatables, and with his friends demolished them; after doing which, he went back with the bones, and placed them, together with some dry horse-dung, under the saddle. Then, finding a bottle with brandy in it, he of course confiscated it.
>
> Next morning Castro, on discovering the trick, looked around with a fierce scowl, using the vilest language, and threatening dire vengeance, but no one paid him the slightest attention. Ever after, on receiving new supplies, he would hold his orderly, Felipe Espinosa Barajas, responsible for them.[5]

Marine Corps lieutenant Archibald Gillespie, who will be discussed at length later on, had a very low opinion of Castro, denouncing him, in an 18 April 1846 letter to U.S. Navy Secretary George Bancroft (1800–1891), in these words:

> Don José Castro, the Commandant General, a man devoid of principal, ... is now endeavoring to get up a revolution to depose the Governor of California, Don Píco, who resides some four hundred miles south ... at the Pueblo de Los Angeles.
>
> General Castro has no force, say, twenty-five men, called Soldiers,

composed principally of degenerated Indians; but he can gather some two or three hundred Californians of Spanish blood, who have a holy terror of the American rifle, and will never expose themselves to make an attack.[6]

The military impact of the presidios in Alta California may have been very slight but their social impact was certainly considerable. As Professor Emeritus Sasha Honig, website editor of the California Mission Studies Association, has pointed out,

> The soldiers and their offspring became a major portion of the later rancho elite of California, along with the civilian settler families with whom they intermarried. These people were the seedbed of the Hispanic population of California, and even today in former presidio towns such as Santa Barbara, their descendants form an active part of community life.[7]

• 4 •

Preludes to War

On 13 May 1846, the U.S. Congress would declare war on Mexico but, in California itself, preludes to this gathering storm had long been evident.

Politically, California was very unstable: it would have no fewer than 12 governors and 15 administrations between 1822 and 1846.[1] Dorotea Valdez was a *Californio* servant who in 1874 had been given permission by her employer to talk frankly with an interviewer. She told him what, in her opinion, had happened when Pío Pico became governor and José Castro become the senior military commander. She said:

> The interests and private views of these men were completely opposite. This situation produced bad feelings to an alarming extent among the Californios of the north and the south. Pío Pico used every means within his power to move the Customs House from Monterey to San Pedro, which was the port for Los Angeles. Castro wanted the Customs House moved to San Francisco [both moves so that he could profit from them].
> Don Pío Pico was conspiring with Forbes [Alexander Forbes, an English or Scottish writer who urged Britain to colonize California] to turn the territory into an English protectorate.[2] Meanwhile Castro, with the assistance of General Vallejo, was doing his best to have the country annexed to the United States.
> To make a long story short, I will conclude by saying that if the Americans had not taken the country in 1846, by 1847 every *Californio* would have been killed in a civil war due to the bitter hatred that existed. No matter how much preaching was done by good men, nobody was willing to listen to the voice of reason.[3]

To add fuel to these political fires, California had by 1846 become a semi-independent republic which very much wanted "home rule," i.e., self-government, in its internal affairs—a state of affairs which the weak central government in distant Mexico City had no choice but to tolerate. In fact, the central government itself seemed to have little interest in retaining California—a distant and impoverished region that was more trouble than it was worth. Thus, despite vague promises to the contrary, the central government would do nothing of substance to help California during the war with the United States.

The *Californios* themselves could not agree on a single political leader. Political confrontations and armed clashes occurred frequently in Alta California between the *Californios* and the Mexican government, on the one hand, and between the competing factions of Alta California itself, on the other.[4] As indicated earlier, Alta California had, in effect, two rival political leaders, neither of whom had much power.

The first of these leaders was Governor Pío Pico, who ruled (after a fashion) from Los Angeles. He was the last Mexican governor of Alta California and asked, rhetorically and prophetically, "What are we to do with them [the American immigrants coming into Alta California]? Shall we remain supine, while these daring strangers are overrunning our fertile plains, and gradually outnumbering and diminishing us? Shall these incursions go unchecked, until we shall become strangers in our own land?"[5]

The other political leader was *comandante-general* of the Mexican army José Antonio Castro, who ruled (again, after a fashion) from Monterey. Like Pico, he was worried by the ever-increasing American presence and wanted Alta California to have a permanent semi-independent status under Mexican—not under foreign—rule.[6] Each man controlled different parts *of the region.* Pico was dominant in the south; Castro held sway in the north. U.S. Consul Larkin reported that

> the cause of the dispute between Pico and Castro is on account of the inhabitants of Monterey and the pueblo de los Angeles [i.e., the small city of Los Angeles] wishing to have their respective towns the capital, each aiming for the custom house to be in their vicinity, making two parties in California, and until the Governor and General reside in the same town, it will continue so.[7]

The net result was that at this time, as another contemporary observer would put it, Alta California "seemed a derelict on the Pacific."[8] Because it was too weak, too lightly populated, and disorganized to defend itself, the region now appeared, especially to the United States, to be exceptionally vulnerable to a possible takeover by a foreign power, e.g., most probably by Great Britain. (In 1841, the British had briefly considered trying to buy San Francisco Bay from Mexico because it would make such a fine port, but nothing came of this idea. Later, the British also considered bringing settlers to the San Joaquin Valley, thereby establishing a foothold in California, but this plan was dropped as California descended into political chaos before the U.S.–Mexican War.)

To make sure that no foreign country did in fact intervene in Alta California, the United States decided not to stand idly by and risk watching local disputes blossom into a pretext for foreign military intervention, either by Great Britain, the most likely candidate, or possibly—if much less likely—by France. In April 1840, Castro, in his capacity as chief magistrate of the province, had ordered the arrest of about 60 American and British nationals living in California, e.g., traders, farmers, and businessmen.[9] Of this group, 47 were found guilty of the trumped-up charge of inciting rebellion and were thrown into jail. One of these men, an American, died as a result of the harsh treatment he received there.

To free these prisoners and to forestall any further coercive acts by Castro or other Mexican officials, the American sloop-of-war *St. Louis*—127 feet long and with a complement, that is, a crew, of 125 officers and men—was ordered to Monterey. (A sloop-of-war was a three-masted vessel; a civilian sloop had only one mast. Unless otherwise stated, all references to sloops in this book are to sloops-of-war.) Although Monterey had long been the capital of Alta California, it did not impress two foreign visitors. One (who was not identified) described it simply as "a mean, irregular collection of mud huts, and long, low, adobe dwellings, strewn promiscuously over an easy slope, down to the water's edge."[10]

Another visitor—Marine Corps lieutenant Archibald Gillespie—wrote to the secretary of the navy on 18 April 1846:

> The Country in this vicinity is beautiful, and presents to the sea one of the most beautiful landscapes I have ever seen. The verdure is very rich, and the hills are covered with groves of pines, free from undergrowth, giving the ensemble the appearance of an extensive park.

> The town of Monterey is small, not containing over one hundred houses, built upon streets running back from the beach, but are in some cases far apart. Everything about the town has a primitive aspect, and nothing is to be met with, that will remind the traveler of the refinements of long settled countries.[11]

The *St. Louis* dropped anchor there on 15 June 1840 and her captain, Commander French Forrest, quickly landed his Marine Guard under Orderly Sergeant James Robinson. (The Marine Corps provided small infantry units, known as Marine Guards, for duties aboard U.S. Navy vessels. These men were trained to conduct offensive and defensive combat operations, both at sea and ashore. They were also ordered to protect the ship's officers in case the crew mutinied.)

As soon as Castro understood that the United States was ready and willing to use force to protect both its own citizens and other foreigners, he quickly backed down. He freed the captives and promised that henceforth he would respect the rights of foreigners. Thus, with his assignment so quickly and so easily accomplished, Commander Forrest set sail from Monterey on 5 July 1840.[12]

The next prelude to war came in 1842.[13] The secretary of the U.S. Navy had, the year before, assigned Commodore Thomas ap Catesby Jones ("ap" means "son of" in Welsh) to command the U.S. Pacific Squadron, which then consisted of the frigate *United States* (his flagship)[14]; the sloops-of-war *Cyane*, *Dale*, and *Yorktown*; the schooner *Shark*; and the storeship *Relief*.[15]

A frigate was a very powerful warship—a battleship, to use a much later term. Because the frigate *United States* carried a big crew (up to 600 officers, enlisted personnel, plus 50 Marines), was very well-armed (32 24-pounders and 24 42-pounders), and was so famously described in print by one of the seamen who served aboard her (Herman Melville, the future author of *Moby-Dick*), her story deserves to be briefly recounted now. It is relevant here because it gives such a unique "I-was-there" insight into some of the duties of the ordinary seamen of the Pacific Squadron during the U.S.–Mexican War.

The *United States* was a wooden-hulled, three-masted, 175-foot-long heavy frigate launched at Philadelphia in 1797. She would play active roles in the 1798–1800 "Quasi-War" with France; in the War of 1812; in the Second Barbary War of 1815–1816; in the U.S.–Mexican

War; and, finally, in the American Civil War. Herman Melville came aboard her as an ordinary seaman on 17 August 1843 at Honolulu. His novel *White-Jacket*, named for the ill-favored white jacket he made for himself to wear while on the ship, was published in 1850 and is a fictionalized account of his experiences on board the *United States*, which he renames the USS *Neversink*.

Melville had many good things to say about some of his fellow shipmates but he was highly critical both of the captain of the *United States*, who often appeared on deck intoxicated, and of flogging. Flogging consisted of repeatedly lashing the bare back of a fettered prisoner with a nine-braided whip known as "the cat o' nine tails." When not in use, the "cat" was kept in a cloth bag which was only opened so that flogging could begin: hence the expression "to let the cat out of the bag."

It was a joyous time for the whole crew when a far-ranging ship was homeward-bound at last. Melville gives us a very fine nautical description of the scene aboard the *United States* as she leaves for Boston, which she would reach in 1844. He writes:

> "All hands up anchor!"
> When that order was given, how we sprang to the bars [of the capstan, a device used to raise the anchor], and heaved round that capstan; every man a Goliath, every tendon a hawser ... till the [anchor] cable was straight up and down, and the ship with her nose in the water.
> "Heave and pall! Unship your bars, and make sail!"
> It was done: bar-men, nipper-men, tierers, veerers, idlers and all, scrambled up the ladder to the braces and halyards; while, like monkeys in palm-trees, the sail-loosers ran out on those broad boughs, our yards; and down fell the sails like white clouds from the ether—topsails, topgallants, and royals; and away we ran with the halyards, till every sheet was distended.
> "Once more to the bars!"
> "Heave, my hearties, heave hard!"
> With a jerk and a yerk, we broke ground; and to our bows came several thousands pounds of old iron, in the shape of our ponderous anchor.
> Where was White-Jacket [Melville, who wore an awkward white jacket he had made for himself] then? It was White-Jacket that loosed the main-royal, so far up aloft there, it looks like a white albatross' wing. It was White-Jacket that was taken for an albatross himself, as he flew out on the giddy yard-arm![16]

4 • Preludes to War

To return now to Commodore Jones: his ships mounted (carried) a total of 116 guns (cannons). Jones was instructed to protect American commerce at sea, to hone the discipline of his men by this active-duty service, and to collect any information that might affect the Pacific Squadron. His orders, however, did not say anything at all about *attacking* Alta California. Indeed, the secretary of the navy had specifically warned Jones that

> nothing but the necessity of prompt and effective protection of the honor and interests of the United States will justify you in either provoking hostility or committing any act of violence toward a belligerent ... especially a state [Mexico] with which our country is at peace.[17]

Nevertheless, Jones and his officers were quite aware of the lively rumors which were forecasting that Mexico would become part of the United States, and sooner rather than later. They also guessed that both France and England might have their own designs on California, too. Thus when Jones reached Callao, Peru, he learned there that a "formidable" French fleet had sailed from Valparaiso, Chile, in March 1842 towards an unknown destination—conceivably, he thought, as a possible first step toward a French occupation of Alta California.

In this connection, it should be noted that Count Eugène Duflot de Mofras—a young French diplomat, explorer, and mapmaker—had been sent out from Mexico City in 1841 to assess the potential of California and Oregon for French business interests and—perhaps for French colonial interests as well. De Mofras himself believed that both Britain and the United States would like to possess California. It was very evident to him, however, that undefended California could be taken by "whatever nation chooses to send there a man-of-war and two hundred men."[18] De Mofras very much hoped that France might somehow acquire California but he knew that the United States was so far ahead of any other country in the race that in the end the Americans would certainly prevail.[19]

On 5 September 1842, Jones heard in Callao that three English ships had left that port on a secret mission. The British had acquired Canada in the 1763 Treaty of Paris and were thought by the Americans to have designs on Alta California as well. To increase his growing concern, at about the same time Jones also received a message from the

U.S. consul in Mazatlán, Mexico, claiming that the United States was about to declare war with Mexico over the issue of Texas.

As a result of all these straws in the wind, Jones decided to sail from Callao to California at once. He put to sea on 7 September 1842, together with the *Cyane* and *Dale*, leaving instructions for the *Yorktown* to follow him. The next day he polled his officers, who agreed that if war had in fact been declared, it was clearly their duty to seize every port in California. Jones sent the *Dale* to Panama to learn if there was any news from Washington and ordered the *United States* and the *Cyane* head for California. They arrived at Monterey on 19 October 1842.

There, two Mexican officers approached them in a small boat and said that they had no knowledge of war having broken out. However, the mate of the American ship *Fama*, which was moored nearby, said that reports of war were current in Hawaii and that he had also heard rumors that England planned to take possession of California.

In Monterey, the Americans clearly had the upper hand in military terms. They had at their disposal about 800 men and 80 cannons; the Mexicans had no troops or weaponry of any military value. Given the reports and rumors that he had heard, Jones decided that, under these circumstances, *doing something* was better than doing nothing. So at 4:00 p.m. on 19 October 1842 he sent ashore Captain James Armstrong, commander of the *United States*, to demand that the Mexican authorities surrender to the American force off their port.

Armstrong accordingly delivered to Governor Juan B. Alvarado an ultimatum demanding that he surrender by 9:00 a.m. the next day. In this ultimatum, Jones awarded himself a sonorous, newly-minted title which lacked any legal basis: "Commander-in-chief of the United States naval forces on the Pacific station and of the naval and military expedition for the occupation of Old and New California, etc."

Two Mexican officials duly came on board the *United States* on 20 October 1842 an hour and a half before the deadline. Since nothing could be settled on the spot, however, in the middle of the morning and in keeping with the threat stated in the ultimatum, 150 American troops (i.e., three divisions of Jones's troops, known as "Stormers," plus the Marines on board) went ashore and marched up a hill to a small fort, which the Mexicans had just vacated. There was no fighting

4 • Preludes to War

whatsoever, and when Jones went ashore himself the next day, he discovered that the mails, i.e., orders and letters sent by sea, had been delayed but made no mention of hostilities. It was clear, in short, that war between the United States and Mexico *had not been declared.*

Jones therefore apologized profusely to the Mexican officials and, on the afternoon of 21 October 1842, the Americans quietly returned to their ships. After friendly farewell parties and other U.S.–Mexican festivities, Jones and his men sailed from Monterey. Jones himself was temporarily recalled by his government for his unwarranted attack but would return to Alta California at the end of the war as commodore of the Pacific Squadron.

Here it is worth adding something more about U.S. Consul Larkin. He was an American businessman who, after several financial ups-and-downs elsewhere, had arrived in Monterey (the "jumping-off place of the world," as he put it sarcastically) in the ship *Newcastle* to seek his fortune. Before he arrived in California, he had been very prejudiced against the Mexicans, writing to his cousin in 1831 that they were "a people I always dispised and detested."[20] Nevertheless, he was extremely eager to make money and he quickly understood that he would in fact be able to do so in California—but only if he overcame his own prejudices. This he managed to do, writing in 1842 to his wife Rachel (spelling and punctuation as in the original): "[I do not] look on the Mexicans so ill as many foreigners do—I have lived to long with them not to have some good feelings for them, and believe they return that feeling towards me."[21]

Larkin was an intelligent, upwardly-mobile man who could swim with the current. That same year he wrote to a merchant friend:

> I am remarkably well situated with this Government and its people; I never meddle seriously in their policies. I never speak against their laws, modes or religion. In my travels I have found almost all the people have some habits to be praised as well as to blame. They appear to be satisfied with me & why should I not be so with them.[22]

The able and affable Larkin prospered in his new homeland. In 1835, for example, he built a fine two-story house in Monterey that tastefully combined New England and California architecture, using both New England designs and California adobe bricks and redwood. Known as Larkin House, it is now a National Historic Landmark and

California Historical Landmark. Larkin also constructed the first wharf in Monterey (a welcome step to improve the loading and off-loading of ships); rebuilt the Customs House there; and successfully engaged in trade with Mexico, the Sandwich Islands (Hawaii), and China.

What is more important in terms of this book, however, is that Larkin had also impressive political skills, which he used in 1842 to help smooth out U.S.–Mexican relations during Jones's precipitous military intervention. Larkin's success in this endeavor brought him to the attention of the Tyler Administration in Washington, D.C., and in 1843 President Tyler appointed him as the first (and last) American consul to Alta California.

Larkin was a very well-informed observer of conditions in Alta California and in 1845 correctly predicted that "the pear [California itself] is near ripe for falling."[23] To lessen his consular duties, he hired a vice consul—William Leidesdorff (c. 1802–1848)—in San Francisco. Leidesdorff became the wealthiest man in San Francisco, was extremely active in civic works, and was hailed by his contemporaries as being "liberal, hospitable, cordial, confiding even to a fault." On the day of his burial, the town was in mourning, the flags were at half-mast, and business was suspended.[24]

When President Polk assumed office in 1845, most observers thought that war with Mexico was virtually certain. Indeed, early in 1846, Secretary of State James Buchanan instructed Larkin to pass the word—secretly—to all interested parties that the United States was ready to support any attempt by Alta California to cut its ties with Mexico.

Always quick off the mark, Larkin had already begun discussions with Mexican general Mariano Vallejo in hope of arranging a peaceful annexation of California. However, before the talks could make any headway, the Bear Flag Revolt broke out on 14 June 1846; a settler from Vermont, William B. Ide, was named commander-in-chief; and Vallejo was imprisoned by a band of Americans.

Larkin believed that California would surely pass into the hands of the Americans because of the great economic advantages this would entail for the United States. He argued that

> with a better state of affairs [under an American government] and an industrious race of inhabitants [the Americans], Upper California could

supply all the Polynesian Islands, San Blas [Mexico], Acapulco [Mexico], and the Northwest Coast, with wheat, beans, peas, flour, fat, tallow, butter, cheese, pork, bacon, salmon, horses, mules, ships' spars, boards, shingles, staves and vessels [and with gold, silver, lead, sulfur, coal, slate, and mercury as well].

The magnificent waters of San Francisco could this day harbor all the vessels afloat in the world. Many whale ships visit it for supplies, and more would do so, were it not for the vacillating laws and desertion of the men from their vessels, favored by those on shore. And the Anglo-Saxon race would soon send their exports over the whole Pacific ocean. It must and will be the medium stopping-place from New Orleans and New York to the China ports, now open to the world.[25]

Larkin's role in the U.S.–Mexican War will be discussed in the coming chapters. His successes thereafter can be briefly traced as follows.[26]

Once the war was over, Larkin focused on new commercial opportunities. In a partnership with another man, he established a settlement at Carquinez Straits (located about 30 miles northeast of San Francisco) that grew into the present city of Benicia. Larkin's main business interests were in San Francisco itself, however, so after a few years he sold his holdings in Benicia. He was well-placed in San Francisco to profit from the economic and political boom that followed the Gold Rush. When the 1849 Constitutional Convention was held in Monterey, he served as a representative from San Francisco.

Larkin built the first brick building in San Francisco in 1850 and then moved temporarily to New York that same year with his family. He later petitioned the U.S. government, unsuccessfully, for repayment for funds he said he had spent on naval supplies and for work he had done on the Monterey Customs House and on the wharf.

Once back in California, he had a fine 18-room brick house built for his family on Stockton Street in San Francisco. It had three stories facing Stockton Street and five stories to the rear, which overlooked a garden of 300 plants. The family's lifestyle was one of conspicuous consumption, opulence, hospitality, and gentility. At a time when common laborers were making only $1 day, the grocer and butcher bills for the Larkin household came to $377.20 in May 1857; sherry was ordered by the gallon.

Larkin acquired at least six land-grant ranches in California; engaged in land speculation; and at that time was believed by some to be the richest man in the United States. As he grew older, however, his love for the simple life of early California days grew stronger. He wrote Abel Stearns, one of his dearest friends from those times: "I begin to yearn again after the times prior to July 1846 and all their honest pleasures and flesh pots of those days. Halcyon days they were. *We* shall not enjoy their like again."[27]

In January 1857, Larkin wrote to President-elect Buchanan seeking a political appointment, either a post in Mexico or the position of United States marshal for San Francisco. However, Larkin did not receive any reply from the new administration, probably because he had supported Frémont, Buchanan's Republican opponent in the recent Presidential election. He made no further effort to return to public life.

In 1858, Larkin contracted typhoid fever when he went out to the Sacramento River to inspect his holdings there, despite the fact that he had been warned that many of the ranch workers there were sick. He died within a week at his home in San Francisco and is now buried in Colma, California.

• 5 •

A Secret Mission to California

U.S Marine Corps lieutenant Archibald Gillespie is sent out on a secret mission to California, after first meeting with President Polk in Washington, D.C., on 30 October 1845.

One of the earliest and most significant milestones in the Pacific Coast campaigns was evident well before the United States-Mexican war was formally declared in 1846. A key figure on this stage, and later as well, was Archibald Gillespie (1810–1873)—an upwardly-mobile 33-year-old U.S. Marine Corps lieutenant who would play a major role in the conquest of Alta California.[1]

Given Gillespie's importance at that time, it is surprising that not more has been written about him. The Department of Special Collections at the Los Angeles library of the University of California holds the Archibald H. Gillespie Papers. These are described by the University of Virginia's Institute for Advanced Technology in the Humanities as follows:

> Being the private and public papers of Archibald Hamilton Gillespie, special messenger from the President of the United States to Fremont, Captain and Brevet Major of the California Battalion of Mounted Riflemen, and Commandant of the Southern Department of the territory of California during the conquest.
>
> A magnificent collection of almost 500 documents concerned with the Conquest of California and its aftermath, and over five hundred pages concerned with Gillespie's private life. Neither Bancroft nor Hittell [Theodore Henry Hittell, 1830–1917] had access to these documents nor have they been used by any historian…. [The Institute mentioned above does not explain why these documents have not been used by

scholars.] No life of Archibald Gillespie, one of the most important figures in the Conquest of California, has ever been written.[2]

Commissioned in the Marine Corps in 1832, Gillespie's first assignments were routine and probably very boring, commanding (successively) the Marine Guards aboard the U.S. Navy ships *Fairfield*, *Vincennes*, *North Carolina*, and *Brandywine*. When he finally returned to the main naval base at Hampton Roads, Virginia, after these tours of duty he was not in good health, so he asked for a very low-key, non-strenuous posting, merely to be in charge of the clothing store at the base. The commandant of the Marine Corps had very different plans for him, however, and ordered Gillespie to report in person to George Bancroft, the secretary of the navy, in Washington, D.C.

At his interview with Gillespie, George Bancroft asked him if he could speak and write Spanish well. When Gillespie confirmed that indeed he could, Bancroft assigned him to carry secret dispatches from Washington, D.C., to California—but only after first meeting with President Polk. This meeting was duly arranged for 30 October 1845.

Following his meeting with Gillespie (which, alas for future historians, was not recorded in any further detail) President Polk made this intriguing entry in his diary:

> I had a confidential conversation with Lieut. Gillespie of the Marine Corps, at about eight o'clock p.m. on the subject of the secret mission on which he was about to go to California. His secret instructions and the letter to Mr. Larkin, United States Consul at Monterey, in the Department of State, will explain the object of his mission.[3]

The net result of the meeting was that Gillespie was ordered to travel, incognito, to California as a merchant going there for his health and for his business interests. In the best cloak-and-dagger fashion, he was given false identity documents drawn up for this purpose, showing him to be not a Marine Corps officer but rather a member of the respected Boston firm of William Appleton & Company, which traded regularly along the California coast.

Of course, this flimsy and transparent disguise fooled no one in California. For example, Angustias de la Guerra Ord,[4] a Mexican lady who will be quoted again in this book, told an interviewer many years later:

5 • A Secret Mission to California

Larkin, the American Consul, introduced Gillespie to the upper crust of Monterey society at a dance he hosted in his home. He told us that Señor Gillespie was an ill man who had come to travel through California to see if his health might improve. He arrived in San Francisco on an American warship. I must confess that neither I nor Señora Spence was deceived by that so-called introduction. We found it difficult to understand why the U.S. government would send an entire warship just to bring an ill young man to California. I must point out that nothing was mentioned about Gillespie being an officer on that ship.[5]

In any case, it was widely rumored, both then and later, that what the President really wanted Gillespie to do was to encourage the *Californios* to revolt against the Mexican government—so that, before too long, California would become part of the United States.

There is no direct documentary proof to support this assertion but some indirect evidence does exist. For example, a 17 October 1845 dispatch from Secretary of State James Buchanan, which reached Larkin on 17 April 1846 in Monterey, says in part: "While the President will make no influence to induce California to become one of the free and independent States of the Union, yet if the People should desire to unite their destiny with ours, they would be received as brethren."[6]

At the same time, Larkin was also instructed "to inspire them with a jealousy of European domination and to arouse in their bosoms that love of liberty and independence so natural to the American Continent."[7]

Gillespie himself wanted to read between the lines and was therefore quick to conclude that getting the *Californios* to rebel was in fact the real reason for his mission to California. What is clear is that, at Polk's instigation, Gillespie suddenly became a secret agent for the U.S. government. He was so pleased by this assignment that on 16 November 1845 he confidently wrote a quick thank-you note to George Bancroft, which reads in part:

> To you, Sir, I cannot say what I would wish at a moment like this [Gillespie was then leaving New York by ship en route, by stages, to California, his final destination], setting forth on an adventurous enterprize; but I can assure you, you will not regret having named me for this service, & that it will ever be borne in grateful remembrance, & I trust, that should I be successful I may not be forgotten,—& will then receive the only reward a Soldier aspires to obtain—[a promotion].

We will soon discharge our pilot [ships had to hire a pilot when coming into a major port like New York], and the Brig Petersburgh [carrying Gillespie] will be well on her road to Vera Cruz.[8]

Later pages of this book will chronicle Gillespie's activities in the California campaigns themselves. Suffice it to say here that the Treaty of Cahuenga (signed on 16 January 1847) brought peace to Alta California but not, alas, to Gillespie himself. Indeed, for him the Alta California campaigns turned out to be the high point of a very promising career that subsequently went sharply downhill.

Gillespie returned to the United States in 1847. Promoted for his valiant service in California, he later held a variety of Marine Corps assignments in the United States but he was always hounded by ill health and, it appears, by a lack of honesty as well. He was assigned as the senior Marine officer in the Pacific Squadron under Captain Mervine, who was then commanding the *Independence*. Before this ship could set sail from New York, however, Mervine charged that Gillespie had "swindled his messmates and brother officers out of money paid him by them for the mess stores."[9] Gillespie therefore resigned from the Marine Corps in October 1854 in order to escape a court-martial.

His life then went from bad to worse. His wife, whom he had met and married in about 1848, left him. He went to San Francisco, arriving there in February 1855, but soon afterwards Mervine published an article in the *San Francisco Chronicle* denouncing him as a thief. Gillespie then moved to the Sacramento area, where he held a series of low-level political appointments. He eventually died in obscurity in San Francisco in 1873 at the age of 61.

• 6 •

The Californios *Expel an American Expedition*

An American expedition, led by the explorer and U.S. Army captain John Charles Frémont and guided by the famous scout Kit Carson, comes down into Alta California from the Sierra Nevada mountains. On 5 March 1846, however, the Mexicans order them to leave, so they slowly move toward Oregon and set up camp there, just north of the California border, on 9 May 1846.

The official goal of this U.S. government expedition was to discover the source of the Arkansas River on the eastern slope of the Rockies. The river, which begins in the Arkansas River Valley in Colorado, formed part of the U.S.-Mexico border established in 1821 by the Adams-Onís Treaty. However, apparently without any official authorization, the leader of the expedition—John Charles Frémont (1813–1890), then a captain in the U.S. Army's prestigious Corps of Topographical Engineers—led his men very far into the west, namely, over the crest of the Sierra Nevada mountains and then down to Sutter's Fort in the Sacramento Valley of central California.

Frémont was energetic, physically fit, intelligent, and entirely self-serving. His own ambition—and thus the reason for this unique journey—was to be able to push himself forward as a Presidential candidate if war with Mexico finally broke out.[1] Because he is by far the most controversial and most colorful American character of the U.S.–Mexican War era, he merits being discussed now in some detail.

A complex personality, Frémont was hailed as the "Pathfinder" by his many contemporary admirers. That said, however, he has not fared so well at the hands of later biographers. In 1943, for example, the

The California Campaigns of the U.S.–Mexican War, 1846–1848

Pulitzer Prize and National Book Award-winning historian Bernard DeVoto had very negative things to say about Frémont in his carefully-researched book *The Year of Decision: 1846*. DeVoto concluded that Frémont "repeatedly jeopardized the United States.... He was worse than a fool, he was an opportunist, an adventurer, and a blunderer on a truly dangerous scale ... he made a play for every opportunity that would serve John Charles Frémont."[2]

Frémont was a master of the art of self-justification. Perhaps as a result of this questionable skill, he was also very prone, especially in his later years, to make ill-fated career and financial decisions. Nevertheless, his personal story is so interwoven with the conduct of the war itself that it is important to recount some of it here.[3]

Frémont's father died when Frémont was still a child. Gifted with a good mind, no shortage of self-confidence, and an ability to find protectors wherever he went, he got a job at the age of 13 as a clerk with a Savannah lawyer. Impressed by the lad's intelligence, the lawyer helped Frémont get an education. After studying mathematics and astronomy (he would find these skills very useful later in his life as he explored and wrote about some of the many unmapped portions of the American West), Frémont was hired to teach mathematics to U.S. Navy cadets aboard the sloop *Natchez*. Then, in 1838, he was appointed a second lieutenant in the U.S. Corps of Topographical Engineers and he led surveying expeditions into the West.

On a visit to Washington, D.C., Frémont fell in love with pretty, 15-year-old Jessie Benton, the highly intelligent daughter of the influential Missouri senator Thomas H. Benton (1782–1858), the chairman of the Military Affairs Committee of the Senate, and eloped with her. At first, Benton was furious, but the charming young couple soon won him over and Benton quickly became Frémont's most powerful supporter.

The Benton-Frémont relationship was based on mutual needs. The Senator needed a handsome man with excellent outdoor and public relations skills to win public support for the doctrine of Manifest Destiny.

Frémont, for his part, needed a well-placed, powerful politician through whom he could be in close contact with the President, the Congress, and the American public. Moreover, this well-placed politician

(Benton) could also help him get the plum assignments which would lead to rapid promotion. Thanks to Benton's help, in 1842 Frémont was given command of an expedition to explore the Rocky Mountains. Together with Kit Carson, who will be discussed presently, Frémont reached the Rockies and symbolically planted an American flag on the summit of a high peak. This publicity stunt would be featured later in Frémont's campaign posters when he ran, unsuccessfully, for the U.S. presidency in 1856.

When he returned to Washington, D.C., at the end of the Rocky Mountain trip, Frémont wrote a report on the expedition. Studded with tables of geographical data which he had calculated based on his own astronomical readings, it contained a narrative of high literary quality. This was in part due to his wife Jessie, who not only edited her husband's work but who also played an important role by drawing out and helping to shape his memories of his travels and adventures. The report was published by the U.S. Senate in March 1843 and was read by a public eager to know much more about and—in many cases, eager to move into—the American West.

From 1842 to 1846, Frémont was guided by the celebrated frontiersman and Indian fighter Kit Carson (1809–1868), who first achieved international fame through Frémont's accounts of their expeditions along the Oregon Trail and into the Sierra Nevada mountains. Carson's own story—his nickname, "Kit," was a family abbreviation of his first name, "Christopher"—is so remarkable and so extensive that only a few of his adventures can be mentioned here.[4] Writing in 1922, the historian Charles L. Camp summarized them in these words in an article in the *California Historical Society Quarterly*:

> From his home in Taos, New Mexico, Carson made no less than six journeys to the Pacific, and engaged in events which brought California under the wing of our republic, participating in the Bear Flag revolt and in Fremont's military activities during 1845–46. He guided Kearny's army of the West down the Gila [River] and across the Colorado Desert and played a notable part in the battle of San Pasqual. As official messenger he carried to the States the first news of the acquisition of California, and two years later, news of the gold discovery. He helped establish the direct route across the Great Basin followed by the emigrants of 1846 and the gold rush days. All this gives Christopher Carson a lasting place in the history of California.[5]

Because his frontier family was so poverty-stricken (his father had been killed by a tree he was felling), Carson was forced to go to work at the age of 14 as an apprentice saddle maker in Missouri. He never learned to read and write, although he could eventually sign his own name. Not wanting to spend his whole life making saddles, however, at the age of 16 he quit and got a job helping to manage the horses, mules, and oxen of a large trading caravan heading for Santa Fe. Later, he became a beaver trapper in the Rockies, where he honed his outdoor skills and began to learn Spanish and seven Indian languages.

Carson married two Indian women—first an Arapaho lady whose name in English was "Singing Grass" (by whom he had a daughter) and later, when she died of a fever following childbirth, a Cheyenne woman known in English as "Making-Our-Road," who left him to follow her own tribe's travels. His third and last wife was 14-year-old Josefa Jaramillo, the daughter of a prominent Mexican family in Taos, New Mexico, by whom he had eight children.

By about 1842, beaver trapping had become a moribund profession due to over-trapping and the change in men's fashions: hats made of beaver felt were no longer in demand and were replaced by top hats made of silk. Beaver trappers, grumbling, "Hell's full of high silk hats,"[6] were forced to look for new jobs. Fortunately for Carson, in 1842 he met Frémont on a Missouri River steamboat. Frémont was then looking for a guide for his expedition to South Pass on the Continental Divide of the Rockies. Carson was ideally suited for this job because he had already spent some time in that region. Their five-month-long expedition was a great success. Frémont's report on it was published by Congress, and it set in motion nearly endless lines of covered wagon caravans taking pioneer families into the West.

In 1843, Frémont and Carson embarked on a second expedition, in part to determine whether the fabled "Buenaventura River" really existed. This was a long-sought but mythical river allegedly flowing west from the Rockies into the Pacific Ocean. If such a river had indeed existed, it might have been used to carry American goods to the Pacific and thence, by sea, for sale in China. The expedition proved that the Buenaventura did not exist. In 1845, Congress published Frémont's account of this second expedition, further burnishing both his and Carson's reputations.

6 • *The* Californios *Expel an American Expedition*

In 1845, Frémont left St. Louis on his third expedition, again with Carson as his guide. This expedition, ostensibly undertaken to find the source of the Arkansas River on the eastern side of the Rockies, would enmesh both men very deeply in the Pacific Coast campaigns of the U.S.–Mexican War. As stated earlier, to further his own chances for glory, Frémont, ably supported by Carson, led this expedition far into the west, i.e., down the western slopes of the Sierra Nevada mountains and into California. It is clear that he had glory on his mind then: he wrote that "in arranging the expedition, the eventualities of war were taken into consideration."[7]

To avoid repetition, most of the activities of these two men in the Pacific Coast campaigns will be covered later in this book. Now, due to limitations of space, it is necessary here to summarize very briefly the remainder of Carson's remarkable career, between the end of the U.S.–Mexican War in 1848 and his own death twenty years later.

In 1849, the first of many "blood and thunder" action novels starring Carson appeared. In fact, the "real" Kit Carson, according to U.S. Army lieutenant George Douglas Brewerton, who rode east with him along the Old Spanish Trail in 1848, was not, on the surface, an impressive figure. Brewerton knew him well and describes him as

> a plain, simple, unostentatious man; rather below the medium height, with brown, curling hair, little or no beard, and a voice as soft and gentle as a woman's. In fact, the hero of a hundred desperate encounters, whose life had been mostly spent amid wildernesses, where the white man is almost unknown, was one of Dame Nature's gentlemen—a sort of article which she gets up occasionally, but nowhere in better style than among the backwoods of America.[8]

Another Army lieutenant—William T. Sherman—wrote of Carson along the same lines in 1848:

> I well remember the first overland mail that reached us in Alta California. It was brought by Kit Carson in saddle-bags from Taos in New Mexico. We heard of his arrival at Los Angeles, and waited patiently for his arrival. His fame was then at its height, from the publication of Frémont's books, and I was anxious to see a man who had achieved such feats of daring among the wild animals of the Rocky Mountains, and the still wilder Indians of the Plains. At last his arrival was reported at the tavern at Monterey, and I hurried to hunt him up.
> I cannot express my surprise at beholding a small, stoop-shouldered

man, with reddish hair, freckled face, soft blue eyes, and nothing to indicate extraordinary courage or daring. He spoke but little, and answered in monosyllables.... He remained at Los Angeles for some months, and was then sent back to the United States with dispatches, traveling two thousand miles almost alone, in preference to being encumbered by a large party.[9]

There seems to be almost no end to Carson's exploits. He helped defeat the Jicarilla Apaches in 1854. In 1858 he concluded a peace treaty between the Pueblo of Taos and the local Indians. When the Civil War began in 1861, Carson became a colonel of the New Mexico volunteers. In 1864, he sent his military unit deep into the Canyon de Chelly, the last Navajo stronghold, to force the Navajos there to surrender. Later, he became a rancher in Colorado. It was there, at the age of 59, that he died in 1868. His last words were addressed, both in English and in Spanish, to the doctor who attended him on his death-bed: "Doctor, *compadre, adios.*"[10]

To backtrack now and return to Frémont's and Carson's descent into California from the Sierra Nevada mountains in 1845: while the expedition itself had initially included only about 15 men, this number gradually rose to the point where Frémont now had nearly 70 heavily-armed frontiersmen under his command. They were all excellent shots and were tough-as-old-leather. Had the need arisen, they would have constituted a very potent fighting force. Indeed, Larkin described them as having "from three to six guns, rifles, and pistols each."[11] In fact, Larkin was quite sure that the men of Frémont's band were the only significant armed force in the whole of Alta California.

These men were much stronger, much better equipped, and much more experienced than the rag-tag Mexican army of Alta California. The Mexican army there was tiny and ineffective: it seldom exceeded 100 badly-trained and badly-armed men.[12] It should be noted here that, unlike their American counterparts, *Californio* civilians usually did not carry firearms in private life. The muskets, carbines (short-barreled muskets), and pistols used by Mexican soldiers tended to be archaic, heavy, and unreliable.

Some *Californio* gentlemen did carry a brace of heavy single-shot pistols in closeable leather holsters slung over the pommels of their saddles. These could be for hunting: indeed, Colton gives his readers a very exciting account of *Californio* men and women who used pistols to kill a bear.[13] In general, however, *Californio* men usually preferred, both as a matter of convenience and of personal honor, to rely instead on their long-bladed knives. Fighting with a knife was considered more "noble" than using a firearm because it required much more courage and skill. The knife was carried in a scabbard which was thrust inside the garter on a rider's right leg.[14]

When the *Californios* saw how strong Frémont's band was, they feared that it was only the advance wave of a forthcoming American invasion of Alta California. On 5 March 1846, the Mexican prefect, Manuel Castro, therefore ordered Frémont and his men, who were then camped in the vicinity of Monterey, to leave California immediately. All that Frémont did, however, was simply to move his camp six miles or so to Gavilán Peak (now named Fremont Peak, it is located 25 miles northeast of Monterey).

There he built a rough but strong fort of solid logs, cut from the abundant trees growing on the ridge, and—in a calculated insult to Mexican dignity—he raised aloft an American flag at the end of a long pole. In response to Larkin's messages to him, sent via courier and keeping him informed of *Californio* troop movements, Frémont replied to Larkin: "If we are unjustly attacked, we will fight to extremity and refuse quarter, trusting our country to avenge our death.... If we are hemmed in and assaulted here, we will die, every man of us, under the flag of our country."[15]

Despite his heroic posturing, however, Frémont realized that he could not stay on this peak forever. On his third day there, the pole so proudly bearing the American flag tumbled to the ground of its own accord. Taking this incident as a sign that it was now time to move on, Frémont and his men left the peak on the night of 9 March 1846 and set up camp again on lower ground only three miles away. Wisely, Castro did not try to attack him there, realizing that his troops would be met by blistering gunfire from Carson and from Frémont's backwoodsmen. However, the very fact that he had been forced by Castro to retreat would make Frémont even more eager to take military action in the coming months to salve his wounded pride.

Slowly and grudgingly, Frémont, Carson, and the rest of the men finally complied with Castro's order to leave Alta California. They made their way to Upper Klamath Lake in the Oregon Country, i.e., a region which was not under Mexican jurisdiction but which was jointly controlled by Britain and the United States.[16] Frémont later claimed that his purpose in going there was to connect this survey-trip with one he had made in 1843–1844 (when he had visited Klamath Lake from the north) and to penetrate the Cascade mountains. In fact, he simply wanted to be as close as possible to California—so that he could play a starring role if war broke out.[17]

• 7 •

Frémont Prepares for War

Gillespie, who has been trying to deliver official dispatches and private letters to Frémont, finally catches up with him at Upper Klamath Lake, Oregon, on 9 May 1846. That night, a band of Klamath Indians[1] attack their camp, killing three of Frémont's men. After burning some Indian villages in retaliation, the Americans return to Sutter's Fort, where Frémont—without any official authorization—begins to prepare for war with Mexico. To be ready to support Americans rebelling against Mexican rule, on 24 May 1846 he orders Gillespie to obtain military supplies from Captain John B. Montgomery, commander of the sloop USS Portsmouth, *which is moored in San Francisco Bay.*

When Gillespie left New York en route to Monterey, he had been given official dispatches from the State Department, which he was to deliver to Larkin. He first memorized them and then he destroyed them—a wise move because during the trip Mexican officials would search his luggage carefully. He rewrote the dispatches aboard the ship taking him to California (this was the 18-gun sloop *Cyane*, commanded by Captain William Mervine) and presented them to Larkin.

These dispatches were very far from being a clarion call to war. Instead, they simply directed Larkin to work quietly and peacefully to encourage the *Californios* to secede from Mexico. He was then to nudge them along gently to the point where they finally concluded that their own best interests in the future lay not with Mexico but with the United States.

Gillespie was also instructed to report to Washington any possible English or French plans to establish a protectorate in Alta California.

He was told to deliver to Frémont a packet of personal letters from Frémont's wife, Jessie. Moreover, he was also to give to Frémont some letters from Frémont's politically-influential father-in-law, Senator Thomas H. Benton, who was a strong supporter of Manifest Destiny.

However, at about same time as Frémont was reading his dispatches and letters at Upper Klamath Lake, far to the east in Concord, Massachusetts, the celebrated American essayist, lecturer, and poet Ralph Waldo Emerson (1803–1882) had just finished reading Frémont's book on his earlier travels in Oregon and California. Emerson sarcastically noted in his own journal:

> The stout [self-confident] Frémont, in his Report of his Expedition to Oregon and California is continually remarking on "the group" or "the picture," etc., "which we make." Our secondary feeling, our passion for seeming [sic; Emerson means "our passion for entering into the spirit of Frémont's account"] must be highly inflamed if the terrors of famine and thirst for the camp and for the cattle, terrors from the Arapahos and Utahs, anxieties from want of true information as to the country and the trail, and excitement from hunting, and from the new and vast features of unknown country, could not repress this eternal vanity of *how we must look*.[2]

In any case, after finishing the dispatches and letters, Frémont concluded that war was in the wind. He certainly believed that his own moment for personal glory had come at last. He therefore decided to reverse course, to return to Sutter's Fort with his expedition, to prepare for war, and to be ready to take some kind dramatic and provocative action against Mexico, even though the United States and Mexico were still at peace then.

First, however, Frémont, Kit Carson, and the other men had to survive a sudden Indian attack that night at Upper Klamath Lake. Since Carson tells this story so well, it is best to use his account here, which has been lightly edited to make it easier to read. Carson said:

> Shortly after Frémont lay down I heard a noise like the stroke of an axe. Jumping up, I saw that there were Indians in the camp, and gave the alarm. They had already tomahawked two men, Basil Lejeunesse and a Delaware, and were advancing to the fire, where four Delawares were sleeping. [The Delawares were Frémont's personal bodyguards.] They heard the alarm in time, and one of them named Crane got up and seized a gun. Unfortunately, it was not his own gun and was not

7 • Frémont Prepares for War

loaded. He did not know this, and kept standing erect trying to fire. He fell with five arrows in his breast, four of the wounds proving mortal.

The evening before I had fired off my gun for the purpose of cleaning it. In doing so I had accidently broken the tube [a metal tube which projected from the barrel of the rifle and channeled the explosive flame of a cap down onto the powder charge], and now had nothing but my pistol. I rushed upon the leader, and fired, cutting the string that held his tomahawk. Having no other weapon, I was now compelled to retire.

Maxwell [one of Frémont's men] next fired on him, hitting him in the leg. As he was turning around, Step [another one of Frémont's men] fired; the ball struck him in the back, passing near the heart, and he fell. The balance of his party then ran. He was the bravest Indian I ever saw. If his men had been as brave as himself, we surely would all have been killed. We had three men killed and one slightly wounded.[3]

Frémont and his men then "threw a blanket over Crane and hung blankets to the cedar boughs and bushes nearby, behind my camp-fire, as a defence against the arrows."[4] No more arrows were fired at them but they remained awake for the rest of the night, huddled down behind their "blanket defenses."

The next morning, Carson noted that the dead Indian had carried an English-made hatchet. Enraged, Carson used this hatchet to beat the Indian's head into pieces; one of the Delawares then scalped the skull. Frémont noticed that the dead Indian was carrying arrows with long "lancet-like" metal points, which Frémont thought might have come from a nearby Hudson's Bay Company trading post. American frontiersmen deplored the fact that private companies could, quite legally, sell items to the Indians which could easily be turned into weapons that could be used against the frontiersmen.

Frémont and his men were further angered when they concluded that the Indians who had attacked them were in fact the same Indians to whom they had given meat, tobacco, and knives a few days earlier. To get revenge, Frémont decided to kill some local Indians. Accordingly, Frémont's party spent the next several days making a clockwise circuit of the lake, killing any Klamath Indians they encountered on the way. They killed both individual tribesmen and small groups of them, leaving 14 Indians dead in one of the villages. The stated purpose of this slaughter was to discourage the Indians from ever attacking an exploring party again. It is not clear, however, how many—if any—

of the Indians they murdered had anything to do with the above attack.

On their way back to California, further adventures awaited Carson and Frémont. They wanted to attack an Indian town on the other side of a river, which they would have to cross to do so. Carson and his party therefor rode along the bank until Carson called out, "Here is a good place" to cross. He and the other riders promptly forced their horses to jump into the river. Instead of finding very shallow water, however, they discovered that it was 10 or 12 feet deep. All the riders promptly went in over their heads, wetting their gunpowder and thus making their guns useless in the face of the enemy. Luckily for them, Frémont and his party arrived just at that time and rescued them.[5]

After crossing the river, Carson and his men approached the Indian camp. Carson remembered that

> as we neared the camp we saw only one Indian, and immediately charged him. I was in advance. When I got within ten feet of him my gun snapped [the hammer of Carson's weapon duly flew forward when the trigger was pulled but the powder charge in the barrel was not ignited and thus the weapon failed to fire] and he drew his bow to fire on me. I threw myself to one side of my horse to save myself. Frémont saw the danger I was in, and ran his horse over the Indian, throwing him on the ground. Before he could recover he was shot.
>
> I consider that Frémont saved my life on this occasion, for, in all probability, if he had not run over the Indian as he did, I would have been killed.[6]

Frémont pressed on to California because, as he writes in his memoirs, "I saw the way opening clear before me. War with Mexico was inevitable."[7] He would later try to justify his actions there by asserting that the "private" or "secret" instructions he had allegedly received from Benton or from other unidentified higher authorities had ordered him to take military action to foil any possible English plot to seize Alta California. He claimed that he was simply trying to be a good soldier by obeying orders. He would write that

> the letter of Senator Benton ... was a trumpet giving no uncertain note. Read by the light of many conversations and discussions with himself and with other governing men in Washington, it clearly made me know that I was required by the Government to find out any foreign schemes in relation to California and to counteract them so far as it was within

7 • Frémont Prepares for War

my power. His letters made me know distinctly that at last the time had come when England must not get a foothold; that we must be first. I was to act discretely but positively.[8]

Frémont claimed that he had been ordered to accomplish this feat by carrying the war with Mexico into Alta California itself, even though he had no official instructions to do so. He knew that the United States wanted to possess California and understood that war was now inevitable. He would write melodramatically: "Then I knew that my hour had come. I resolved to return forthwith [from Oregon] to the Sacramento Valley and bring all the influence I could command. This decision was the first step in the conquest of California."[9]

However, as DeVoto explains, Frémont's repeated insinuations that he had received secret instructions invariably dissolve when the facts are studied. There were in fact no secret instructions of any kind: Frémont was simply making up a story to justify his actions, which were solely designed to further his own career. According to DeVoto,

> Frémont ultimately rests on the private letters from his wife and from Benton (neither of them qualified to give him orders or in this instance even advice), which, he says, were a kind of family cipher. (This cipher, we are to understand, consisted of oblique allusions to earlier conversations.) It all boils down to the fact that Benton again advised him to watch out for foreign intervention in California if war with Mexico—which Benton did not favor and did not expect—should break out, or the negotiations over Oregon should reach a crisis (as he did not think they would).[10]

The historian Bancroft reached a similar conclusion. He wrote:

> An impression has been prevalent that Frémont engaged in the revolt by reason of secret instructions from the United States, conveyed to him by Gillespie either in writing or verbally, or indirectly through private letters from Senator Benton. Frémont has never stated that he received such instructions: having of course no right to do so even if it were true. On the contrary, he has often denied it more or less directly.
>
> But in his testimony and that of Gillespie in 1847–8 room was left, designedly I think, for an inference that they could say more if at liberty to do so; and the spirit of this testimony, given at a time when he sought to legalize against the United States certain claims for supplies taken by Frémont's men, together with the secrecy observed by the government respecting the written instructions to Gillespie, Larkin, and Frémont, originated, as I suppose, the current theory to which I have alluded

[that he had received secret instructions], but which.... I regard as without foundation in fact.[11]

En route from Oregon back to Sutter's Fort, as soon as Frémont learned that the U.S. Navy sloop *Portsmouth*, captained by Commander Montgomery, was moored in San Francisco Bay, he sent Gillespie to the ship with a requisition for a large amount of military supplies, which could only have been needed in case of war with Mexico. Commander Montgomery would send an official letter to William Ide, the leader of the Bear Flag revolt, denying Ide's request for weapons. Some *Californios*, however, insisted that the *Portsmouth* was in fact helping arm the insurgents. Indeed, Manuel Castro, the Mexican prefect, even wrote to the minister of war in Mexico City on 19 June 1846, complaining that the ship was giving weapons to the rebels.[12]

In any case, Gillespie's shopping list of 24 May 1846 included the following items:

- 8,000 percussion caps. (At one cap per shot, this translates into 8,000 musket or rifle shots.)
- 1 keg of gunpowder.
- 300 pounds lead. (Melted down and cast into molds, this would make as many as 9,600 bullets.)[13]
- Food.
- Salt.
- Soap.
- Canvas (for tents).
- Iron (to be forged into horseshoes).

Frémont may have been self-serving but he was also prescient. Less than one month after Gillespie's visit to the *Portsmouth*, the American revolt against the Mexicans would begin in earnest in Sonoma.

• 8 •

The Bear Flag Revolt

During the short-lived Bear Flag Revolt, in which both Frémont and Gillespie play key roles, American settlers in California free themselves from Mexican rule on 14 June 1846.

The background of this revolt was that, in April 1846, Mexican Governor José Castro proclaimed that the purchase or acquisition of land in Alta California by foreigners who had not become Mexican citizens "will be null and void, and they will be subject (if they do not retire voluntarily from the country) to be expelled whenever the country might find it convenient."[1]

Rumors began to spread among American settlers that this edict would soon be enforced. Moreover, the settlers also feared that, as part of this process, the *Californios* would encourage the local Indians to set the settlers' crops on fire in order to drive the settlers away. Some of the settlers were sufficiently alarmed by these reports that they formally raised the issue of "Mexican aggression" in a meeting with Frémont. Although he did not promise to provide any military assistance to them himself, Frémont did tacitly encourage them to resist Mexican demands.

Using his own words, it is worthwhile here learning what the historian Bancroft had to say about the men who took an active part in the Bear Flag Revolt. His account of this event (contained in Volume V of his magisterial *History of California*) is still one of the best and most detailed. He says that "the revolution broke out soon after Frémont's return from Oregon; and it would not have broken out at all had it not been for the presence and cooperation of that officer and his hardy followers."[2]

Bancroft goes on to divide the Bear Flag revolutionaries into three different groups of what he terms "filibusters," using a historical definition of this term which means "persons engaging in unauthorized warfare against a foreign state."[3]

- The first group were those who

engaged in the revolt honestly as a measure of self-defense, whose fears of danger to life and property though unfounded were to some extent real.

- The second group

was a class—among the overland immigrants, deserters from vessels who had come up to New Helvetia [Sutter's Fort] from the bay [San Francisco Bay], and Frémont's men—composed of adventurers pure and simple. Reckless, daring, and unprincipled men, with nothing to lose, they were eager for a fight with the Californians, partly for the mere excitement of the thing, just as they were always eager for a fight with the Indians. In the turmoil of a revolution, something might occur to their advantage; at least, they could gratify certain personal dislikes [against the *Californios*]; and especially did they have an eye on the herds of the native rancheros.

- The third group consisted of

political adventurers, whose reward was to be not plunder in the vulgar sense, but glory and office and wealth under a reformed political system. Some were enthusiastic Americans, who believed in the manifest destiny of their nation to raise the stars and stripes anywhere in America without regard to the wishes of the natives.... Some of these leaders looked forward to official prominence in an independent California republic; others looked further, to contracting of debts, the issuance of bonds, and to future profitable negotiations with the United States; while still others looked upon the movement as but the beginning of a war in favor of the United States, from the government and people of which nation they expected great honor, and in which war they hoped to secure a more prominent position than if they waited for the [American] naval forces to begin hostilities.

Matters came to a head in June 1846, when General Mariano Vallejo offered 170 horses to Castro, who was then in Santa Clara. The American settlers heard—incorrectly, as it turned out—that these horses would be ridden by *Californio* troops whom Castro would send out to attack the American settlers. (The horses were in fact destined for use by Castro in central California against Governor Pico, his rival.)

Under the fiery leadership of Ezekiel Merritt, a former Rocky Mountain trapper, the angry settlers began to mobilize an armed force to stop the transfer of the horses. Merritt himself held a deep grudge against Vallejo because the latter had allegedly struck him at some point. Marius Duvall, a U.S. Navy surgeon in California in 1846–1847, described Merritt as "a brawny, stern man of forty years of age; he is hard featured, has bloodshot eyes and a peculiar stuttering speech. His whole appearance was that of a man moved by some revengeful intoxicating passion."[4]

The cumulative result of all these hostile feelings was that on the morning of 9 June 1846, a group of about 10 settlers, with Merritt in the lead, rode out to capture the horses and to prevent them from reaching Castro's forces in Santa Clara. Merritt's men were successful in this mission and brought the horses to Frémont's camp. They then sent Castro's men, who had been guarding the horses and some of whom they had captured, back to him with an insulting message: that if he wanted the horses back, "he must come and get them."[5]

About 10 more settlers joined the tiny American force, which then proceeded to attack Sonoma in the early hours of 14 June 1846 in order (as they saw it) to protect American lives and property there—which were not in fact in any danger whatsoever. It is important to note here that the settlers took this dramatic step long before news of the outbreak of the U.S.–Mexican War on 13 May 1846 had reached them. This news would not get to California until 2 July 1846, when three American Navy ships—the frigate USS *Savannah* and the sloops USS *Cyane* and USS *Levant*—brought it with them when they captured Monterey.

Early in the morning of 14 June 1846, Vallejo was rudely awakened from sleep when his home was surrounded by the insurgents—a motley band of armed men. When he understood what they wanted, he gallantly offered to surrender his sword to them. They refused to accept it, so instead he offered them some good brandy from his own cellar, which they accepted with evident pleasure but nevertheless still kept him prisoner.

Since Sonoma was not garrisoned by any Mexican troops, there was no fighting at that time. In a later skirmish, however, on 24 June 1846 Mexican captain Joaquín de la Torre would try to drive the insurgents out of Sonoma. His ill-considered effort resulted in the death of one of his own men and the wounding of several others, after which he and the remaining *Californio* troops retreated.

The insurgents held General Vallejo and a few other *Californios* as prisoners in Sutter's Fort and proclaimed their own independence from Mexico by establishing what is known, perhaps too grandiosely since it lasted only 26 days, as the Bear Flag Republic. In the process, they ran up the Bear Flag, which the settler John Bidwell described as follows:

> Another man left at Sonoma was William L. Todd, who painted, on a piece of cotton, a yard and a half in length, with old red or brown paint that he happened to find, what he intended to be a representation of a grizzly bear. This was raised to the top of the [flag]staff, some seventy feet from the ground. Native Californians looking up at it were heard to say "Coche," the common name among them for pig or shoat.[6]

The insurgents were accordingly dubbed the "Bears" and their movement has gone down in California history as the Bear Flag Revolt. This name may also be a play on the fact that some of these men may have lived along or near the Bear River, which rises in what is now Tahoe National Forest and flows into the Feather River near Yuba City, California. The original flag was destroyed in the San Francisco earthquake and fire of 1906, but today the state flag of California displays some of its features, e.g., the image of a grizzly bear.

One of the insurgents, William Ide, was a very energetic man with literary ambitions. According to one of his colleagues, he "was seized with a fit of writing, which continued almost incessantly for several days, all the time keeping his own counsel."[7] The result of Ide's labors was a "Proclamation of the Bear Flag Revolt," which listed not only the American settlers' grievances against the Mexican government but also his own promises for the future—in his new and self-appointed capacity as the "Commander in Chief."

The full text of this remarkable document reads as follows:

> To all persons, citizens of Sonoma, requesting them to remain at peace, and to follow their rightful occupations without fear of molestation.
> The Commander in Chief [Ide himself] of the Troops assembled at the Fortress of Sonoma gives his inviolable pledge to all persons in

California not found under arms that they shall not be disturbed in their persons, their property or social relations to one another by men under his command.

He also solemnly declares his object to be First, to defend himself and companions in arms who were invited to this country by a promise of Lands on which to settle themselves and families who were also promised a "republican government," who, when having arrived in California were denied even the privilege of buying or renting Lands of their friends, who instead of being allowed to participate in or being protected by a "Republican Government" were oppressed by a "Military Despotism," who were even threatened, by "Proclamation" of the Chief Officer of the aforesaid Despotism, with extermination if they would not depart out of the Country, leaving all their property, their arms and beasts of burden, and thus deprived of the means of flight or defense. We were to be driven through deserts, inhabited by hostile Indians to certain destruction. To overthrow a Government which has seized upon the property of the Missions for its individual aggrandizement; which has ruined and shamefully oppressed the laboring people of California, by their enormous exactions on goods imported into this country; is the determined purpose of the brave men who are associated under his command.

He also solemnly declares his object in the Second place is to invite all peaceable and good Citizens of California who are friendly to the maintenance of good order and equal rights (and I do hereby invite them to repair to my camp at Sonoma without delay) to assist us in establishing a "Republican Government" which shall secure to all: civil and religious liberty; which shall detect and punish crime; which shall encourage industry, virtue and literature; while shall leave unshackled by Fetters, Commerce, Agriculture, and Mechanism.

He further declares that he relies on the rectitude of our intentions; the favor of Heaven and the bravery of those who are bound to and associated with him, by the principle of self determination; by the love of truth; and by hatred of tyranny for his hopes for success.

He further declares that he believes that a Government to be prosperous and happyfying in its tendency must originate with its people who are friendly to its existence. That its Citizens are its Guardians, its officers are its Servants, and its Glory their reward.

William B. Ide
Head Quarters Sonoma
June 15, 1846[8]

A riveting firsthand account of the Bear Flag Revolt comes from Mrs. Rosalía Leese, sister of General Mariano Guadalupe Vallejo.

Known to her contemporaries as "a woman full of spirit" and interviewed in Monterey in 1874, she said in part:

> On June 14, 1846, at about 5:30 in the morning, an old man named Don Pepe de la Rosa came to my home and told me that a group of seventy-two ragged desperados had surrounded General Vallejo's house. Many of those men were sailors from whaling ships who had jumped ship. They arrested General Vallejo [and two other *Californio* leaders].
>
> Some of the men were wearing caps made from the skins of coyotes or wolves. Others were wearing slouch hats full of holes or straw hats as black as charcoal. Most of these marauders had on buckskin pants, but some wore blue pants reaching only to the knee [these were the breeches worn by deserters from Navy ships]. Several of the men were not wearing shirts, and only fifteen or twenty of the whole bunch were wearing shoes.
>
> After the General was hurriedly taken away, the marauders who had stayed behind in Sonoma raised a piece of linen cloth on the flagpole located in the corner of the plaza near the old mission church. The cloth was about the size of a large towel, and they had painted a red bear and one star on it. John C. Frémont was the man who had planned this all-out robbery of California. Even though he was an officer of the U.S. army, it is fair to assume that Frémont was afraid to compromise the honor of his government. He was not about to let his thieves steal California while waving the flag [the American flag] lovers of liberty throughout the world hold dear. This was why he adopted a flag [the Bear Flag] unknown to civilized nations.
>
> A few days after my husband was taken away, John C. Frémont arrived in Sonoma. Many paid writers have characterized Frémont with a great number of endearing qualities, but he was a tremendous coward. Listen to me! [Here Mrs. Leese recounts how, when Frémont was worried that a contingent of *Californios* might capture him] Frémont changed out of his fancy uniform into a blue shirt. He put away his hat and wrapped an ordinary handkerchief around his head. He decided to dress like this so that he would not be recognized. Is this the way a brave man behaves?
>
> I could tell you about the many crimes committed by the Bear Flag mob, but since I do not wish to detain you any longer, I will end this conversation with this: these hateful men instilled so much hate in me for the people of their race that, even though twenty-eight years have gone by since then, I still cannot forget the insults they heaped upon me. Since I have not wanted to have anything to do with them, I have refused to learn their language.[9]

The Bear Flag Revolt caught the usually well-informed Larkin entirely by surprise. He wrote, "Captain Fremont and Mr Gillespie ...

are supposed by the Californians to be at the springing of this business and fanning it on.... They have started the big Ball to roll.... I can not stop it."[10]

Frémont, for his part saw in the Bear Flag Revolt a golden opportunity for himself. He quickly abandoned any pretense of neutrality; arrived in Sonoma on 23 June 1846 at the head of about 60 soldiers; and took command of the Bear Flag Revolt in the name of the United States. Other settlers joined the Bears at Sonoma, bringing their total number to about 90 men.

James W. Marshall, who would later discover gold at Sutter's Mill in 1848, described this motley force thus:

> There were Americans, French, English, Swiss, Poles, Russians, Chileans, Germans, Greeks, Austrians, Pawnees [Indians from present-day Nebraska and Kansas], native Indians [California Indians], etc. Some wore relics of their homespun garments, some relied on the antelope and bear for their wardrobe, some [were] lightly dressed in buckskin leggins and a coat of war-paint, and their weapons are equally various.[11]

With such men in their ranks, Frémont's and the Bears' control over the lands north of San Francisco Bay was assured. It would pave the way for the Americans to seize control of the California coast shortly thereafter.[12]

Both the flags of the United States and of the Bear Flag Republic were raised at Sonoma on 4 July 1846 to celebrate the independence of both the United States and California. Following these festivities, Frémont proposed to the settlers that a volunteer militia should be organized under his leadership. Discussions continued the next day (5 July 1846) with the Bear Flaggers' initial commander, William Ide. It was agreed that such a 250-man militia should be formed immediately.

An agreement was therefore drawn up for all the volunteers to sign. With the signatures or marks of these newly-minted soldiers, what might be called Frémont's "California militia-battalion" was thereby born. Frémont was its chief and Gillespie was his adjutant.[13] The historian David Nevin gives this account of Frémont's speech when he accepted command of the unit:

> Frémont outlined his intentions, which were nothing less than to march south to seize the whole of California. No longer was this a simple uprising of men in the Sacramento Valley interested only in their own

protection [from Indians and from *Californios*]. Now they were a conquering force, committed to making California their own. *Without knowing that his country was at war and without authority, Frémont had precipitated a revolution and then had assumed its command.*[14]

• 9 •

The "Battle of Monterey" and the End of the Bear Flag Revolt

The "battle of Monterey" in California described here was merely a skirmish and must not be confused with the very bloody battle of Monterrey in Nuevo León, Mexico, which also took place during the U.S.–Mexican War and in which 488 Americans and 367 Mexicans were killed or wounded. In the unopposed "battle of Monterey" in California, a landing party from the U.S. Navy ships Savannah, Cyane, *and* Levant, *led by Captain William Mervine, occupies Monterey on 7 July 1846. Four days later, on 11 July 1846, the American flag is raised at Sutter's Fort, thus ending the Bear Flag Revolt.*

Monterey was the capital of Alta California from 1777 to 1846 under both Spain and Mexico and was the only legal port of entry for taxable goods. All shipments to Alta California by sea had to pass through the Customs House, which was built and modified in three phases: first by the Spaniards in 1814; then by the Mexicans in 1827; and, finally, by the Americans in 1846. It is now the oldest government building in the state and is California's Historic Landmark Number One.

On 4 July 1846, the harbor of Monterey was calm but the local *Californios* were anxious, having heard unsettling rumors of American aggression. One of the upper class *Californios* who supported the American invasion was a Mexican lady named Angustias de la Guerra Ord. Dictating her reminiscences in 1878 at the age of 62, she has left us such an outstanding firsthand account of the American capture of Monterey on 7 July 1846 that it deserves to be quoted here extensively.

Mrs. Ord said:

> If I remember correctly, there were one or two American warships in the port on July 4, 1846. A few days earlier, there already was talk that those ships were going to take the plaza on July 4, 1846. So with that in mind, the priest was told to finish the afternoon prayer very early. The people of the town believed so firmly that the plaza would be taken during that prayer, at about five-thirty or six o'clock a rumor spread through the church that the Americans were landing. The people left the church in a mad rush and one poor woman was injured.
>
> When the news of the taking of Sonoma was received, the superior officer of the American ships was informed. The ships had either entered the port after the event or were already here. The superior officer said that the incident had no connection with him or his authority.
>
> Finally the memorable 7th of July [1846] arrived. On the morning of that day, I well remember, there were in Monterey harbor 3 American warships, one of which flew the ensign of Commodore Sloat [John Drake Sloat, 1781–1867].
>
> During the morning the preparations could be seen. Many armed boats [ships' boats, not surfboats, which were not used until the battle of Veracruz on 9 March 1847] filled with men, came ashore and took possession without any interference. There was no garrison, and I believe that the only Mexican officer present was old Captain Mariano Silva.
>
> The taking of California was not at all to the liking of the Californians, least of all the women.[1] It must be confessed, however, that California was on the road to the most complete ruin. On one hand, the Indians were out of control, committing robberies and other crimes on the ranches, with little or nothing being done to curb their depredations. On the other hand, there was discord between the people [the *Californios*] of the north and of the south. In addition, both north and south were against the Mexicans from the mainland. But the worst cancer of all was the widespread plundering, which was carried on widely. There had been so much such looting of government resources that the funds in the treasury had bottomed out.
>
> General Castro maintained a corps of officers sufficient for an army of 3,000 men; all, good or bad, drew their salaries. These officers had no other use for the money than to grease the palms of their supporters, who would help them achieve their personal goals. Of these officers, very few offered their services when the hour came to defend the country against a foreign invasion. The greater part performed no more service than the figurehead of a ship.[2]

9 • The "Battle of Monterey" and the End of the Bear Flag Revolt

The Americans attacked Monterey at 7:00 a.m. Captain Mervine of the USS *Cyane* presented a formal demand to Mexican Captain Mariano Silva, the commandant of Monterey, stating that the United States and Mexico were now at war and that Silva must therefore immediately surrender all the forts, troops, arms, and public property under his control to Mervine and his men.

At 8:00 a.m. Silva replied that he could not surrender anything because he had no orders to this effect. He suggested instead that Mervine discuss the matter with the Mexican commandant general, to whom Mervine's summons was being forwarded. He said that he himself was leaving the town immediately. He wrote to Mervine that Monterey was in point of fact "peaceful and without a soldier; nor, according to information from the treasurer, is there any public property or munitions.... God and liberty!"[3]

At 9:30 a.m. a general order was issued by Commodore Sloat to the officers and men of his invasion force. Other regulations stressed that although the United States was now at war with Mexico, Mexican citizens must be treated with the greatest possible respect, for otherwise "eternal disgrace would be attached to our names ... by [any] indignity offered to a single female," and severe penalties were prescribed in any cases of plunder.[4]

The decks of the American ships were cleared for action and before 10 a.m. six landing boats from the USS *Cyane*, *Levant*, and *Savannah*, led by Mervine's gig (a gig is a long, light ship's boat reserved for use by the captain), approached the customhouse wharf, where at 10:20 a.m. about 250 sailors and Marines disembarked. A short proclamation by Sloat was read and was posted in English and Spanish. The American flag was raised and was welcomed by cheers from sailors and Marines. For their part, the American ships in the harbor fired celebratory 21-gun salutes. These ceremonies were over by 11:00 a.m. and the Americans settled into a peaceful and undemanding occupation of Monterey, which had surrendered without offering any resistance.

Not long thereafter (on 9 July 1846), 75 Marines and sailors from the USS *Portsmouth*, under Captain John B. Montgomery, landed at Yerba Buena (a little port in San Francisco Bay with about 900 inhabitants which in January 1847 the Americans would rechristen as "San

Francisco") and raised the American flag there.[5] Two days later (on 11 July 1846), the American flag was also raised over Sutter's Fort, thereby officially converting the short-lived Bear Flag Revolt into a formal United States military occupation of California.

It is worthwhile pausing here to learn what Edwin Bryant (1805–1869), a former newspaper editor and an *alcalde* (mayor) of San Francisco who will be quoted again later and at greater length, had to say about San Francisco when he visited it in September 1846 and in June 1847. He wrote:

> The water at the entrance [to San Francisco Bay] and inside is of sufficient depth to admit the largest ship that was ever constructed; and so completely land-locked and protected from the winds is the weather that vessels can ride at anchor at perfect safety in all kinds of weather. The capacity of the harbour is sufficient for the accommodation of all the navies of the world.
>
> The town of San Francisco is situated on the south side of the entrance, fronting the bay, and about six miles from the ocean.... A more approachable harbour, or one of greater security, is unknown to navigators. The permanent population of the town is at this time [September 1846] between one and two hundred, and is composed almost exclusively of foreigners. [In a footnote, Bryant adds, "In June 1847, when I left San Francisco, on my return to the United States, the population had increased to about twelve hundred, and houses were rising in all directions."] There are but two or three native Californian families in this place.
>
> The houses, with a few exceptions, are small adobes and frames, constructed without regard to architectural taste, convenience, or comfort. Very few of them have either chimneys or fireplaces. The inhabitants contrive to live the year round without fires, except for cooking.
>
> This place is, doubtless, destined to become one of the largest and most opulent commercial cities of the world, and under American authority it will rise with astonishing rapidity.[6]

Frémont's men, accompanied by a group of American settlers and by a company of American dragoons (light cavalrymen), dramatically rode into Monterey on 19 July 1846. They were about 160 in number. By combining, annotating, and editing several first hand contemporary accounts and a few modern versions, their travels and their entry into the little capital city of Alta California can be described along the following colorful lines.

9 • The "Battle of Monterey" and the End of the Bear Flag Revolt

Frémont himself wrote:

> Our cavalcade made a strange and grotesque appearance; and it was impossible to avoid reflecting upon our position and composition ... [our group was] guided by a civilized Indian, attended by two wild ones from the Sierra, a Chinook from the Columbia [River], and our mixture of American, French, German [frontiersmen]—all armed—four or five languages heard at once—above a hundred horses and mules, half-wild—American, Spanish, and Indian dresses [men's clothing], could be seen and equipments intermingled—such was our composition. Our march was a sort of procession. Scouts ahead and on the flanks; a front and rear division; the pack-animals, baggage, and horned cattle in the center, and the whole stretching a quarter of a mile along our dreary path. In this form we journeyed, looking more as if we belonged to Asia than to the United States of America.[7]

Another account of this same event comes from Lieutenant Frederick Walpole, an officer of the 80-gun British ship *Collingwood*, which had entered Monterey Bay only hours after Sloat had raised the American flag there. Walpole has this to say:

> During our stay in Monterey, Captain Frémont and his party arrived. They naturally excited curiosity. Here were true trappers, the class that produced the heroes of Fennimore Cooper's best works. These men had passed years in the wilds, living upon their own resources; they were a curious set.
>
> A vast cloud of dust appeared first, and then in a long file emerged this wildest wild party. Frémont rode ahead, a spare active-looking man, with such an eye! He was dressed in a blouse and leggings, and wore a felt hat. After him came five Delaware Indians, who formed his personal bodyguard, and have been with him through all his wanderings; they had charge of two baggage horses. The rest, many of them blacker than the Indians [due to their years under the sun], rode two by two, rifle held by one hand across the pommel of the saddle.[8]
>
> Thirty-nine of them are his regular men, the rest are loafers picked up lately; his original men are principally woodsmen, from the State of Tennessee and the banks of the upper Missouri. He has one or two with him who enjoy a high reputation in the prairies; Kit Carson is as well known there as "Duke" is in Europe [here "Duke" probably refers to the British duke of Wellington, Arthur Wellesley (1789–1852), who defeated Napoleon I at Waterloo].
>
> The dress of these men was principally a long loose coat of deer skin, tied with thongs in front; trowsers of the same, of their own manufacture which, when wet through, they take off, scrape well inside with a

knife, and put on as soon as dry; the saddles were of various fashions, though these and a large drove of horses, and a brass field-gun [a cannon], were things they had picked up about California. They are allowed no liquor—tea and sugar only; this, no doubt, has much to do with their good conduct; and the discipline, too, is very strict.[9]

Most of Frémont's men were a very rough group. With 300 extra horses in their *caballada* (a *caballada* was a herd of horses from which riders selected their mounts), the earth seemed to tremble as they passed. Variously armed with single-shot rifles or muskets, with five-shot Colt revolvers,[10] and with Bowie knives,[11] these men, with their long hair and black bushy beards framing keen eyes, "made a strong impression," thought Frémont approvingly, as they moved through the streets of Monterey. They stopped in groups of six or seven and chatted with admirers from the U.S. Pacific Squadron, from the British ship *Collingwood*, and from Monterey itself. Their numbers, their formidable appearance, and their splendid marksmanship, "astonished all and made the Englishmen stare."[12]

• 10 •

The California Battalion

The California Battalion is formed on 23 July 1846 and sets sail from Monterey to conquer Southern California. It will be disbanded by Frémont in April 1847 in the Sacramento area.

Commodore Robert Field Stockton (1795–1866), commanding officer of the U.S. Navy's Pacific Squadron, officially authorized the formation of the California Battalion, a 250-man military unit, on 23 July 1846. The modern historian Neal Harlow described this ambitious, egotistical, and very combative officer as follows:

> Commodore Robert F. Stockton, a person of very considerable wealth and fame, energy and imagination, had volunteered for service in the Pacific, hoping to fall in with some rewarding action.
> Though short in stature, he was of somewhat lordly mien, self-centered, with an appetite for adventure and a taste for glory. He ... had fought pirates, served in the War of 1812, and earned the sobriquet of "Fighting Bob" through a propensity for dueling. In 1843–1844 he had supervised the development of an experimental low-lying, sail-and-steam-driven naval vessel, the *Princeton*, which carried among its armament two great cast-iron guns, one of which burst during a demonstration on board, killing the Secretaries of State and Navy.
> Afterwards he had accompanied what was reputedly his own "navy" to Texas to foster annexation and to urge its President ... to start a war with Mexico.[1] [The president of the Republic of Texas was the head of state when Texas was an independent republic from 1836 to 1846.]

Stockton's California Battalion, also variously known as the first California Volunteer Militia and as the U.S. Mounted Rifles, was the successor to the earlier and more informal California militia-battalion. Even though the California Battalion was in fact a land force, officially it was considered to have been a naval unit because it was organized by Stockton and served as part of his naval command.[2]

An excellent firsthand account of the men in this unit comes from the U.S. naval officer and writer Henry Augustus Wise (1819–1869), who during the U.S.–Mexican War served as a lieutenant aboard the razee *Independence*. (A razee was a ship that had been modified to reduce the number of her decks.) In his book *Los Gringos: An Inside View of Mexico and California, with Wanderings in Peru, Chili* [sic], *and Polynesia*, which was published in 1849, Wise describes these men in such vivid terms that it would be a shame not to record them here (with "translations" where needed) for the benefit of modern readers who are not familiar with the unique speech of the mountain men.

Wise wrote:

The *cavallada* [sic] of spare horses were driven into the corral near by, and we were presented in due form to the riders. It was the most impressive little band I ever beheld; they numbered sixty, with heavy beards and unshorn faces, had gaunt bony frames like steel, dressed in skins, each man with his solid American rifle, and huge [Bowie] knife at the hip.

With all their wildness and ferocious appearance they had quite simple manners, and were perfectly frank and respectful in bearing. Their language and phraseology were certainly difficult for a stranger to comprehend, for many of them had passed the greater portion of their lives as trappers and hunters among the Rocky Mountains; but there was an air of indomitable courage hovering about them, with powers to endure any amount of toil or privation—men who wouldn't stick at scalping an Indian or a dinner of mule meat;—and you felt assured that with a score of such staunch fellows at your side you would sleep soundly, even though the forest was alive with an atmosphere of Camanche yells.

They were the woodsmen of our far west, who on hearing of the disturbances in California enrolled themselves for service in the Volunteer Battalion—more by way of recreation, I imagine, than for glory or patriotism. In truth, the natives [*Californios*] had good reason to regard them with terror...

[During a dinner of fried beef, biscuits, and whiskey] one stalwart bronzed trapper beside me, [and] finding an attentive listener, began:

"The last time, Captin, I cleared the Oregon trail, the Ingens fowt us amazin' hard.... Pete [here the trapper is addressing a friend who is also sitting around the campfire], do you notice how I dropped the red skin who pit the poisoned arrer in my moccasin! Snakes [this is a misspelling of the contemporary expression "Sakes alive!"—a mild oath], Captin, the varmints [Indians] lay thick as leaves behind the rocks; and bless ye, the minit I let fall old Ginger [the trapper's pet name for his rifle] from my jaw, up they springs, and lets fly their flint-headed arrers in amonst us, and one on 'em wiped me right through the leg.

I tell yer what it is, hoss, I riled, I did, though we'd had tolerable luck in the forenoon—for I dropped two and a squaw and Pete got his good six—barrin' the darned villains had hamstrung our mule, and we were bound to see the thing out.

Well, Captin, as I tell ye, I'm not weak in the joints, but it's no joke to hold the heft of twenty-three pounds[3] on a sight for above ten minutes on a stretch; so Pete and me scrouched down, made a little smoke with some sticks, and then we moved off a few rods, whar we got a clear peep...

For better than an hour we seed nothin', but on a suddin I seed the chap—I know'd him by his paintin'—that druv the arrer in my hide; he was peerin' around quite bold, thinkin' that we'd vamoosed; I jist fetched old Ginger up and drawed a bee line on his cratch, and, stranger, I give him such a winch in the stomach that he dropped straight into his tracks; he did! in five jumps I riz his har, and Pete and we warn't troubled agin for a week."[4]

The men of the California Battalion were paid $25 per man per month. They included 190 California settlers, many of them former Bear Flaggers; 34 of Sutter's best-trained Indians, who were, as was then customary, paid in trade goods rather than in cash; and even a few *Californios*, who were eager to help break Alta California loose from the incompetent and corrupt rule of the Mexican government. All these men were volunteers. They had to agree not to violate the chastity of women; to conduct their revolution honorably; and to obey their officers' commands. With the exceptions of Frémont and Gillespie (see below), the men of the California Battalion could choose their officers from their own ranks.

Commodore Robert F. Stockton, whose 44-gun frigate USS *Congress* was then anchored in Monterey Bay, replaced Sloat. This was another stroke of good luck for Frémont for two reasons: (1) Stockton was, to use a modern military phrase, more "forward leaning" than Sloat; i.e., he was more energetic and much more willing to risk taking military action[5]; and (2) Stockton was not likely to raise any awkward questions about the official authorization—or, more accurately, the *lack* of official authorization—for Frémont's aggressive actions in California.

(When Sloat, a very cautious and conservative career naval officer, had raised this subject with Frémont earlier, Sloat had been genuinely shocked to learn that Frémont had acted without any orders—i.e., he had acted entirely on his own initiative and volition.)

Stockton immediately promoted Frémont, who would be in command, to the rank of Major, and Gillespie, his deputy, to the rank of Captain. Shortly thereafter, when the California Battalion was officially mustered into (became part of) the U.S. Army, Frémont and Gillespie were given the brevet ranks of Lieutenant Colonel and Major, respectively. (A brevet was a warrant authorizing a commissioned officer to hold a higher rank temporarily, but without receiving the pay of that rank except when actually serving in that role.)

To begin the conquest of Southern California, the California Battalion filed aboard the *Cyane*, now commanded by Captain Samuel F. DuPont, and set sail for San Diego.[6] This would not be a pleasant passage for these landlubbers: most of them were violently seasick, including the indomitable Carson. Later, Frémont would write about this voyage, with considerable understatement, that then "we were all very low in our minds."[7]

Landing at San Diego, DuPont and his men captured the Mexican hermaphrodite brig *Juanita* and her cargo. (A hermaphrodite brig is a two-masted sailing ship with a square-rigged foremast and, on the mainmast, a square topsail above a fore-and-aft gaff mainsail.) The Mexicans, being hopelessly outgunned, made no effort to save the *Juanita* or to oppose the American landing at San Diego.

Edwin Bryant, the former Kentucky newspaper editor and *alcalde* of San Francisco, wrote a popular book in 1848 with the sonorous title of *What I Saw in California: Being the Journal of a Tour, by the Emigrant Route and South Pass of the Rocky Mountains, Across the Continent of North America, the Great Desert Basin, and through California, in the Years 1846, 1847*. Selections from this firsthand account give such an excellent picture of these times that they deserve to be quoted here at some length. Bryant wrote:

> November 30 [1846]—The battalion of mounted riflemen, under the command of Lieutenant-Colonel Frémont, numbers, rank and file, including Indians, and servants, 428. With the exception of the exploring party, which left the United States with Col. F. [Frémont], they are

composed of volunteers from the American settlers [in California], and the emigrants who have arrived in the country [in California] within a few weeks. The latter have generally furnished their own ammunition and other equipments for the expedition. Most of these are practised riflemen, men of undoubted courage, and capable of bearing any fatigue and privations endurable by veteran troops. The Indians are composed of a party of Walla-Wallas from Oregon, and a party of native Californians. [The Walla-Walla Indians lived in Oregon and Washington bordering the Walla Walla River and the Columbia River.] Attached to the battalion are two pieces of artillery, under the command of Lieutenant McLane, of the navy.

In the appearance of our small army there is presented but little of the "pomp and circumstance of glorious war." There are no plumes nodding over brazen helmets, nor coats of broadcloth spangled with lace and buttons. A broad-brimmed low-crowned hat, a shirt of blue flannel, or buckskin, with pantaloons and moccasins of the same, all generally much the worse for wear, and smeared with mud and dust, make up the costume of the party, officers as well as men.

A leathern girdle surrounds the waist, from which are suspended a bowie and a hunter's knife [a Bowie knife was big and was designed for fighting, while a hunter's knife was much smaller and was used for a variety of non-lethal purposes], and sometimes a brace of pistols. These, with the rifle and holster-pistols, are the arms carried by officers and privates.

A single bugle (and a sorry one at that) composes the band. Many an embryo Napoleon, in his own conceit, whose martial spirit has been excited to flaming intensity of heat by the peacock-plumage and gaudy trappings of our militia companies, when marching through the streets to the sound of drum, fife, and brass band, if he could have looked upon us, and then consulted the state of the military thermometer within him, would probably have discovered that the mercury of his heroism had fallen several degrees below zero.

Thirteen beeves are slaughtered every afternoon for the consumption of the battalion. These beeves are generally of good size, and in fair condition. Other provisions having been exhausted, beef constitutes the only subsistence for the men, and most of the officers. Under the circumstances, the consumption of beef is astonishing. I do not know if I shall be believed when I state a fact, derived from observation and calculation, that the average consumption per man of fresh beef is at least ten pounds per day.

A cold rain fell upon us during the entire day's march. We camped at four o'clock, p.m.; but the rain poured down in such torrents that it was impossible to light our camp-fires and keep them burning. This continued nearly the whole night, and I have rarely passed a night more uncomfortably.

The men composing the Californian battalion, as I have stated before, have been drawn from many sources, and are roughly-clad, and weather-beaten in their exterior appearance; but I feel it but justice here to state my belief that no military party ever passed through an enemy's country, and observed the same strict regard for the rights of its population. I never heard of an outrage, or even a trespass being committed by one of the American volunteers during our march. Every American appeared to understand perfectly the duty which he owed to himself and others in this respect, and the deportment of the battalion might be cited as a model for imitation.[8]

Frémont left about 40 men to garrison San Diego and then continued on to Los Angeles, which on 13 August 1846 surrendered peacefully to his and Stockton's combined forces. Four days later, on 17 August 1846, Stockton issued the following proclamation, which formally solidified American rule: "Having by right of conquest taken possession of the territory known by the name of Upper and Lower California [I] now do declare it to be a territory of the United States under the name of the Territory of California."[9]

• 11 •

Naval and Amphibious Operations I
From the Establishment of the American Blockade to the Capture of La Paz

As mentioned earlier, due to their complexity these operations are condensed and are studied in their entirety in this chapter and in the next chapter.

On 19 August 1846, the commanding officer of the U.S. Navy's Pacific Squadron, Commodore Robert F. Stockton, declares that all the ports on the west coast of Mexico are now subject to an American blockade. Its purpose (and that of its two successors in 1847 and 1848, respectively) is to prevent any trade goods, food supplies, and war material from reaching Mexican forces. To give boots-on-the-ground support to these blockades, American sailors and Marines conduct numerous small-scale naval and amphibious raids in both Alta and Baja California.

The Pacific Squadron of the U.S. Navy had been established in 1821 with the broad but undefined mandate of "protecting American shipping interests" in the Pacific Ocean off South America, North America, and Hawaii. Its area of operations was expanded further in 1835, when the East India Squadron was formed and became part of the Pacific Squadron. Later, as war with Mexico looked increasingly likely, more ships were assigned to the Pacific Squadron.

Since at that time there were no American ports in the Pacific, the Pacific Squadron had to obtain its naval supplies from storeships afloat. Food and water, however, could be obtained in sizeable quantities only ashore, i.e., from local ports of call in the Hawaiian Islands or from seaside towns along the Pacific Coast. For example, the log of the U.S. Navy's sloop-of-war *Dale* during the U.S.–Mexican War shows that she spent five days "watering ship" at the island of Toboga near modern-day Panama City. Writing in 1939, the U.S. Navy historian Captain Dudley W. Knox explained the procedure in these words:

> This laborious process normally had to be done with the ship's boats and was one of the chief bug-bears of sailing-ship days. The very limited amount of water that could be carried severely restricted the daily allowance for each man and was a governing consideration in the operations of men-of-war with their large crews. Every convenient opportunity was taken to replenish the supply of water carried in wooden casks in the hold, which otherwise would be empty in about three months, unless the crew was put on a reduced allowance.[1]

The naval and amphibious policies of the United States during the California campaigns had been summarized concisely in the instructions sent to General Kearny from Secretary of War Marcy on 3 June 1846. Marcy wrote:

> It is expected that the naval forces of the United States, which are now, or will soon be, in the Pacific, will be in possession of all the towns on the seacoast and will cooperate with you in the conquest of California. Arms, ordnance, munitions of war, and provisions, to be used in that country, will be sent by sea to our squadron in the Pacific, for the use of the land forces.[2]

In retrospect, it can be seen that the Pacific Squadron played a useful but not a crucial role in the Americans' capture and holding of the two Californias. During the early months of the war, the 350 to 400 Marines and sailors serving aboard American ships near California were in fact the only highly-trained military force along the California coast south of Oregon. Later, during the American operations in or near Baja California itself, probably only about 300 Marines were involved, but they were usually more than a match for the local Mexican seamen and soldiers.

Ships of the Pacific Squadron with Marines on board included the frigates *Congress* and *Savannah*; the sloops *Cyane, Dale, Levant, Warren,*

11 • Naval and Amphibious Operations I

and *Portsmouth*; and the razee *Independence*.[3] Marines could be landed from these ships at any of the ports, towns, or over the beaches of the coasts of the Californias. In most cases, however, a landing was merely a show of force: the Navy simply did not have enough Marines in this theater of war to keep troops ashore for any considerable period of time. The Mexicans cleverly played upon this American weakness. The most effective defense that the badly-outgunned *Californios* could muster was simply to melt away into the hinterland and wait there until the Americans ran low on food and water and had to sail away.

Since the Marines' high degree of mobility both on land and sea allowed them to move quickly, this fact probably made their numbers appear to the Mexicans much greater than they actually were. Moreover, unlike sailors, the Marines were well trained in land warfare, especially in the use of muskets. They were thus a very effective combat force ashore. The net result was that, along the coasts of the Californias, the few hundred Marines of the Pacific Squadron could effectively dominate large swatches of Mexican territory, if only temporarily.[4]

The American naval and amphibious operations in the western waters of Mexico did not have a major impact on the course of the war as whole but they did effectively transport U.S. forces along the west coast. They also tied down Mexican troops who otherwise might have either been used in Alta California itself or perhaps even sent eastwards, overland, to help defend Mexico City. Finally, the western blockade may also, in some small way, have helped General Scott in the east by depriving Mexican forces there of any munitions which might otherwise have been sent to them from the west coast.[5]

It must be understood here that the American naval and amphibious operations in the Pacific theater were not part of a carefully-choreographed seamless master plan to win the war, but were instead chiefly ad-hoc attacks against Mexican targets of opportunity. This fact gives any chronological account of these operations the same "choppy" quality that they must have had in real life.

This is first evident in the formal approval of these operations in November 1845, when Commodore John Drake Sloat arrived at Mazatlán on the west coast of Mexico to take command of the Pacific Squadron. Sloat was carrying secret orders from Secretary of the Navy George Bancroft to use the Pacific Squadron to the fullest extent feasible in the war with Mexico. Bancroft's orders to Sloat of 12 July 1846 and 13 August 1846 included the following general points, which are quoted here verbatim:

> The object of the United States is, under its rights as a belligerent, to possess itself entirely of Upper California. When San Francisco and Monterey are secured, you will, if possible, send a small vessel of war to take and hold possession of the port of San Diego; and it would be well to ascertain the views of the inhabitants of Pueblo de los Angeles, who, according to information received here, may be counted upon as desirous of coming under the jurisdiction of the United States. If you can take possession of it, you should do so.
>
> The object of the United States has reference to ultimate peace with Mexico [the long-term strategy of the United States is peace with Mexico]; and if, at that peace, the basis of *uti possidetis* [Latin for "as you possess"—a principle in international law stating that territory and other property remains with its possessor at the end of a conflict, unless otherwise provided for by treaty] shall be established, the government expects, through your forces, to be in actual possession of Upper California.
>
> After you shall have secured Upper California, if your force is sufficient, you will take possession, and keep the harbours on the Gulf of California as far down, at least, as Guaymas.
>
> As to the ports south of it [Guaymas], especially Mazatlan and Acapulco, it is not possible to give you special instructions. Generally, you will take possession of, or blockade, according to your best judgment, all Mexican ports as far as your means will allow.
>
> Generally you will exercise the rights of a belligerent; and bear in mind that the greater the advantages you obtain, the more speedy and more advantageous will be the peace.[6]

The first use of the Pacific Squadron in the California campaigns dates from 7 July 1846, when the men of the USS *Savannah*, USS *Cyane*, and USS *Levant* took part in the American capture of Monterey. Two days later, on 9 July 1846, the USS *Portsmouth* under Captain John B. Montgomery landed 75 Marines and sailors at Yerba Buena and took possession of it without firing a shot.

On 11 July 1846, the 26-gun royal navy sloop *Juno* sailed into San Francisco Bay and anchored at Sausalito, while at roughly the same time the British man-of-war *Collingwood*, flying the flag of Admiral Seymour, commander of the British Pacific Squadron, turned up outside Monterey Harbor. Neither of these British ships took any action to help or hinder the Mexican side or the American side during the war, but their very presence raised concerns among American officials who were under instructions to be on the lookout for any signs of foreign intervention in Alta California.

Seymour's mission was, in part, to gauge the strength of any sentiment among the *Californios* for a British protectorate over the area. Contemporary correspondence, however, suggests that the real assignment of the British fleet in the Pacific at this time was to prevent any encroachment by France on British interests in the Pacific Islands. In California itself, British ships focused on the narrower mandate of gathering intelligence and being ready to protect British nationals if this should ever become necessary.

Frémont, Sloat, and many other observers, however, were convinced that this was simply a smokescreen: they believed that the British fleet was merely biding its time, waiting for the best moment to seize California. Nevertheless, it had become clear to the British that now the United States could never be displaced as the "new owner" of Alta California.[7] As a result, the *Collingwood* quietly spent a week in Monterey fitting new spars made from trees cut on the nearby hills, rather than vigorously investigating any latent pro–British sentiments.[8]

Ships of the Pacific Squadron sometimes served as floating warehouses for Frémont's California Battalion, supplying it with gunpowder, bullets, and other military goods. The Squadron also transported American forces to other California ports during the war. For example, the USS *Cyane* carried Frémont and about 160 of his men to San Diego on 29 July 1846, and the city was captured without a shot being fired.

On 6 August 1846, the USS *Congress* was credited with capturing the undefended harbor of Los Angeles, while on 19 August 1846, as mentioned earlier, Stockton declared that the ports (and harbors, bays, outlets, and inlets as well) on the west coast of Mexico south of San Diego were now subject to blockade by the Americans.

In practice, however, Stockton could assign only two of his ships— the sloops *Cyane* and *Warren*, each carrying 20 guns—to this blockade duty. He ordered Samuel F. DuPont, commander of the *Cyane*, to blockade the Mexican naval base at San Blas, and Joseph B. Hall, commander of the *Warren*, to blockade Mazatlán. (Mazatlán was tactically important because it was the major resupply base for Mexican forces in the Californias.)

In a message formally advising all ships in the area that the United States and Mexico were at war, Stockton stated that because California now belonged to the United States, a safe anchorage for non–Mexican ships could be found at all seasons in San Francisco Bay.[9]

In broader terms, his strategic goal was to seize Acapulco eventually and to use it as a base from which to send American troops to attack deep into mainland Mexico. However, he himself did not have enough troops at hand to mount such an extensive overland campaign. Moreover, it proved to be quite impossible to recruit enough local Americans for this task: they simply did not want to go to war any distance beyond Alta California. As a result, this proposed campaign never even began.

On 2 September 1846, USS *Cyane* captured two Mexican vessels at San Blas without meeting any resistance. Five days later, on 7 September 1846, the USS *Warren* seized the Mexican brig *Malek Adhel*, which was moored at Mazatlán.[10] The story of this latter capture gives a good insight into the remarkable state of unpreparedness of Mexican shipping during the California campaigns.

As a first step in this attack, Lieutenant William Radford positioned the *Warren* so that her starboard battery bore on the city (i.e., so that her starboard cannons were directly aimed at Mazatlán). He and 69 of his men then embarked in four ship's boats and rowed to the *Malek Adhel*. Since it was siesta time, the *Malek Adhel*'s crewmen were all asleep when Radford and his men suddenly appeared alongside their vessel and boarded her. Caught entirely off-guard, the Mexican crew dove overboard and swam to shore.

After raising the American flag, the American boarding party got the brig loose from her two anchors and kedged her out of the harbor toward the open sea. (To kedge a ship was to move her by means of a small anchor dropped some distance away and in the direction of travel desired. The ship was then hauled up to the anchor by means of a windlass. The anchor could be repositioned in the same or in a different direction.) This prize, the *Malek Adhel* herself (a ship captured in wartime was known as a prize), proved to be a valuable and handy vessel for her new owners—the Americans. Eighty feet long on deck, she

11 • Naval and Amphibious Operations I

was armed with two iron 9-pounder cannons and ten brass 6-pounders. Taken to Monterey by her American captors, she proved to be a good sailor and good sea boat (that is, she handled very well in rough weather).

On 1 October 1846, the *Cyane* seized two Mexican schooners at Loreto, about 150 miles north of La Paz, and on 7 October 1846 she cannonaded Guaymas on the mainland. In that same month, the *Warren* left for San Francisco, and *Cyane* left shortly thereafter. The result was that this first blockade of Mexico's west coast only lasted about four weeks. It had very little effect because their need for more supplies, food, and water prevented the American ships from remaining on station any longer. Moreover, the continuing demands of the Alta California campaign ashore made it impossible for the U.S. Navy to keep its storeships in Baja California waters, so far from the scene of more important military action.

To retake Los Angeles, which the Americans had initially captured on 13 August 1846 but had then lost on 29 September 1846 during the *Californio* uprising (this event will be discussed shortly), about 360 Marines and sailors, supported by four artillery pieces, were used in a joint operation with about 70 of Kearny's cavalrymen and part of Frémont's California Battalion of some 450 men. Faced with this overwhelming force, the Mexican residents and armed forces of Los Angeles surrendered to the Americans, quickly and peacefully, on 10 January 1847.

A remarkable footnote on the history of the war is how news of victory or defeat was sometimes quickly relayed. Colton could write from Monterey:

> We have no intelligence, as yet, from the seat of war [Los Angeles]. The solicitude of the public to know the result is at the highest pitch. No one doubts that the issue [the outcome of battle] has been very decisive. A report reached us today that the town of los Angeles had been taken by our troops, and that a large percentage of the Californians had laid down their arms.
>
> This rumor comes through the washerwomen of this place. They get their intelligence from the Indians, who cross the stream in which they wash their clothes. Singular as this sort of mail may seem, it very often conveys news, not only with wonderful dispatch, but with extraordinary accuracy.

The first capture of Los Angeles by Com. Stockton, was announced by these washerwomen; they were also the first to spread the news of the breaking out of the insurrection at the same place, and knew of the retreat of the Americans at San Pedro before any other class of people in Monterey. So much for a wash-tub mail. You may think lightly of it as of the soap-bubbles that break over its rim; but if you are wise you will heed its intelligence.[11]

A major result of the Los Angeles campaign was the Treaty of Cahuenga, which will also be described later. Thus, by mid–January 1847, the situation in Alta California seemed to be peaceful and stable. Stockton could therefore begin to plan a better-organized blockade of some of the ports on the west coast of Mexico.

To strengthen the Americans' naval hand in the Pacific theater of the war, the retired ship of the line USS *Independence* (a ship of the line was a large, heavy vessel carrying powerful guns) was recalled to active duty. She was rebuilt and recommissioned as a razee frigate in 1846. She entered Monterey Bay on 22 January 1847 after a quick (146-day) voyage around Cape Horn and became the flagship of the new commander of the Pacific Squadron, Commodore William Branford Shubrick, who had replaced Stockton in a routine personnel shuffle. In Monterey, Shubrick quickly demonstrated his good sense and naval courtesy by inviting General Kearny aboard and by pledging his own willingness to cooperate fully with him.[12]

In addition to using its own ships, the U.S. Navy also chartered merchantmen (privately-owned commercial ships) to carry American forces in the Pacific theater of the war. A good example here is the New York Volunteers, who were recruited with the understanding that they could remain in California for as long as they liked after their tours of duty there were finished. They were shipped around Cape Horn to Alta California, where they staffed garrisons in Monterey, Santa Barbara, Los Angeles, and San Diego, and fought against the Mexicans at La Paz and Todos Santos in Baja California. To get them to California, the Navy hired the merchantmen *Thomas H. Perkins*, the *Loo Choo*, and the *Susan Drew*. The USS *Preble* protected this convoy while it was underway, while the small storeship USS *Brutus* took aboard 50 men who had been left behind for various reasons.

Other vessels involved in this movement of men and material

11 • Naval and Amphibious Operations I

included the ships *Isabella* and *Sweden*. A total of about 850 soldiers were transported to California in such vessels. These newly-arrived troops took over many of the on-shore naval and military garrisoning and Baja California assignments previously held by the men of the Pacific Squadron, the California Battalion, and the Mormon Battalion.

As soon as the Americans had won the war in Alta California itself, they turned their full attention to taking control of Baja California's towns and, in the process, to destroying as many of the Mexican vessels they could find moored or underway along the California coast.

On 2 March 1847, U.S. Navy captain James Biddle arrived in California aboard the *Columbus* on his way from Japan back to the United States. Since he was the senior naval officer, he temporarily took charge of the entire American naval force in the Californias. Shortly thereafter, the *Portsmouth*, under the command of U.S. Navy lieutenant John Missroon, was ordered to sail to Baja California and to capture—more for symbolic reasons than for anything else—two of the towns of Baja California.

Upon reaching San José del Cabo, Missroon therefore demanded that the local Mexicans surrender. They refused, so 140 Marines and sailors were sent ashore without encountering any resistance and raised the American flag. Once this was done, they quietly returned to their ship, which then remained offshore for a few days before sailing for San Lucas.

On 3 April 1847, the *Portsmouth* arrived at San Lucas, where the Marine detachment landed and raised the American flag without meeting any opposition. The same thing happened yet again on 13 April 1847 at La Paz: the Marines and sailors landed, raised the American flag, and left without firing a shot. The next day, Colonel Francisco Palacios Miranda, the governor of Baja California, quietly surrendered La Paz to the Americans. A committee of local Mexican residents there signed articles of capitulation, by which they were granted American citizenship and were permitted to keep their own officials and their own laws.

On 30 May 1847, Kearny sent U.S. Army lieutenant colonel Henry S. Burton (1819–1869) and two companies of the 1st Regiment of the New York Volunteers aboard the storeship *Lexington*. Their mission was to secure the American military possession of Baja California and establish an American presence there, showing their skills and good will by undertaking various construction projects. These volunteers did an excellent job. For example, in a letter of 22 June 1847 an American resident of Los Angeles wrote of them:

> The regiment of New York volunteers is now very much scattered, being distributed among different posts, from Sutter's settlement on the Sacramento to La Paz in Lower California—a distance of 1500 miles. The regiment will never probably be together again while in service. They will dearly earn all they receive from the government [their very modest wages]. The hand of American industry and enterprise is plainly to be seen wherever our troops are stationed.
>
> Bricks are burned [manufactured], ovens are built, chimneys erected, saw-mill put into operation, and comfortable houses constructed wherever timber can be had. Watches and clocks, too, are sent to these stations from a distance of fifty miles, to be repaired; cloths bought to be made into clothing; leather to be made into boots and shoes, and at one of the posts two of the New York volunteers have opened a stall at which beef, lamb, veal, and mutton can be purchased dressed in Fulton market style [offered for sale as done at the Fulton market in New York].
>
> These are specimens of what is going forward by way of civilization and improvement under the sway of the United States government and its arms. All can do well here who choose to help themselves and become useful.[13]

After the USS *Independence* left for San Francisco on 3 June 1847, the *Cyane* was the sole American warship left on the west coast of Mexico. To provide the pro–American inhabitants of La Paz and San José del Cabo with at least a fig-leaf of protection, Commander Du Pont simply sailed the *Cyane* back and forth between San José del Cabo and Mazatlán. This maneuver effectively spelled the end of the blockade, however, because Mexican trade could resume as soon as the *Cyane* was out of sight over the horizon.

Upon meeting the *Cyane* at San José del Cabo on 20 June 1847, Commander Montgomery, in charge of the *Portsmouth*, learned that Mazatlán was now open to commercial shipping. After discussing this issue with Commander Du Pont, on 28 June 1847 Montgomery returned to San Francisco for instructions. The *Cyane* then left California to obtain in Hawaii the supplies she needed. The net result was that this second blockade proved to be as ineffective as its predecessor.

11 • *Naval and Amphibious Operations I*

By July 1847, however, Biddle was satisfied with the military and naval situation on the Pacific Coast, so he turned the Pacific fleet over to Commodore William B. Shubrick and sailed for the United States aboard the *Columbus*. On 21 July 1847, the storeship *Lexington*, carrying from Alta California two companies of New York Volunteers, arrived in La Paz. These troops landed there unopposed and went ashore to set up a small garrison.

• 12 •

Naval and Amphibious Operations II
From the Capture of La Paz to the Return of the Sloop *Cyane* to Norfolk, Virginia

On 10 August 1847, Commodore Shubrick sent the USS *Portsmouth* and *Congress* to begin a new blockade of Mazatlán, Guaymas, and San Blas. Moreover, when the *Dale* reached La Paz in mid–September 1847, Burton ordered her commander, Thomas Selfridge, to set sail for Loreto and Mulegé to prevent supplies from being landed there and to get a pledge of neutrality from the inhabitants.

On 30 September 1847, to avoid a hostile reception, the *Dale* entered the port of Mulegé flying the *British* flag rather than the American flag. This was in fact a time-honored and legitimate naval tactic: it was not illegal, so long as the vessel hoisted its real flag when military action actually began. As soon as the *Dale* anchored, she lowered the British flag and raised the American flag. U.S. Navy lieutenant Tunis Augustus Macdonough Craven, whose journal is of great historical interest and will be quoted here, tried to go ashore himself but a hostile group of Mexicans prevented him from doing so.

Craven then decided to try to capture the unmanned Mexican schooner *Magdalena*, which lay at anchor there. He sent 50 of his men in four of his ship's boats to tow the *Magdalena* out to the *Dale*. In the process, however, the Americans discovered that the hull of the *Magdalena* was so rotten that she was leaking very badly. Since this vessel could be of no use to them, they burned her.[1]

On 1 October 1847, upon learning that there were 200 armed Mexicans in the vicinity of Mulegé, Commander Selfridge decided to begin offensive operations there. He had a letter delivered to the Mexican authorities in Mulegé, directing them to lay down their arms, to remain neutral, and not to try to contact their colleagues on the mainland. In reply, Mexican army Captain Don Manuel Pineda refused to remain neutral. Moreover, he strenuously protested against the *Dale's* sailing under false colors, i.e., by flying the British flag in order to deceive the Mexicans. Pineda also boasted that he would recapture La Paz.

The Americans did not let his defiance rattle them. Early that afternoon, Craven and 17 Marines and sailors entered their ship's boats and rowed up the Rio de Santa Rosalía, a small river that ran through the town. They landed on the right bank of the river and exchanged shots with some of Pineda's men, who were drawn up on the opposite bank and who then retreated to the hills behind Mulegé. This was an effective defense against the Americans because there were too few Marines and sailors to follow them. In the late afternoon, Craven's men returned to the *Dale*, having accomplished nothing of significance.

There were no casualties on either side, but the American inability to capture Mulegé was the first American failure in the Baja peninsula conflict and was counted by the Mexicans as a victory for their own side. Trade between Guaymas on the mainland and Mulegé in Baja California continued unabated, despite the efforts of the *Libertad*, a schooner charted by the U.S. Navy from Captain Peter Davis, an American citizen living at La Paz, to suppress it. The *Libertad* was put under the command of Lieutenant Craven but seems to have accomplished nothing of substance.

On 17 October 1847, the *Congress* and the *Plymouth* anchored at Guaymas. When the fortress there and its garrison of 600 men refused to surrender, the guns of American ships began firing at it. Most of the townspeople fled during the night, followed by the garrison itself. The Marines, reinforced by sailors, landed and raised the American flag, but since there were too few of them to occupy the town, they had to be withdrawn. On 20 October 1847, however, the presence of Captain Elie A.F. La Vallette and the sailors and Marines of the USS *Congress* forced the remaining Mexican defenders to evacuate Guaymas.

Pineda and his fellow officers had alienated most of the local population of San José del Cabo by forcing the men into military service; by demanding, but not paying for, supplies; and by stealing the property of those who had collaborated with the Americans. Nevertheless, despite their disillusionment with Pineda himself, on 23 October 1847 some Mexican patriots at San José del Cabo proclaimed that rule by the Americans was now at an end. Their purely verbal opposition, however, ended as soon as the USS *Cyane*, *Congress*, and *Independence* all arrived at that port five days later. The Mexicans saw that they had no hope of prevailing against such naval and amphibious forces, so American rule continued unchallenged.

Upon learning that anti–American activity was also going on at Todos Santos, about 90 miles away on the Pacific coast, Commodore Shubrick sent U.S. Navy lieutenant Montgomery Lewis, U.S. Army lieutenant Henry W. Halleck, and 30 seamen to investigate the situation. For Lieutenant Halleck, the highlight of this trip was his meeting with five pretty Mexican girls at a small ranch on the outskirts of Todos Santos. He describes them in these words:

> Wearing dresses without sleeves and low in the bosom, like our belles at home when they wish to display their charms in the ballroom, and being too poor to afford *rebosas* [long woven scarfs, often of fine material, worn over the head and shoulders by women] with which Mexican ladies usually conceal their budding beauties, these belles of Pescadero in their simple calico robes, without the wild grass, cotton, bran, or whalebone [without the fashion aids used by American women], presented us as lovely figures as the eye could ever wish to gaze upon.[2]

As was the case in Alta California, there were anti–American and pro–American factions among the people of Baja California. For example, at the mission in Todos Santos, Father Gabriel González, chief of the Dominican missions in Baja California and the official for the management of a large ranch there, entertained the Marines with rum and light conversation while he secretly sent a rider to warn Pineda's insurgents, who were 30 miles away, advising them to attack as soon as the Marines were off-guard and were making their way back to San José del Cabo.

Lieutenant Lewis and his men did not encounter Pineda's forces and they returned safely to San José del Cabo on 7 November 1847, but Lewis could not know that Pineda was about to attack La Paz and San José del Cabo. To retain the American hold on San José del Cabo, Shubrick left Lieutenant Charles Heywood, four midshipmen (i.e., junior naval officers), and 20 Marines there. These men, armed with one 9-pounder carronade (a small cannon firing a projectile weighing 9 pounds) and 75 carbines, occupied the barracks in an old mission located on a rise of land at the north end of town.

On 8 November 1847, the *Dale* arrived and would remain in the harbor almost continuously for the next eight months to prevent Mexican forces from returning to the town. That same day, the *Independence, Congress,* and *Cyane* left San José del Cabo and headed for Mazatlán. On 11 November 1847, with some of the cannons of the Pacific Squadron trained on the city, a landing force of 750 Marines and sailors, under Shubrick's command, called on the city of Mazatlán to surrender. Since its garrison had fled the night before, it was an easy decision for the inhabitants to agree to surrender. The Americans would hold Mazatlán until the end of the war.

On 16 November 1847, Pineda's forces, which were estimated to total 300 men, attacked the American garrison at La Paz. Under Burton's command, 112 Americans occupied a position on the south side of a gulch, overlooking La Paz. There they piled palm logs around their adobe barracks and around an emplacement for their two 6-pound field pieces. These cannons poured a hail of canister shot upon the Mexican troops, forcing them to withdraw to La Laguna. (Canister shot was a type of anti-personnel ammunition for cannons. Similar to naval grapeshot, which consisted of a mass of metal balls tightly packed into a canvas bag but with smaller and more numerous balls, it was very effective against soldiers at close range.) To prevent Governor Miranda's townhouse from being used by the Americans as a headquarters, the Mexicans burned it as they retreated. In this skirmish, four or five Mexicans, and one American, were killed.

At the same time that Pineda began his attack on La Paz, he also sent a force of about 150 men, led by three of his lieutenants, to attack Heywood's force of 25 Marines and sailors and 25 California volunteers, who were stationed in the barracks at San José del Cabo. On 19 November 1847, Heywood refused the Mexicans' demand that he surrender, so the Mexicans commenced their attack. On 21 November

1847, however, two American whalers—the *Magnolia* and the *Edward*—suddenly appeared offshore. Thinking that these vessels were U.S. Navy ships, the Mexicans quickly withdrew. In their aborted assault at San José del Cabo, the Mexicans lost at least six men killed; Heywood's forces suffered no losses.

Pineda's forces were subsequently augmented by other Mexican troops and on 27 November 1847 he led a second attack, with about 500 men, on La Paz. The Mexicans advanced toward the American position, using ravines and cacti to shield their movements, but were driven back by American musket fire.

On 8 December 1847, a launch (a small boat designed to carry personnel or supplies) sent to the American fleet at Mazatlán by Burton arrived in La Paz with more provisions and ammunition. That same day, the *Cyane*, under Commodore Shubrick's orders, arrived from San Blas and lifted the siege. While the number of Mexican casualties during the second attack on La Paz is not known, Burton reported finding 38 graves. No Americans had been killed. Lieutenant Craven described the appearance of the ruined town: "All that part of the town that was not protected by the [American] garrison's muskets was burned, the vine and the fig tree as well as the graceful palm—all being devoured. Such are the beauties of war."[3]

A month later, on 12 January 1848, at the fortress of San Blas on Mexico's west coast, Lieutenant Frederick Chatard of the barque *Whilton* removed the cannons of the fortress from that city. (A barque has three or more masts, with the foremasts rigged square and the aftermast rigged fore-and-aft.) Six days later, on 18 January 1848, Chatard also spiked the three fortress guns at Mazatlán. (Spiking involved hammering a barbed piece of steel into the touchhole of a cannon so that it could not be fired.) As a result of his actions, the only useable fortress guns still available to the Mexicans were now those located about in Acapulco, about 300 miles to the southeast.

In the meantime, at San José del Cabo, with the departures of both the *Portsmouth* and the *Southampton*, the American outpost there was left without any naval support. At that point, Heywood's garrison consisted only of 27 Marines, 16 sailors, 20 California volunteers, and three artillery pieces.

On 22 January 1848, about 300 Mexicans and a number of Yaqui

Indians attacked Heywood's camp. They captured eight of Heywood's men, who had been in the process of transporting, from the beach to their barracks, some supplies left for them by a schooner. In addition to trying to decide what they could do to rescue their eight comrades, Heywood's remaining men also had to take care of nearly 50 local women and children who had fled to the barracks when the fighting erupted.

While Heywood persevered at San José del Cabo, in the early morning darkness of 30 January 1848 Lieutenant Craven and 12 Marines from the *Dale* attacked the little Mexican garrison at Cochori, Sonora, located about eight miles east of Guaymas. This fight is an unusually good example of the many small-scale skirmishes that characterized the American naval and amphibious operations in Baja California. Lieutenant Craven recounts the story in these words, beginning when he and his men set off from the *Dale* in the ship's boats:

> We went about four miles in our boats, and landing through the surf on the beach some three miles from the village, with quick step and profound silence marched upon the place. On getting near the village, I detached the Marines, twelve in number, with orders to get near the outpost and lie concealed until I had reached the barracks, that our assault might be made simultaneously.
>
> Lieut. Fabius Stanly led the advance, and we pushed through thicket and hedge until within 100 yards of the barracks undiscovered. We now divided into two parties, Stanly leading on the right, I filing to the left, that we might surround the barracks before assaulting it. As my company were filing around the corner of the barracks we were discovered and fired at by the sentry on the house. Stanly had reached the front of the barracks, surprising the sentry there and seizing him with his own hands, not however, until he had given the alarm.
>
> In an instant a number of the guard rushed out from the rear and fired in the faces of my men. I ordered a charge but as it was pitchy dark some escaped, while others were shot down while flying. As soon as we fired I had the satisfaction of hearing a volley from the Marines, who rushed upon the picket guard and overpowered it. Lights were struck and found that we had captured Captain Mendoza and his lieutenant, with their mistresses, all in charming dishabille; the fair ones, thus by the rule "larums" [alarms] of war roused from their repose, seemed in nowise agitated, but "au contraire" were interesting indeed.
>
> We captured, I say, the captain, lieutenant and eleven privates; in the assault five [Mexicans] were killed and two wounded. Twenty stands of

arms, 500 rounds of ball cartridges, a stand of colors and a quantity of provisions also fell into our hands, as well as the guard boat.[4]

A month later, back at San José del Cabo, the Mexicans had solidified their hold on all of this area except for the barracks. Low-level clashes continued. On 11 February 1848, the young American officer who was Heywood's second-in-command was killed by a Mexican sniper. That same day the Mexicans also captured the garrison's water supply. To the desperate people inside the barracks, their only choices now seemed to be either dying of thirst or surrendering.

Upon learning of the plight of the San José del Cabo garrison, Shubrick ordered the *Cyane* to the rescue. This ship reached the port at sundown on 14 February 1848 and, the next morning, 102 American officers and men stormed ashore. They advanced down a two-mile-long road near the hamlet of San Vicente, where Mexican forces were waiting for them. As the Americans moved forward, Heywood and 30 of his men sallied out from the barracks to join them. When the Americans opened fire, the Mexicans turned and fled. During this 21-day siege, the Americans lost three men and the Mexicans lost between 13 and 35.

Once San José del Cabo was in American hands, at dawn on 16 March 1848 the Americans attacked Pineda's headquarters in the hamlet of San Antonio (near La Paz) and put the Mexicans there to flight. Pineda himself escaped in his night clothes. The Americans lost one man in this encounter, but they managed to rescue the eight men who had previously been captured.

One of the more colorful U.S. Army officers was Captain Henry M. Naglee of the New York Volunteers. He was known as "Black Jack" Naglee—possibly a reference to the easily-concealed club weapon now spelled "blackjack." Naglee may have earned this nickname because of the stern discipline he imposed on his troops and the harsh punishments he meted out to them if they misbehaved. On 22 March 1848, he and 114 men from the First Regiment of New York Volunteers arrived at La Paz aboard the storeship *Isabella*. Burton could now pursue Mexican forces without leaving La Paz itself exposed to attack.

On 26 March 1848, Burton and 217 men therefore marched to Todos Santos, about 55 miles southwest on the Pacific coast. William

R. Ryan, who was one of these Volunteers, left this description of his fellow soldiers at the beginning of the march:

> We had all sorts of costumes, some military, some Californian, some wearing a hybrid of the two, others after a fashion decidedly more brigandish than anything else, but the majority of us appearing much the worse for wear for our rough journey through the thorns, whilst many were literally in rags.[5]

On 22 March 1848, an advance party of 15 American troops captured Pineda at San Antonio. During this engagement, some 200 to 300 Mexicans and Yaqui Indians had positioned themselves on a hill directly in the path of Burton's advancing troops. When they fired on Burton's men, Naglee's company attacked them from the rear. Burton reported that in this engagement 10 Mexicans, and no Americans, were killed. He then led his remaining troops back to La Paz, arriving there on 7 April 1848. He brought with him a large number of Mexican prisoners, i.e., Pineda himself, six other officers, and 103 non-commissioned officers and privates.

Burton is remembered by historians not only for his military role but also for his romantic prowess. This is what Bancroft has to say about him:

> Captain H.S. Burton fell in love with the charming Californian, María del Amparo Ruiz, born at Loreto, and aged sixteen. She promised to marry him. The servants reported this to a certain ranchero who had unsuccessfully been paying his addresses to her, and he informed Padre Gonzáles, saying that a Catholic should not marry a Protestant. The padre thanked the man in a letter, which the latter hawked about offensively, out of spite, because his suit had been rejected. But for all this, the Loreto girl married the Yankee captain.[6]

Naglee, whom Burton had sent towards Magdalena Bay, about 150 miles northwest on the Pacific coast, in hopes of intercepting any Mexican forces in that area, returned to La Paz on 12 April 1848, after having completed a fruitless 350-mile trek over hot, rocky mule paths in pursuit of an elusive enemy who knew that it was wiser to retreat rather than to stand and fight the Americans.

When he was within a mile of La Paz, however, Naglee committed a serious war crime: in direct violation of military orders, he ordered that two prisoners—an Indian and a *Californio*—be executed. For this illegal action, Colonel Richard Barnes Mason (1797–1850), the military governor of California, ordered that Naglee be arrested. Naglee escaped punishment only when President Polk granted a general pardon to military and naval officers who were acting in wartime.

Ironically, the later American successes in Baja California came only after the 2 February 1848 signing of the Treaty of Guadalupe Hidalgo, which officially ended the war. Under the terms of this treaty, Baja California would not become part of the United States but would remain Mexican territory. This decision was not popular among the American officers who had served there. For example, after the end of the war ex-lieutenant Edward Gould Buffum would write:

> Never in the history of wars among civilized nations was there a greater piece of injustice committed, and the United States deserves for it the imprecations of all who have a sense of justice remaining in them. The probability is that some ignorant scribbler, who had cast his eyes upon the rugged rocks that girdle her seacoast, had represented [Baja] California as a worthless country, and, that, forgetting justice and good faith, our government left this compromised people to suffer at the hands of their own.[7]

The lack of military action that followed the signing of the treaty made some of the New York Volunteers feel very bored and restless. They also objected to Naglee's iron discipline and onerous punishments. Many of them believed that since the war was now over, they were entitled to leave military service whenever they wished. Mini-mutinies therefore broke out among the Volunteers, e.g., at San José del Cabo in April 1848 and at La Paz in June 1848. Both of these disturbances were quickly put down by Marines from the *Cyane* and *Independence.*

In early August 1848, Lieutenant William Sherman, the senior adjutant to military governor Mason, ordered the New York Volunteers to return to Alta California to be discharged there. The ship-of-the-line *Ohio* and the sloop *Warren* were assigned to act as troop transports, while the storeship *Southampton* and the sloop *Lexington* would carry any Mexican refugees who wanted to leave Baja California now that Mexico had lost the war.

However, many of the Mexican residents of Baja California who had sided with the Americans now decided to remain in Baja California because they did not want to lose all their land and property there. The *Ohio* left La Paz on 1 September 1848 and San José del Cabo on 6 September 1848 with the last of the volunteers and with 350 refugees on board. She reached Monterey on 9 October 1848.

That same day, the *Cyane*, for her part, returned to Norfolk, Virginia, where she received congratulations from the secretary of the navy for her contributions to the American successes in the California campaigns. She was one of the most famous U.S. Navy ships of the war, having captured or destroyed 30 enemy vessels.

• 13 •

The Californio *Uprising* and Its Aftermath

During the siege of Los Angeles, which begins on 23 September 1846, Mexican general José María Flores takes command of the Californio uprising against the American invaders. U.S. Army lieutenant Talbot recounts his escape from Californio forces.

On 17 August 1846, a ship arrived at Los Angeles, which Stockton and Frémont, leading a force of 50 Marines, had occupied earlier without meeting any opposition from the *Californios*. The ship was bearing dispatches confirming that war between the United States and Mexico had indeed been declared. Stockton thereupon issued a proclamation stating that California now belonged to the United States. He also imposed a 10:00 p.m. to dawn curfew, which stated that any person found armed outside his own home, and without permission from the Americans to be armed, would be subject to arrest and deportation as an enemy.

Frémont had installed Gillespie as the *alcalde* of Los Angeles. Gillespie was an intelligent, brave Marine but he was also quick to take offense, had a hair-trigger temper, and held the Mexican soldiers, including by extension their *Californio* compatriots, in visible contempt.

On 16 January 1846, for example, while in Mexico City he had written to Navy Secretary Bancroft that although some of the Mexican cavalrymen and infantrymen he saw there "were stout men, in pretty good order" and "tall, strong looking men," the great majority were not. Gillespie commented (punctuation as in the original):

> All the others were miserable indeed, and completely worn out by long travel; all very small delicate men, and would not be taken into

service in any other country. The Artillery about 200 strong, was remarkable, only for the very miserable condition of its appointments, and the decidedly ineffective appearance of the whole Corps.... I have no hesitation in saying, it is composed of the most miserable Troops I have ever seen.

As it is a well known fact that in the Spanish Americas the Indian soldier will follow his officer to the death, I was very particular in observing each officer as he passed me, and I must say, a more pitiable collection was never seen with any soldiery—They are generally very young, quite small of stature, appear to have little control over the men and, I am credibly informed, are almost entirely ignorant of the soldier's duties. There is no precision in their movements, nor the least bearing of a soldier about them. The Troops are very seldom drilled, and exercise of any kind is very rare.[1]

The Californios, for their part, did not like Gillespie because he looked down on them as a conquered people. Moreover, he imposed oppressive regulations on them in Los Angeles. For example, to prevent a crowd from forming, no two men were permitted to go about the streets together. Local citizens were forbidden to hold meetings in their own houses. Shops had to be closed at sundown. Liquor could not be sold without Gillespie's express permission. Rather than letting the *jueces de paz* (justices of the peace) resolve petty cases of crime by themselves, Gillespie involved himself in them, too. Houses were searched for weapons and people were jailed on suspicion alone.

Power seems to have gone to Gillespie's head. Benito Wilson, an American resident of Los Angeles, reported that—on the most frivolous pretexts—Gillespie had the most respectable men of the community hauled up before him, apparently only to humiliate them. When he was in Los Angeles, Larkin learned that "it appears even from the Americans that Captain A H G [Archibald H. Gillespie] punished, fined, and imprisoned who and when he pleased without any hearing."[2]

Moreover, many of the local Americans did not like Gillespie, either. They were convinced that firearms were essential for their self-defense and that they had the right to carry them wherever and whenever they pleased.

To make matters even worse, Gillespie himself did not have any confidence at all in the garrison of 48 Americans serving under him in Los Angeles. He wrote of them:

Some very good men but many bad and discontented from having to remain in the South [southern California] until a relief could arrive. They were men unaccustomed to control, perfect drunkards whilst in the *cuidad* of wine & *Aguardiente* [strong liquor], but serviceable Riflemen in the field. They were men for whom the Californians could have no respect, & whom, from the spirit of insubordination they constantly evinced, the Californians thought they could overcome. Every means in my power were tried to enforce discipline, but the men on whom I depended would not do the Soldier's duty.[3]

Matters came to a head on 23 September 1846 when a street hoodlum named Sérbulo Varela and a band of his followers attacked Gillespie's garrison.[4] The Americans easily beat off the assault, killing two of Varela's men, but news of this uprising quickly spread and inflamed many patriotic *Californios*. The next day, about 300 *Californios* came together at a Mexican military camp about a mile from the barracks where the Americans were staying. General José María Flores, who had long been hostile to the American invasion, took command of these insurgents.

In the face of the quickly-mounting opposition and hostility they were facing, Gillespie and his followers felt it would be prudent for them to retreat to a small local prominence which they nicknamed "Fort Hill." There they could easily defend themselves from any *Californio* attacks. It turned out, however, that on Fort Hill they would have very little access to water, the nearest supply being a distant well or spring in a yard at the base of the hill. It became clear that they would soon be forced to move elsewhere. Gillespie therefore decided to send out a rider to get help from Stockton. He chose an expert horseman named John Brown, whom the *Californios* called "Juan Flaco" ("Lean John"), probably because he was so wiry after long years in the saddle.

Carrying an official dispatch to Stockton—and also, as a backup in case he was captured en route, secret messages written on thin cigarette paper and then rolled up and hidden in his long hair—Brown succeeded in slipping through the *Californio* lines and then rode on to San Francisco Bay, a distance of almost 400 miles, in the remarkable time of only 52 hours. He was able to deliver the dispatch to Stockton, alerting him to Gillespie's desperate situation on Fort Hill.

In the meantime, however, with no relief in sight Gillespie had no choice but to yield on 30 September 1846 to Flores, who granted the

13 • The Californio Uprising and Its Aftermath

Americans very generous surrender terms. The Americans were permitted to keep their weapons and to march unopposed to San Pedro, the little port serving Los Angeles, where they could find water and, hopefully, a friendly ship. Accordingly, on 1 October 1846, Gillespie and his men, accompanied by some refugees from Los Angeles, arrived at San Pedro. Three days later, they all boarded the American merchantman *Vandalia* there and waited at anchor for orders.

When Stockton, who was aboard his flagship in San Francisco Bay, learned from hard-riding John Brown that the *Californios* had risen in southern California and that Gillespie and his men were in dire straits, he sent Captain Mervine in the *Savannah* to rescue them. Thus it was that on 7 October 1846 some 225 Marines and sailors from the *Savannah*, backed up by Gillespie's own men from the *Vandalia*, went ashore to try to recapture Los Angeles.

This episode provides some useful insights into both the difficulties of conducting amphibious operations and the personality clashes which could so easily erupt in the process. As a career seaman, Mervine was an expert on naval operations but he had no firsthand experience conducting land campaigns.

In this particular case, he apparently did not realize that to attack Los Angeles with the greatest hope of success he first needed to have in place—that is, right at hand—some assets which he did not then possess, namely, ambulances, supplies, and artillery. Gillespie, for his part, knew very well, as an experienced Marine Corps officer, precisely what was needed. So, unleashing his always-quick temper, Gillespie bitingly criticized Mervine's attack as being "irrational."

This accusation must have infuriated Mervine, but relations between the two men would grow even worse. For example, as the battle progressed near Rancho de los Palos Verdes (a cattle ranch whose name in Spanish means "the ranch of the green trees"), the *Californios* opened fire on American troops as they were filing through a narrow canyon. Gillespie's sharpshooters soon cleared the heights of the *Californio* riflemen, but this incident led to furious words from Mervine. Indeed, Gillespie would write that "Captain Mervine now began to holler after me, 'Captain Gillespie, you are wasting ammunition. We can't spare the caps!'—repeating this and a variety of like expressions of displeasure, discouraging to my men."[5]

After having four of his men killed and several wounded, Mervine broke off this joint effort to retake Los Angeles and on 8 October 1846 he ordered all the remaining troops to withdraw to San Pedro. Gillespie was greatly angered by this retreat: he felt that if the Americans had held their ground and continued to fight, they would have won decisively. From this time on, these two men would be bitter enemies.[6]

The *Californio* uprising had forced Mervine, Gillespie, and their men to leave Los Angeles. By December 1846, however, Stockton felt that his own forces were now strong enough to recapture the city. He therefore decided to form a remarkable corps of Horse Marines, simply by putting the Marines under his command on horseback.

This was not, in fact, a brilliant idea. Marines were sea-going infantrymen. They had been carefully taught how to fight valiantly both on land and at sea, but they had never been taught how to manage horses. Nevertheless, they were trained to obey orders, and obey orders they did. One eyewitness—Ordinary Seaman Joseph T. Downey of the *Portsmouth*—described the first and only outing of Stockton's Horse Marines.

Downey wrote:

> The crowd was waiting with gaping mouths to see how the Horse Marines would work. "Mount!" was the word and mount they did, and no sooner were they mounted than a number of them were dismounted again. Then commenced a scene which soon convulsed the bystanders with Laughter, and convinced the Old Commander [Stockton] that his scheme would not work.
>
> I have said that a number were dismounted. I might have said "a great number," but shall not, nor shall I say that they were not at all particular how they dismounted, nor shall I say that some came over the head, and some over the stern, of the Horses, some on the right, and more on the wrong side, nor how many legs were seen at once in the air, as their owners were describing involuntary sommersets, nor how muskets flew in all directions nor how some of the Horses ran away with their Riders and more without their Riders, how Marines, Muskets, caps [the cloth caps worn as part of the Marine uniform] and Horse Equipage was strewed in promiscuous heaps from one end of town to the other.[7]

Needless to say, the idea of Horse Marines was quickly scrapped. Stockton prudently decided that if the Marines were ever going to

13 • The Californio Uprising and Its Aftermath

recapture Los Angeles, they would have to march there, not ride there.

On a personal level, the *Californio* uprising can probably best be summed up by quoting at some length the experiences of U.S. Army lieutenant Theodore Talbot. Referring to events which had taken place the autumn before, he wrote on 15 January 1847:

> My position [in Santa Barbara] was a very pleasant one; Santa Barbara being the residence of some of the stateliest Dons and prettiest Señoras in all California. I had been here, however, but a few days when I received a *correo* [a letter], post-haste from Capt. Gillespie, bringing news of a rebellion in the south—the City of Angels being surrounded by 500 Californians under arms. The courier had barely escaped with his life, and brought me Gillespie's motto seal, concealed in a cigarita, to vouch for the truth of what he said.
>
> Although my position was very precarious, I kept a firm upper lip in order to keep down the people of Santa Barbara, which had some 70 fighting men and several resident Mexican officers, until aid could be received from the north. I succeeded in this until the City of the Angels was taken, and Gillespie forced to capitulate. Manuel Garpis, the commander, then marched with two hundred men on Santa Barbara. They surrounded the town, and sent in a letter demanding my surrender, and guarantying our lives, etc., etc. They gave us two hours to deliberate.
>
> We had all determined not to surrender our arms; and, finding the place we then occupied untenable, with so small a force, we determined to push for the hills (our best ground for fighting), or die in the attempt. I accordingly marshalled my little force and marched out of the town without opposition—those who lay on the road [the *Californio* troops stationed along the road], retreating to the main force which was on the lower side of the town.
>
> Having so unexpectedly been allowed to pass their force, I camped in the hills overlooking the town, and determined to remain there a few days, and co-operate with any force which might be landed at Santa Barbara.

The Mexican soldiers, however, set fire to the hills where Talbot and his men were hiding. This forced them to flee for their lives and try to make their way to Monterey. Talbot wrote:

> After a month's travel [from the Tulare Valley in central California], coming some 500 miles, mostly afoot, enduring much hardship and suffering, we at length effected a junction with Col. Frémont at Monterey.

They were very glad to see us, for certainly they thought we had all been killed. In fact, the Californians had circulated that report. You must excuse me for dwelling on my little adventure; for the fact is, I have suffered more from downright starvation, cold, nakedness and every sort of privation than in any trip I have yet had to make, and I have made some rough ones.[8]

• 14 •

The Army of the West and the Mormon Battalion

While the Californio uprising is going on, U.S. Army brigadier general Stephen Watts Kearny leaves Santa Fe with the Army of the West on 25 September 1846, bound for San Diego. He will be followed by the Mormon Battalion, which will build a wagon road along the Gila River route in order to transport military supplies to California. Once in California, the men of the Mormon Battalion will support other American forces during the war.

After the United States declared war on Mexico on 13 May 1846, the initial American strategy was to field three armies: (1) the Army of Occupation, which was assigned to capture coastal northeast Mexico; (2) the Army of the Center, which was to take the key cities of north-central Mexico; and (3) the Army of the West under General Kearny, which is the most important army for the purposes of this book. However, several months into the war, the Americans realized that a fourth army would be needed as well. This last force, led by General Winfield Scott, was ordered to capture Mexico City itself, beginning with an amphibious landing in the east near Veracruz.[1]

The Army of the West had two major goals. The first goal was to seize Santa Fe, the territorial capital of Nuevo México (New Mexico). Once this had been done, the next objective was to march across the Southwest, capture San Diego, link up there with the U.S. Navy and Marine forces of the Pacific Squadron, and then take control of the major coastal ports of California.

As Kearny and his dragoons advanced from Santa Fe toward San Diego, on 6 October 1846 they met Kit Carson and his band of about

15 men near Socorro, New Mexico. Carson was carrying sealed dispatches from California to Washington. He told Kearny that California was now entirely pacified and was totally under American control; a civilian government was being organized and would be headed by Frémont as the first governor. This was disheartening news both for Kearny's dragoons and for Kearny himself.

The dragoons were very disappointed. They were trained to fight and were itching for a fight. Indeed, they told Dr. Griffin, an Army surgeon on Kearny's staff, that they had "hoped when leaving Santa Fe that they might have a little kick up with the good people of California but this blasted all our hopes, and reduced our expedition to one of mere escort duty."[2]

Kearny, for his part, must have been happy to learn that from a military point of view the war in California had been going so well, but its very success suggested that there might be nothing for him to do once he finally got to San Diego. For this reason, he decided to send 200 of his 300 dragoons back to New Mexico, thus keeping only 100 men for service in California.

He also prevailed on Carson to give his dispatches to another rider (Thomas Fitzpatrick, one of Kearny's scouts), and then turn around to retrace his own steps in order to lead Kearny and his remaining dragoons to California. Carson agreed to do so without any protest, despite what must have been his keen disappointment at this unexpected turn of events. Had he been allowed to deliver his dispatches to Washington as planned, he knew there was an excellent chance that he would have met President Polk and other high-ranking government officials—a singular and well-deserved honor for him. But as U.S. Army captain Abraham R. Johnson later wrote,

> The general [Kearny] told him [Carson] that he would relieve him of all responsibility, and place the mail in the hands of a safe person to carry it on. He [Carson] finally consented, and turned his face to the west again, just as he was on the eve of entering the settlements, after his arduous trip, and when he had set his hopes on seeing his family. It takes a brave man to give up his private feelings thus for the public good; but Carson is one such. Honour to him for it![3]

As Kearny and Carson and their combined forces continued their westward trek, on 23 November 1846 Kearny learned from an intercepted

Mexican courier, who was part of a Mexican unit driving horses to Sonora, Mexico, that the *Californios* had risen in revolt against American rule. This came as a great shock to Kearny because the 100 dragoons he still had with him would now not be enough for his military needs in California. Nevertheless, he had no alternative but to press on towards San Diego.

In this process, Carson would play a vital role. At one point in the journey, Kearny and his forces had camped on a hill near Rancho San Bernardino, a 35,000-acre Mexican land grant located about 90 miles from San Diego. There they were surrounded by hostile *Californio* patrols and did not have enough water for themselves or enough fodder for their horses. Kearny therefore decided to send out, on foot, three of his best men—namely, Carson himself, Lieutenant Edward F. Beale, and Beale's Indian servant Che-muc-tah—to make contact with other American forces and get help.

Senator Benton, who may have learned about this event from his son-in-law Frémont, describes the meager preparations of their trip (punctuation as in the original):

> The brief preparations for the forlorn hope [that these three men could somehow get through the *Californio* lines and arrange for help to be sent] were soon made; and brief they were. A rifle each, a blanket, a revolver, and a sharp knife, and no food; there was none in the camp. General Kearny invited Beale to come and sup with him. It was not the supper of Antony and Cleopatra; for when the camp starves, no general has a larder. It was meager enough.
>
> The General asked Beale what provisions he had to travel on; the answer was, nothing. The General called for his servant to inquire what his tent afforded; a handful of flour, was the answer. The General ordered it baked into a loaf and be given to Beale. When the loaf was brought, the servant said that was the last, not only of bread but of everything; that he had nothing left for the general's breakfast.
>
> Beale directed the servant to carry back the loaf, saying that he would provide for himself. He did provide for himself; and how? By going to the smoldering fire where the baggage [*sic*; here Benton must mean the scraps left over from the evening meal] had been burnt in the morning, and scraping from the ashes and embers the half-burned peas and grains of corn which the conflagration had spared, filling his pockets with the unwanted food. Carson and the faithful Indian provided for themselves with some mule meat.[4]

This was such a death-or-glory odyssey that here it is best to let Carson recount it in his own words. He told an interviewer:

> As soon as it was dark [on the night of 8 December 1847] we started on our mission. To avoid making a noise when crawling over the rocks and brush, we [Carson and Beale] took our shoes off [the Indian had never worn shoes and thus went barefoot], and fastened them under our belts.[5]
>
> We could see three rows of *Californio* sentinels, all mounted, and would have to pass within twenty yards of one of them. We finally got through, but we had to crawl about two miles, having the misfortune to lose our shoes, we had to travel barefoot over a country covered with prickly pear and rocks. We reached San Diego the next night, and Commodore Stockton immediately ordered 160 to 170 men to march to General Kearny's relief.
>
> I remained behind in San Diego, and Lieutenant Beale was sent aboard the frigate *Congress*. He had become deranged from his excessive exertions and did not entirely recover his health for two years.[6]

This ordeal was so exhausting that it had a very heavy impact even on wilderness-hardened Carson. With his usual gift for understatement, however, he would only admit that after the trip he had "felt poorly for several days."[7]

As all this was going on, the Mormon Battalion—the first and only religious unit in American military history—was also heading toward California.[8] One of its duties was to build a road for the wagons of the Army of the West. This road would later be used by some of the pioneers heading for the California gold field, by the Butterfield Stage Line, and by the Southern Pacific Railroad. Another important duty of the battalion would be to provide the troops needed by the Americans to occupy San Diego and Los Angeles.

The Mormons had recently been expelled from their settlement in Nauvoo, Illinois, and wanted help from the United States to move further west. President Polk was willing to assist them (he did not forget that he had received Mormon votes) and suggested that they enter the military service of the United States.[9] Instructions were accordingly issued to Kearny to enlist them in the Army of the West.

The newly-formed Mormon Battalion marched out of Santa Fe on 19 October 1846, just when Kearny and the Army of the West were getting close to the Gila River. With too many wagons and not enough food, the trip was already very hard on the Mormons. One of them—Robert L. Bliss—wrote this on 6 November 1846, just before the battalion turned westward from the Rio Grande. Spelling and punctuation are as in the original:

> [W]e are now on half rations & have only 60 days Rations from Santa Fee & [w]e expect it will take us at least 120 days to go to the Pacific or Bay of San Francisco ... our teams are tiring out & we expect a hard time if we are not intercepted by an Enemy [Bliss had heard rumors that the Mexicans might attack the battalion]; we are cheerful & happy notwithstanding we have to carry our Guns accoutrements Napsacks Canteens haversacks & push our Waggons over hills which are not few nor far between & we expect still greater difficulties when we leave this River to cross the Mountains.[10]

As if this were not enough, in southeast Cochise County, Arizona, the Mormons also had to fight a running battle with wild cattle. The leader of the battalion, Lieutenant Colonel Philip St. George Cooke, has left this remarkable account:

> One [bull] ran on a man, caught him in the thigh, and threw him clear over his body lengthwise; it then charged on a team, ran his head under the first mule, tore out the entrails of the one beyond, and threw them both over. Another ran against a sergeant, who escaped with severe bruises, as the horns went on either side of him. A third ran at a horse tied to a wagon, and, as it escaped, the great momentum forced the hind part of the wagon from the road. I saw one rush at some pack mules and gore one so that its entrails came out broken.
>
> I also saw an immense coalblack bull charge on Corporal Frost of Company A. He stood his ground while the animal rushed on for one hundred yards. I was close by and believed the man was in great danger of his life and spoke to him. He aimed his musket very deliberately and only fired when the beast was within ten paces; and it fell headlong, almost to his feet.
>
> One man, when charged on, threw himself flat on the ground, and the bull jumped over him and passed on. I have seen the heart of a bull with two balls through it, that ran on a man with these wounds, and two others through the lungs![11]

Cooke writes with such enthusiasm that it is fitting to end this chapter by quoting his Order Number 1, issued from the Headquarters of the Mormon Battalion, Mission of San Diego, on 30 January 1847, the day after the battalion finally arrived there. He wrote in part:

> The lieutenant-colonel congratulates the battalion on their safe arrival on the shore of the Pacific Ocean, and the conclusion of the march over two thousand miles. History may be searched in vain for an equal march of infantry. Nine-tenths of it has been through a wilderness where nothing but savages and wild beasts are found, or deserts where, for want of water, there is no living creature. There, with almost hopeless labor, we have dug deep wells which the future traveler will enjoy.
>
> Without a guide who had traversed them, we have ventured into trackless prairies where water was not found for several marches. With crowbar and pick and ax in hand we have worked our way over mountains which seemed to defy aught save the wild goat, and hewed a passage through a chasm of living rock more narrow than our wagons.... Thus, marching half naked and half fed, and living upon wild animals, we have discovered and made a road of great value to our country.[12]

The men of the Mormon Battalion were discharged at Los Angeles on 16 July 1847. They had managed to bring their wagons all the way from Fort Leavenworth, Kansas, to the Pacific Ocean. Later, and after some modifications, the route they pioneered would become the most heavily traveled road to California across what is now the American Southwest.[13] They did an excellent job, too, in California itself. An American living in Los Angeles wrote of them in a letter of 22 June 1847:

> The Mormon force here and at San Diego consists of about 360 men. Their term of service expires on the 17th of July [1847]. They have been invited to re-enter the service for another year, but at present there is not much prospect of their doing so. This is extremely to be regretted, for they are an orderly, quiet, and peaceable set of men, submitting without resistance or a murmur to the severest discipline, and altogether a most useful and efficient body of men.[14]

• 15 •

The Battle of San Pascual

Californio lancers defeat American soldiers at the battle of San Pascual on 6 December 1846.

Small as it was when compared to the battles of other wars, the battle of San Pascual, which took place eight miles east of what is now Escondido, California, which in turn is about 30 miles from San Diego, was the most noteworthy *Californio* victory and the greatest American defeat of the war.

On 3 December 1846, after a hard two-day ride through cold, rainy weather, Gillespie and his men finally made contact with Kearny. They discovered, however, that Kearny's dragoons were not ready to fight the *Californios* because their long ride across the deserts towards California had exhausted them and their horses. In fact, many of their best horses had died en route and had been replaced with half-wild horses picked up from local ranches.

Despite these setbacks, however, Kearny, Gillespie, and Carson agreed that the poorly-trained and badly-led *Californios* could not possibly defeat their own corps of well-trained, highly-motivated American soldiers serving under able and experienced officers. Kearny therefore decided to move forward and to attack, at dawn on 6 December 1846, the 80 to 100 *Californio* lancers led by Captain Andrés Pico, who were known to be camped close to the nearby Indian village of San Pascual.

Such lancers were the elite arm of the Mexican cavalry—a fact which, never having seen them in action and having a low opinion of Mexicans in general, the Americans entirely failed to understand. Most of the lancers had first learned their trade as *vaqueros* by using their spears to slaughter the large number of half-wild and unwanted cattle that were consuming valuable pasturage in Alta California. In combat, these lancers carried long, wooden-hafted spears with iron tips and fitted with cross-toggles to prevent the spears from penetrating the body of an enemy too deeply. If the spear did penetrate deeply, it would be difficult or impossible for the lancer to retrieve his weapon quickly and use it again on another target. The lances often had small red pennons attached near their tips. These were designed to flutter before the eyes of enemy horses and thus frighten them.

At the battle of San Pascual, American military pride would outstrip American military might. The first portent of trouble was a bungled American pre-attack reconnaissance mission launched at night. Led by Lieutenant Thomas C. Hammond, this foray made so much noise, thanks to its clanking sabers, that the *Californios* quickly woke up and rode out to meet the Americans, shouting at them: *"Viva California. Bajos los Americanos, hijos de putas"* ("Long live California! Down with the Americans, sons of whores!").[1]

Nevertheless, despite this inauspicious beginning, at 2:00 a.m. on 6 December 1846, Kearny ordered his dragoons to move forward through the cold rain that was falling and wetting the gunpowder in their firearms. Kearny told Gillespie to stay in the rear of the American column to supervise the troops guarding the artillery, baggage, and supplies. At the same time, the dragoons at the head of the column were instructed to ride forward and attack the lancers led by *Californio* Captain Andrés Pico.

To narrow the considerable distance (more than 1,000 yards) then separating the Americans and the *Californios*, Kearny gave the order for his dragoons to break into a trot. However, Captain Johnson, who was leading an advance guard with Carson and about 40 other men, misheard this command. He thought that it was an order to *gallop*, so he, Carson, and about 12 dragoons, all of whom were mounted on good horses in good condition, immediately rushed forward at top speed. They made the fatal mistake, however, of charging without any support from the main body of Kearny's force, which was very poorly mounted and was now strung out a mile and a half behind them.

The *Californios*, who were then retreating before the attack of the

15 • The Battle of San Pascual

advance guard, paused just long enough to put a bullet through Johnson's head. Seeing this, Captain Pico and his lancers (these men were probably the best light horsemen in the world at that time) quickly wheeled around and attacked the now-disorganized dragoons.

Just before this happened, Gillespie had ordered his own riflemen to dismount and to open fire on the *Californios*. When he saw Johnson fall, however, he immediately galloped forward himself to try to organize the dragoons to fight effectively.

Because of damp gunpowder, the Americans' muzzleloading muskets would not always fire.[2] As a result, the Americans were reduced to fighting with their sabers, which were entirely ineffective against the long lances of the *Californios*, and to swinging their now-useless muskets as clubs. Felicita, an Indian woman of the San Pascual tribe, watched the battle. She later recalled that

> the Americans did not shoot their guns many times; perhaps the rain had made the powder wet. They struck with their guns and used the sword, while the Mexicans used their long lances and their *riatas* [lariats]. The mules that the Americans rode were frightened and ran all through the willows by the river. After them rode the Mexicans on their swift horses, striking with the lance and *lassoing* with the *riata*; it was a very terrible time.[3]

Another firsthand account of the battle comes from the *Californio* lancer José P. Palomáres, who reported,

> With our lances and swords we attacked the enemy forces, who could not make good use either of their firearms or of their swords.... We did not fire a single shot: the combat was more favorable to us with our sidearms (swords) [because of the thick press of battle, the *Californios* found it better to use their swords rather than their muskets]. Quickly the battle became so bloody that we became intertangled one with the other and were barely able to distinguish one from the other by voice and by the dim light of dawn which began to break.[4]

Gillespie, for his part, was a very hard-charging Marine. He parried six lance thrusts but then was hit on the back of his neck, perhaps by the butt of a lance; toppled off his horse; and was then pinned to the ground by a lance thrust that left such a deep gash in his back that it nearly penetrated his lungs. His horse had to leap over him. A second lance-thrust went through one of his lips and broke a tooth.

Nevertheless, despite his wounds, he managed to struggle to his feet and make his way toward Kearny's two howitzers. The *Californios* had already captured one of them, but the other stood loaded and ready to fire. The American artillerymen around the gun did not have any matches to use to fire it, so Gillespie used his own cigar lighter to set off the powder charge and fire the howitzer. He then collapsed from loss of blood. Midshipman James N. Duncan quickly had another howitzer wheeled up; his troops fired it and its charge of grapeshot scythed down some of the attacking *Californios*.

Carson himself had a very narrow escape during this fight. He had been in the advance guard galloping toward the *Californio* camp and remembered that

> when we were within one hundred yards of their camp, my horse fell and threw me, and my rifle was broken into two pieces. I barely escaped being trodden to death, since I was in advance and the whole command had to pass over me. I finally saved myself by crawling out of the way. I then ran on about one hundred yards to where the fight had commenced. I saw a dead dragoon and taking his gun and cartridge box I joined in the melee.[5]

In this battle, the *Californios* were clearly victorious, although at the end of the day the Americans still held the field and on this technical ground they tried to claim a victory. Kearny himself, however, wrote to his wife: "We gained a victory ... but paid most dearly for it."[6]

The battle of San Pascual was the bloodiest battle of the California campaigns. Out of a total of 153 Americans involved, 18 were killed and 13 were wounded—including not only Gillespie but also Kearny himself. The 75 *Californios*, for their part, had 13 men wounded and one taken prisoner, so, with reason, they considered this fight to have been a *Californio* victory.

• 16 •

The Treaty of Cahuenga

Two California *defeats near Los Angeles lead to the Treaty of Cahuenga, which is signed on 16 January 1847 at Campo de Cahuenga, the site of an abandoned adobe ranch-house. As Frémont will boast at his court-martial in 1848, "It put an end to the war [in Alta California but not in Baja California] and to the feelings of war. It tranquilized the country, and gave safety to every American from the day of its conclusion."*[1]

About one month after acquitting themselves so well at the battle of San Pasqual, on 8 and 9 January 1847 the *Californios* lost the last two significant military engagements of the war in California, i.e., the minor battles of San Gabriel and La Mesa, and realized that their situation was now hopeless. They clearly had no alternative but to surrender to the Americans.

In the first of these clashes, on 8 January 1847 a joint Stockton-Kearny army encountered Flores' 500-man force at the San Gabriel River, not far from Los Angeles. The *Californio* artillery opened fire on the Americans but the poor quality of its gunpowder, coupled with the poor aim of its gunners, prevented many American casualties. American troops then waded into the river, crossed it, and attacked the *Californios* on the other bank. Captain William H. Emory, who was Kearny's aide, remembered that "the enemy opened his battery, and made the water fly with grape and round shot. Our artillery was now ordered to cross—it was unlimbered, pulled over by the men, and placed in counter-battery."[2]

Kearny himself personally aimed the American artillery pieces, which, upon firing, silenced two of Flores' cannons. American troops then charged up a hill held by the *Californios* and formed "hollow squares." (A hollow square was a classic close-order combat formation used by an infantry unit when it was threatened by a cavalry attack.) The Americans fired only one or two musket volleys before the *Californios* broke off the fight and retreated towards Los Angeles. Although this battle went on for an hour and a half, on each side only two men were killed and only a few wounded.

The next day, 9 January 1847, the two armies met again, this time on the plain of La Mesa, some six miles up the river. Although some of Flores' force had melted away, he was still able to field about 300 men. The battle persisted for two and a half hours but it was inconclusive. Although Flores' artillerymen fired up nearly all the gunpowder they had, not a single American, and only one *Californio*, was killed in this encounter.

The net result of these clashes was that, since any Mexican defense of Los Angeles had now evaporated, on 10 January 1847 the Americans were able to reoccupy the city. Gillespie himself raised the American flag which had been hauled down in defeat about four months earlier. Four days later, on 14 January 1847, Frémont arrived in Los Angeles at the head of 400 men. Remarkably, he brought with him a treaty of the *Californios'* surrender—namely, the Treaty of Cahuenga—which would be signed on 16 January 1847. Equally remarkable, Frémont had drafted this document himself without consulting either of his superiors—Stockton or Kearny. The remnants of Flores' army had signed it.

This document halted the war in Alta California. Known to the Mexicans as the "Capitulation of Cahuenga," it was not in fact a formal treaty between the United States and Mexico but was rather an informal agreement between two rival military forces (the Americans and the *Californios*), the upshot of which was that the *Californios* agreed to stop fighting in Alta California.[3] This document, drafted by José Antonio Carrillo in Spanish and in English, was approved by Frémont and by Mexican governor Andrés Pico at Campo de Cahuenga in what is now North Hollywood in Los Angeles, California. Frémont later presented the document to Stockton, who formally approved it.

Its provisions included the following items. It called on the *Californios* to give up their artillery. It provided that prisoners on both sides should be freed at once. The *Californios* who promised not to take up arms again and agreed to obey the laws and regulations of the

United States could return peacefully to their own homes and ranches. They would be allowed the same rights and privileges enjoyed by American citizens, but were not compelled to take an oath of allegiance until a peace treaty was signed between the United States and Mexico. They could leave Alta California if they wished to do so. This agreement would later be incorporated into the official Treaty of Guadalupe Hidalgo on 2 February 1848 between the United States and Mexico.

The preamble of the Treaty of Cahuenga, which contains all its essential points, reads as follows[4]:

> To All To Whom These Presents Shall Come, Greeting: Know Ye, that in consequence of the propositions of peace, or cessation of hostilities, being submitted to me, as Commandant of the California Battalion of the United States forces, which have so far been acceded to by me as to cause me to appoint a board of commissioners to confer with a similar board appointed by the Californians, and it requiring a little time to close the negotiations; it is agreed and ordered by me that an entire cessation of hostilities shall take place tomorrow afternoon (January 13 [1847]), and that the said Californians be permitted to bring in their wounded to the mission of San Fernando where, also if they choose, they can move their camp to facilitate said negotiations.
>
> J. C. Frémont
> Lieutenant-Colonel U.S.A. and
> Military Commandant of California

The full text of this document, signed on 16 January 1847, also included eight Articles spelling out its logistical details. It was signed both by Frémont and by *Californio* commander, Andrés Pico. After the 1848 Treaty of Guadalupe-Hidalgo ending the war as a whole, Pico would become an American citizen and later a state assemblyman and then a state senator representing Los Angeles in the California State Legislature.[5]

Thus, in a little more than half a year, a relative handful of American forces, namely, the California Battalion, the naval and Marine forces of the Pacific Squadron, two companies of Kearny's dragoons, and the Mormon Battalion, had managed to seize Alta California. At the same time, however, a legal process would begin which would result in Frémont's conviction by a court-martial in 1848.

• 17 •

The Earliest Days of the Gold Rush

The discovery of gold in California has already been mentioned in this book but further details are needed now to explore the relationship between the California campaigns and the earliest days of the Gold Rush. The underlying issue here is simply stated: an American soldier on active duty in California earned only $7 per month. If he deserted, he could earn $10 to $20 per day in the mines as a common laborer. Skilled men, e.g., drivers of ox teams, could make twice as much as senior U.S. Army officers.

The U.S.–Mexican War was still going on when gold was discovered on 24 January 1848, and the gold frenzy would continue long after the Treaty of Guadalupe Hidalgo finally brought the war to an end on 2 February 1848. The treaty was ratified by the United States on 30 May 1848 and was formally proclaimed (i.e., officially published by it) on 4 July 1848. News of the treaty, however, did not reach California (via La Paz and Los Angeles) until 6 August 1848.[1] By that time, the nascent gold rush was already well underway.

The celebrated author and humorist Mark Twain, who had considerable personal experience with the boom-and-bust psychology of mining in Nevada,[2] was certainly right about the Sierra Nevada mountains. He had one of his fictional characters boast of them, "There's gold in them thar hills!"[3] In many cases, the truth about such mining—or at least what then passed for the truth—was stranger than fiction. Here are some examples[4]:

- A Southerner brought his slave with him to a settlement known as Old Dry Diggins, near Coloma, California. The

17 • The Earliest Days of the Gold Rush

slave repeatedly dreamed about finding gold under a certain cabin there. When his master had a similar dream, the master bought the cabin. Together the two men dug up the dirt floor and panned out $20,000 in gold.
- Another man in the same settlement took out $2,000 in gold from under his own doorstep.
- Three Frenchmen dug out a tree stump in the middle of the Coloma road and retrieved $5,000 in gold from the hole.
- A little girl found a strange-looking, colorful rock and brought it to her mother, who washed it and found that it was a lump of pure gold, weighing between six and seven pounds.[5]
- In the summer of 1848, an ox-team driver named John Sullivan panned out $26,000 in gold dust from a Sierra creek.
- The next summer, a young man staked a claim somewhere between Coloma and the middle fork of the American River. He dug down four feet to bedrock and found gold there in big chunks. In six weeks, he took out $20,000 worth of gold, including one nugget weighing 14 pounds.

All this came about because on 24 January 1848, as John Marshall made his daily inspection of the millrace on the downstream side of Sutter's mill, he found a few bits of gold there. He wrote in his diary:

> I went down as usual and after shutting off the water from the race I stepped into it, near the lower end, and there upon the rock about six inches beneath the water I discovered the gold. I picked up one or two pieces, and examined them attentively. I then tried it between two rocks and found that it could be beaten into a different shape but not broken.[6]

Another man working at the mill with Marshall was Henry Bigler, one of the several Mormon Battalion veterans employed by Sutter. Bigler made this succinct note in his own diary (spelling and punctuation are as in the original): "Monday 24th [January 1848] this day some kind of mettle was found in the tail race that looks like goald discovered by James Marshall the Boss of the Mill."[7]

At Marshall's suggestion, the mill hands pooled all the tiny fragments of gold that they found. They then gave the gold to Bigler, who scattered it in plain sight along the millrace. He did this in the expectation that Sutter would find it and, to celebrate, would give the men a drink from the jug of *aguardiente* which Sutter—being a very jovial man—usually carried with him to share with friends.

Interestingly, this is the first recorded case in California of "salting" a mining claim.[8] In mineral exploration, "salting" was the illegal process of adding gold or silver to an ore sample to make the underlying body of ore appear more valuable than it really was. However, since this was the first time that gold had been discovered in the foothills of the Sierra Nevada mountains, there was no possible way for Marshall and Bigler to know that there was in fact a vast amount of gold there.

Bigler made another entry in his diary on 30 January 1848: "Sunday 30th clear [clear weather]. Our metal has been tride and proves to be gold it is thought to be rich we have pict up more than a hundred dollars woth last week."[9]

In addition to being the most reliable chronicler of the discovery of gold, he was also the first man in the area to go out deliberately looking for more gold. On Sundays and at every other opportunity, for example, he went off looking at likely spots, no longer looking in the millrace itself but now in the many other streams, gullies, ravines, and sandbars threading through the area.

On Sunday, 6 February 1848, he and James Barger, another Mormon Battalion veteran, crossed the river and, using the jackknives Sutter had given them for this purpose, dug into rock crevices and picked out the gold, speck by speck. By nightfall they had collected $10 worth. Increasingly, Bigler now began to go off by himself, claiming that he wanted to hunt ducks or deer alone. In practice, of course, he simply wanted to find more gold. This became a lucrative pursuit for him: by using his jackknife, in one day he could sometimes find as much as an ounce and a half of gold, worth $24.

Sutter himself was a very good natured man and often fell prey to his own boastful impulses. Indeed, he lacked the very caution he urged upon his employees. He even bragged publicly about the gold discovery in a 10 February 1848 letter to General Mariano Vallejo. With the grace for which *Californio* gentlemen were so well known, Vallejo politely remarked that "as water flows through Sutter's millrace, may the gold flow into Sutter's purse."[10]

Not surprisingly, it did not take very long for news of the discovery

17 • The Earliest Days of the Gold Rush

of gold to find its way into print in California. On 15 March 1848, a San Francisco paper, the *Californian*, ran the following story:

> GOLD MINE FOUND.—In the newly made raceway of the Saw Mill recently erected by Captain Sutter, on the American Fork, gold has been discovered in considerable quantities. One person brought thirty dollars worth to New Helvetia [Sutter's Fort], gathered there in a short time. California, no doubt, is rich in mineral wealth; great chances here for scientific capitalists. Gold has been found in almost every part of this country [in California].[11]

There were probably no more than a few hundred gold seekers in the field in May 1848 but by midsummer there were between 8,000 and 10,000 men in the Sierra foothills. Something like $250,000 worth of gold was scooped from the rich California earth in 1848 alone. Army Captain Joseph L. Folsom wrote to a colleague, future Civil War General William Tecumseh Sherman, who had been stationed in Monterey, that he (Folsom) expected soon to be the very last person left in San Francisco: almost all of the other inhabitants had left the town for the gold fields. Folsom joked that "only lunatic asylums can effect a cure of the present ills of the body public—at least until hunger drives all the visionary fools from the gold 'diggins.'"[12]

One of the most readable accounts of the gold rush comes from the former journalist and former lieutenant of the New York Volunteers, Edward Gould Buffum, who has already been quoted. After his discharge in Los Angeles from the New York Volunteers, he decided to stay on in California and to pan for gold in the region around Sutter's sawmill. (To pan for gold is to use water and a shallow metal pan to separate out the tiny particles of gold from the sand and gravel in which they are hidden.)

He was amazed to learn that successful miners could make $100 per day on the average—at a time when common laborers in other parts of the United States were earning only $1 a day. In his excellent 1850 book *Six Months in the Gold Mines* (1850), Buffum gives this account of his first experience panning gold:

> On this visit to Foster's Bar [a spot on the American River where a miner named Foster had been successful] I made my first essay in gold-digging. I scraped up with my hand my tin cup full of earth, and washed it in the river. How eagerly I strained my eyes as the earth was washing

155

out, and the bottom of the cup was coming into view! and how delighted, when, on reaching the bottom, I discerned about twenty little golden particles sparkling in the sun's rays, and worth probably about fifty cents. I wrapped them carefully in a piece of paper, and preserved them for a long time—but, like much more gold in larger quantities, which it has since been my lot to possess, it has escaped my grasp, and where it is now Heaven only knows.[13]

One thing that Buffum and his fellow miners had to learn the hard way was that while earnings from gold mining might be very high, the cost of labor was very high, too. He writes:

> Our teamster's bill was something of an item [something of a shock] to men who were not as yet accustomed to "gold-mine prices." We paid three hundred dollars for the transportation, about fifty miles, of three barrels of flour, one of pork, and about two hundred pounds of small stores [a American naval term meaning personal items], being at the rate of thirty dollars per cwt. [per 100 lbs.] This was the regular price charged by teamsters at that time, and of course there was no alternative but to pay, which we did, although it exhausted the last dollar belonging to our party.
> But then, before us, on the banks of that pretty stream and in the neighboring gorges, lay the treasures that were to replenish our pockets, and the sigh for its departure was changed by this thought into a hope that our fondest wishes might be realized in our new and exciting occupation.[14]

An American military presence in the gold fields was soon evident. The military governor of California, Colonel R.B. Mason, toured the gold fields in June 1848 and then, upon his return to Monterey, drafted a report on his findings. He sent the report to Washington, along with some gold samples and a map dated 20 July 1848 showing where James Marshall had found the gold. President Polk included the map in a message to Congress, thereby officially confirming the discovery.[15]

Linking the gold directly to the war, Mason himself stated, "I have no hesitation now in saying that the country drained by the Sacramento and San Joaquin rivers will pay the cost of the war with Mexico a hundred times over."[16]

For an American public tired of the divisiveness and human and financial costs of the U.S.–Mexican War, the Mason report would provide a welcome bit of good news in Polk's opening message to the second session of the 30th Congress on 5 December 1848. Nevertheless, the gold rush would bring significant problems with it as well as great opportunities. For example, in the 18 months beginning 1 July 1848, the Army in northern California lost, by desertion, 716 men of a total 1,290. So many sailors jumped ship that the Pacific Squadron's commander, Thomas ap Catesby Jones, advised the secretary of the navy: "For the present and I fear for years to come, it will be impossible for the United States to maintain any naval establishment in California."[17]

Desertion was indeed a problem, but it was not the only one in the gold fields which was related to the war.[18] The discovery of gold had created a situation in which thousands of American immigrants were competing with native-born *Californio* miners in the gold fields. Residuals of anti–Mexican war-time patriotism, coupled with xenophobia, nativism, and racism, resulted in violent confrontations between English-speaking immigrants and Spanish-speaking residents. Eventually, most of the latter were driven away from the most profitable gold fields. As a consequence of vigilantism and its attendant lynchings, harassment, and abuse of "foreigners," several countries lodged diplomatic protests and financial claims against the U.S. government, but nothing came of them.

In 1849 the new military governor of California, General Percifor Smith, responding to local fears that foreigners were now sweeping up all the gold, issued "trespass" orders prohibiting non-citizens from mining gold on public property, i.e., virtually anywhere in the uninhabited foothills of the Sierra Nevada mountains. He also appealed to American civilians to help him enforce his policy. The result was that, under the protection of the American military establishment, Anglo-American miners could rob and harass "foreigners" with impunity. Since neither the Americans nor the Mexican government considered *Californios* to be their own citizens, these miners were left without the protection of either nation.

Smith and his wife had arrived in San Francisco on 28 February 1849 and soon heard that no confidence could be placed in either American regular or volunteer troops to stay at their posts and maintain law and order in California. He was told that they would desert in large numbers, along with sailors from naval and commercial vessels alike.[19] Indeed, Smith also learned that some of the most trusted British

Marines had already deserted from British ships, together with their petty officers (noncommissioned officers)—a very rare and perhaps even unprecedented event in British naval history. In fact, however, all vessels, of whatever nationality, which moored in San Francisco Bay during the Gold Rush would lose part or all of their crews.[20]

Brigadier General Bennet Riley, with troops of the U.S. 2nd Infantry, arrived at Monterey on 12 April 1849 aboard the transport *Iowa*.[21] The next day he assumed the duties of being both military governor and commander of the 10th Military Department. By stationing his troops as near the gold mines as possible, he hoped to keep the peace and, at the same time, to minimize defections. Los Angeles and San Luis Rey were therefore abandoned as military posts, and, to mitigate this loss, weapons for defense were supplied to uneasy farmers and other respectable people.

Furloughs continued to be granted to soldiers, allowing them to hunt for gold on their own time, when they were not on duty. Given the very limited forces at Riley's command, he made repeated requests to Washington for additional men, especially for ordnance, medical, and topographical staff officers, but Washington was not very responsive and he had only meager results to show for his efforts.[22]

· 18 ·

Frémont Is Court-Martialed

On 31 January 1848, after a court-martial trial, one year, Frémont is found guilty of mutiny, disobedience to the lawful command of a superior officer, and conduct prejudicial to good order and military discipline. President Polk drops the charge of mutiny (the penalty for which was dismissal from the service) but approves the other two charges. The court-martial had recommended executive clemency, so Polk remits the sentence, releases Frémont from arrest, and orders him to report for active duty. Frémont, however, refuses to accept Polk's pardon, on the grounds that acceptance would be an admission of guilt. He resigns from the Army instead.

When Kearny finally reached California, he was carrying orders from President Polk to set up a civilian government with himself at the helm. But by the time he got there, Stockton had already formed a government on his own authority and refused to surrender command to Kearny. The stage was thus set for an epic legal squabble.

On 16 January 1847, less than one week after the American occupation of Los Angeles, Stockton arbitrarily renewed Frémont's appointment as military governor of California.[1] Quite remarkably, he did so in the face of orders from President Polk stating that *Kearny*, not Frémont, should be the next governor. Stockton would argue, quite inaccurately and unconvincingly, that his own consolidation of political power in California somehow overrode the President's directive.

Kearny thus found himself in an impossible situation. On the one hand, he had no personal desire to become governor; on the other, while he had to obey the President's orders, he had no practical way to do so if Stockton would not agree. The only military force Kearny still had at his own disposal was a small unit of 50 dragoons: it was Frémont who commanded most of the forces, and Frémont had sided with Stockton in hopes of furthering his own career.

On 18 January 1847, the day after a confrontation with Stockton and Frémont, Kearny left Los Angeles for San Diego. There he awaited instructions from Washington. However, this issue began to be resolved early in February 1847, when Commodore Branford Shubrick, Stockton's successor, arrived in California. He lifted the onerous curfew law which Stockton had imposed and which Gillespie had vigorously enforced, and he sent the *Cyane* to bring Kearny to Monterey for a conference.

At that meeting, Shubrick yielded to Kearny's authority but persuaded him not to raise the Frémont issue before the imminent arrival of Richard B. Mason, commander of the 1st Dragoons. When Mason did arrive, he was carrying orders from President Polk to take over the governorship himself whenever Kearny decided that Alta California had been sufficiently pacified to permit this. It was agreed that, with Shubrick's assent, Kearny would be officially confirmed as military commander and as civil governor. Kearny himself was to go east to Fort Leavenworth as soon as California was pacified; Mason would then succeed him in California.

Frémont was so infuriated by this turn of events that he conjured up the image of a non-existent Indian revolt and even challenged Mason to a duel. (Frémont was furious because these events ended his own hopes for high political office in California. Fortunately, Kearny forbade the duel.) But all Frémont's strident defiance came to naught. The California Battalion was quietly disbanded in the Sacramento area. Stockton and Gillespie soon traveled overland back to Fort Leavenworth and in June 1847 both Kearny and Frémont also left for Fort Leavenworth.

There, on 22 August 1847, Kearny formally brought charges against Frémont, accusing him of mutiny, disobedience of orders, assumption of powers, and conduct prejudicial to military discipline. Recalled to Washington for a court-martial which was held from November 1847 through January 1848, Frémont was found guilty of most of the charges. His appointment to take the position of governor of California was revoked and he was sentenced to dismissal from the Army. President Polk approved the conviction for disobedience and mutiny, but remitted the penalty of dismissal from the Army. Nevertheless, Frémont angrily resigned.

During his testimony at the court-martial, Frémont did not make a favorable impression on observers, coming across as unrepentant, greedy, self-centered, rash, insubordinate, and melodramatic.[2] Some of his concluding comments in his 58-page "Defense of Lieut. Col. J.C. Fremont, before the military court martial" bear this out. He stridently told the court-martial:

> I consider these difficulties in California to be a comedy (very near a tragedy) of three errors: first, in the faulty orders sent out from this place [Washington, D.C.]; next, in the unjustifiable pretensions of General Kearny; thirdly, in the conduct of the government in sustaining these pretensions. And the last of these errors I consider the greatest of the three.
>
> Certainly the difficulties in California ought to be inquired into; but how? Not by prosecuting the subordinate [Frémont himself], but the principals; not by prosecuting him who prevented, but him who would have made civil war. If it was a crime in me to accept the governorship from Commodore Stockton, it was a crime for him to have bestowed it; and, in either event, crime or not, the government which knew of his intention to appoint me, and did not forbid it, has lost the right of prosecuting either of us.
>
> My acts in California have all been with high motives, and not a desire for the public service.... I prevented civil war against Governor Stockton, by refusing to join General Kearny against him: I arrested civil war against myself, by consenting to be deposed, offering at the same time to resign my place of lieutenant colonel in the army....
>
> I am now ready to receive the sentence of the court.[3]

After the court-martial, Frémont was still very well-known to the American public and he still wanted to advance much further in the future, by becoming president of the United States. The story of his later—and invariably unsuccessful—adventures is a very interesting one, but this is not the place for it.

Suffice it to say that Frémont's dreams of glory were never realized and that he eventually died in poverty in New York in July 1890. His wife Jessie, who was living in Los Angeles, partially on the charity of friends there, and whose excellent writing was all that had saved the couple from financial ruin, could not even afford to travel east to his funeral. The best she could do was to send by mail, so that it could be buried with him, the miniature of herself which she had sent west with Kit Carson for Frémont to carry on his second expedition.

• 19 •

The Treaty of Guadalupe Hidalgo

The Treaty of Guadalupe Hidalgo ends the war everywhere in Mexico on 2 February 1848. Under the terms of this treaty, the United States acquires more than half a million square miles of Mexican territory and will become a world power in the late 19th century.

The enormous impact of this treaty has been ably summed up by the scholar Richard Griswold del Castillo in these words:

> Beyond territorial gains and losses, the treaty has been important in shaping the international and domestic histories of both Mexico and the United States. During the U.S.–Mexican War, U.S. leaders assumed an attitude of moral superiority in their negotiations of the treaty. They viewed the forcible incorporation of almost one-half of Mexico's national territory as an event foreordained by providence, fulfilling Manifest Destiny to spread the benefits of U.S. democracy to the lesser peoples of the continent. Because of its military victory the United States virtually dictated the terms of settlement. The treaty established a pattern of political and military inequality between the two countries, and this lopsided relationship has stalked U.S.–Mexican relations ever since.[1]

During the U.S.–Mexican War, some Americans expected that Baja California, like Alta California itself, would inevitably—and sooner rather than later—become part of the United States. For example, before leaving with the Pacific Squadron to capture Mazatlán, Commodore Shubrick had proclaimed on 4 November 1847 that "the flag of the United States is destined to wave forever over the Californias. No contingency can be seen in which the United States will ever surrender or relinquish the possession of the Californias."[2]

Moreover, on 7 December 1847, while the Mexicans were trying to recapture La Paz, President Polk said in his annual message to Congress:

> Early in the commencement of the war, New Mexico and the Californias were taken possession by our forces. Our military and naval commanders were ordered to conquer and to hold them, subject to being disposed of by a treaty of peace. These Provinces are now in our undisputed occupation and have been so for many months, all resistance on the part of Mexico having ceased within their limits.... I am satisfied that they should never be surrendered to Mexico.[3]

In addition, on 12 April 1848, U.S. Army lieutenant Henry W. Halleck wrote to Colonel Richard M. Mason, the military governor of California:

> For the United States to voluntarily surrender this country [Baja California] to the Republic of Mexico, and leave the Californians exposed to the loss of life and confiscation of property for having sided with us, under the assurances ... held out to them, would not only be itself a breach of national faith, but would make us appear in the eyes of the world guilty of the most deliberate and cruel deception.[4]

Last but not least, on 29 April 1848 Commander Du Pont wrote to Commodore Shubrick:

> The country [Baja California] is completely quieted, and, from what I can learn and from personal observations, I am impressed with the belief that all men of substance and respectability would decidedly prefer the American government [rather than the Mexican government], and will be much mortified if the territory should not be included in the treaty.[5]

Along these same lines, one can add that most of the Americans who wrote about their own experiences in Baja California during the war seriously questioned the U.S. government's reasoning which resulted in Baja California being excluded from the Mexican Cession. ("Mexican Cession" is a shorthand term for the lands ceded by Mexico to the United States under the terms of the Treaty of Guadalupe Hidalgo.)

There were two important reasons why Baja California was excluded from the peace treaty. The first was that the United States government now very much wanted to end the politically-unpopular

19 • The Treaty of Guadalupe Hidalgo

U.S.–Mexican War, in which the Americans were widely seen, both in the United States and abroad, as being bullies. The second reason was that Baja California itself was such a poor, arid, desolate region with so few natural resources that making it part of the United States did not make any economic sense. It was seen as a distinct liability rather than as an asset.

Probably because the California campaigns were to some extent a side-show of the main theater of U.S.–Mexican War, the treaty did not have much to say about Baja and Alta California themselves. Article V only provided that

> in order to preclude all difficulty in tracing upon the ground the limit separating Upper from Lower California, it is agreed that the said limit shall consist of a straight line drawn from the middle of the Rio Gila, where it unites with the Colorado, to a point on the coast of the Pacific Ocean, distant one marine league due south of the southernmost point of the port of San Diego.[6]

Article VI stated that

> the vessels and citizens of the United States shall, in all time, have a free and uninterrupted passage by the Gulf of California...; it being understood that this passage is to be by navigating the Gulf of California and the river Colorado, and not by land, without the express consent of the Mexican Government.[7]

Once the treaty had been negotiated and signed, it still had to be ratified by the congresses of the United States and Mexico. There was considerable opposition to it in both countries.[8] In the United States, for example, the abolitionist (anti-slavery) faction in the northern states opposed any annexation of Mexican territory, fearing that such a move might usher in the birth of more slave states. In Mexico, a sizeable minority of the congress was actually in favor of continuing the war, despite the crushing military defeats inflicted by the Americans on Mexico—so dramatically illustrated by the American occupation of Mexico City itself.

Nevertheless, in the end, legislative majorities prevailed and both countries decided to ratify the treaty. The Americans wanted a troublesome war over and done with; the Mexicans wanted to get the Americans out of Mexico City, Veracruz, and other major cities so they could resume collecting tariffs and duties and pay the army and government bureaucracy.⁹

The treaty was therefore ratified by the U.S. Senate by a vote of 38 to 14 on 10 March 1848, and by Mexico through a legislative vote of 51 to 34 and a Senate vote of 33 to 4 on 19 May 1848. The Treaty of Guadalupe Hidalgo was then formally proclaimed on 4 July 1848. Writing many years later, Virginia Trist, the wife of Nicolas P. Trist, the chief clerk of the State Department and the official who negotiated the treaty on behalf of the United States, recorded her own feelings:

> Just as [the American and Mexican negotiators] were about to sign the treaty ... one of the Mexicans, Don Bernardo Couto, remarked to him [to Nicholas Trist], "this must be a proud moment for you; no less proud for you than it is humiliating to us." To this Mr. Trist replied "we are making peace, let that be our only thought."
>
> But, said he [Trist] to us in relating it, "Could those Mexicans have seen into my heart at that moment, they would have known that my feeing of shame as an American was far stronger than theirs could be as Mexicans. For though it would not have done for me to say so there, that was a thing for every right-minded American to be ashamed of, and I was ashamed of it, most cordially and intensely ashamed of it."¹⁰

• 20 •

From Military to Civilian Rule

One immediate and major result of the California campaigns was that California was ruled by a series of American military governors from 1846 to 1849. The eventual transition to civilian rule went relatively well and California became a state in 1850. In Southern California, however, a combination of heavily-taxed Californios *and American pro-slavery activists tried three times—and failed each time—to carve out for themselves either statehood or a territorial status separate from that of Northern California.*

All of the seven military governors have already been discussed in this book. To recapitulate briefly, they were: John Drake Sloat (1846), Robert F. Stockton (1846–1847), John C. Frémont (1847), Stephen W. Kearny (1847),[1] Richard Barnes Mason (acting, 1847–1849), Persifor Frazer Smith (1849), and Bennet Riley (1849).

Frémont was clearly the most dramatic and most controversial of these leaders, but Riley had the biggest political impact over the long run: he was largely responsible for California's first constitution and thus for its permanent transition from military to civilian rule.[2] Although some critics would question the legal basis of Riley's sweeping powers, he would be able to show them a 9 October 1848 letter from Polk's Secretary of War proving that he was indeed carrying out the letter of the law. The letter authorized him to respect and to assist the present *de facto* government of California and not to try to change it unless and until it was modified by competent local authority.

There were many serious and unresolved problems in Alta California at this time. *Alcaldes* sometimes ruled according to their personal preferences. In other cases, they simply did not know what to do. Even when they did know their duties, they might be afraid to carry them out because of the danger of retaliation, in the absence of any effective law and order. Private property was not respected. Land titles were clouded or fraudulent. There were raids by the Indians and counter-raids by the settlers. Assault and murder were commonplace but they almost always went unpunished.

An exception to this latter rule was the short but colorful career of Joaquin Murrieta (c. 1829–25 July 1853). He was—depending upon one's point of view—either an evil bandit or an admirable Mexican patriot. Regardless of the sometimes-murky facts about his brief life, he is one of the few individuals from the Gold Rush era who has achieved a lasting international notoriety.

The tale of Joaquin Murrieta is a telling footnote in the Gold Rush history of California. Many of the stories about him vary in details but the main outlines are clear enough.[3] Joaquin was born in Mexico and, hoping to make his fortune, migrated to Saw Mill Flat (or Shaw Flat) at the height of the Gold Rush. There his wife (or his girlfriend) was raped and killed by five American miners; his brother was hanged for a crime he did not commit; and Joaquin himself was tied to a tree and severely whipped for a crime that he did not commit.

Legend has it that, as a result of these insults, Joaquin promised to track down and kill the five miners, which he did. He then swore to take revenge on all Americans. Toward this end, he organized a bandit gang and began a life of robbery and murder throughout the Mother Lode region (the key gold mining area) of the Sierra Nevada mountains. His chief lieutenant was Manuel Garcia, a man locally known as Three Fingered Jack because he had lost one finger in a fight. (Garcia had played a minor but murderous role in the era of the Bear Flag Revolt.) Together, Joaquin and Garcia became so infamous that many mining communities could exchange stories about them during the years 1850 to 1853.

In 1852, a newspaper in Stockton, California, ran this story:

> It is well known that during the winter months a band of Mexican marauders have infested Calaveras county, and weekly we receive the details of dreadful murders and outranges committed in the lonely gulches and solitary outposts of that region. The farmers lost their

cattle and horses, the trader's tent was pillaged, and the life of every traveller was insecure.

The band is lead [sic] by a robber, named Joaquin, a very desperate man, who was concerned in the murder of four Americans, sometime ago, at Turnerville.[4]

Local lawmen considered Joaquin to be one of the most dangerous bandits ever to appear in California. Some of the Mexicans there, however, claimed that he was a modern version of Robin Hood, stealing from the rich and helping the poor. They also saw him as an avenger of the wrongs they had long suffered—and still continued to suffer—under American domination. In any case, all commentators agreed that Joaquin and his band were very good at robbery, murder, and cattle and horse theft.

Their very fame, however, eventually led to their undoing. In July 1853, California Governor Bigler announced that a special unit of California State Rangers, led by Captain Harry Love, had killed both Joaquin and Three Fingered Jack at Ponoche Pass in the Tulare Valley. To prove that these men were dead, the Rangers had cut off Joaquin's head and preserved it in a large jar of alcohol. His colleague's maimed hand was similarly amputated and preserved in alcohol, too. These gruesome trophies were taken to Sacramento, the state capital, and rewards totaling $6,000 were paid to Love. The bandits' deaths were announced publicly and the trophies went on tour throughout California.

Rumors soon began to spread, however, that Love had not in fact killed Joaquin Murrieta but another—and entirely innocent—Mexican by the same name. (To add to this confusion, four of Joaquin Murrieta's robber-companions also had "Joaquin" as their first name.) Some people who claimed they had known Joaquin Murrieta said that the preserved head was not his. Other rumors held that Joaquin Murrieta had retired to Mexico, or that he had appeared in Hornitos, California, to unearth a fortune in gold he had buried there.

In 1854, a San Francisco journalist named John "Yellow Bird" Rollin Ridge, who was an American Indian, published a fictional and highly sensationalized account of Joaquin's life, entitled *The Life & Adventures of Joaquin Murieta* (sic). A flood of other pulp-publications, films, and TV productions followed in due course. The best known of these are founded on the Joaquin legend and focus on the fictional character Zorro, who was created in 1919 by the New York writer Johnston McCulley. Zorro is, of course, firmly on the side of law and order.

As all of this was going on, the Gold Rush was encouraging an immense and totally unregulated migration into California. California's problems gradually multiplied and became so troublesome that the editor of the newspaper *Alta California* was moved to complain in print that "the present state of anarchy (we can call it nothing else) is much to be deplored."[5] Having a duly-elected, responsible civilian government in power seemed to many to be the essential first step needed to address these troublesome issues.

In his capacity as military governor of California, Riley therefore presided over a constitutional convention in Monterey on 1 September 1849. The background to this convention illustrates the power of the people's initiative. Nine months earlier, on 11 December 1848, a large meeting had been held in San Jose; resolutions were adopted in favor of arranging a convention to form a provisional territorial government. Early in March 1849, some of the organizers issued an address to the people of California, which recommended that delegates should meet in Monterey and that they "should be vested with full power to frame a State Constitution to be submitted to the people of California."[6]

Since in 1848 and again in 1849 Congress had refused—because of the enormous divisiveness of the slavery issue—to take any action setting up a civilian government for California, so in 1849 Riley decided to move matters along more briskly. Accordingly, he issued, entirely on his own authority, a proclamation on 3 June 1849 calling for an election of delegates and for "the formation of a State constitution or a plan for a territorial government."[7]

There were to be 37 (later 48) delegates, chosen from selected towns and cities of California. Most of the delegates were pre–1846 American settlers; eight of them were *Californios*. The election of delegates was held in Monterey on 1 August 1849 and a constitutional convention met in Monterey one month later, on 1 September 1849. The historian Hubert Howe Bancroft described this latter meeting (perhaps with some overstatement) as follows:

> Never in the history of the world did a similar convention come together. They were to form a state out of unorganized territory only

lately wrested from a subjugated people, who were allowed to assist in framing a constitution in conformity with the political view of the conquerors.[8]

Bayard Taylor of the New York *Tribune* was an author, traveler, and journalist visiting California at that time. He reported that although the United States had many warm supporters, particularly among the intelligent and influential *Californios*, most of the common people did not "rejoice" at the sudden change which had overtaken California. Losing the war had reduced them, nearly overnight, to a powerless minority. It extinguished their political and social dominance and would now force them to master the new language, new customs, and new laws imposed on them by arrogant foreigners. Nevertheless, Taylor believed that if a new civilian government followed a policy of impartiality and reconciliation, as the military governors had in fact done, any American-Mexican differences would eventually be ironed out through the workings of a shared citizenship.

On 12 October 1849, Riley issued the following proclamation:

> The people are now called upon to form a government for themselves, and to designate such officers as they desire to make and execute the laws. That their choice may be wisely made, and that the government to be organized may secure the permanent welfare and happiness of the people of the new State, is the sincere and earnest wish of the present Executive, who, if the Constitution be ratified, will, with pleasure, surrender his powers to whomsoever the people may designate as his successor.[9]

The final copy of the new Constitution was signed on 13 October 1849. It was ratified by Californians in an election on 13 November 1849 by a vote of 12,061–811. On 1 December 1849, California's first civil governor—Peter H. Burnett, a former judge of the Oregon Supreme Court—was inaugurated. Earlier that same day, Riley had issued a proclamation which read in part: "A new executive having been elected and installed into office ... the undersigned hereby resigns his power as [military] governor of California.... The principal object of all his wishes is now accomplished—the people have a government of their own choice."[10]

In fitting thanks for his successful labors to bring civilian rule to California, Riley received two generous presents from his supporters.

The first was a "large and massive" snuff box with the initial R set in pearls in an oval on the back of the lid. This box was described as being an exquisite piece of workmanship of "novel beauty." The second present was an enormous gold medal, weighing one pound, and a heavy chain of gold nuggets preserved in their native shapes. The box and the chain were presented to Riley at a great banquet in his honor.[11]

Nearly one year later, on 9 September 1850, California would become the 31st state as part of the Compromise of 1850. The Compromise was a set of five laws that dealt with the issue of slavery. California had requested permission to enter the Union as a free state, thus potentially upsetting the balance between the free and slave states in the U.S. Senate. Under the terms of a solution negotiated by Senator Henry Clay to avoid a crisis between North and South, California was able to enter the Union as a free state.[12]

In rural Southern California, however, political conditions were very different from those in relatively more urban Northern California. Dissatisfied with high taxes and with what they considered very unfair land laws, the *Californios* of Southern California made common cause with pro-slavery advocates there and tried to achieve either a separate state for themselves or a new territory, to be known as the "Territory of Colorado," which would be separate from Northern California. They tried three times, and failed each time.

Their last attempt centered around the Pico Act of 1859. In 1843, Antonio María Pico (1809–1869), a former soldier, had received a 35,546-acre Mexican land grant known as Rancho Pescadero, which encompassed what is now Tracy, California. The Treaty of Guadalupe Hidalgo had provided that all such land grants would be honored by the United States. In 1852, Pico therefore filed a claim with the U.S. Public Land Commission to keep his ranch, but this claim was rejected in 1854. Ultimately, his claim would be confirmed by the U.S. Supreme Court in 1865 but in the meantime, like many other *Californio* landowners, Pico found himself in a very difficult financial position because of the high legal fees this litigation entailed.

For this reason, in 1859, together with fellow *Californio* ranchers, he petitioned Congress, protesting that California's stiff taxes and protracted litigation were unfairly depriving him and his colleagues of their property. Pico's petition is too long to be presented in its entirety, but its key points can be quoted here. Pico wrote to Congress and put forth his views in polite but clear terms. He wrote:

> During the war between the United States and Mexico the officers of the United States, as commandants of the land and sea forces, on several occasions offered and promised in the most solemn manner to the inhabitants of California, protection and security of their persons and their property.
>
> [The *Californios*] heard with dismay of the appointment, by Act of Congress, of a Commission with the right to examine all titles and confirm or disapprove them, as their judgment considered equitable.
>
> The undersigned [Pico and his fellow-petitioners], ignorant then of the forms and proceedings of an American court of justice, were obliged to engage the services of American lawyers to present their claims, paying them enormous fees. Not having other means with which to meet those expenses but their lands, they were compelled to give up part of their property, in many cases as much as a fourth of it, and in other cases even more.
>
> The expenses of the new state government were great, and the money to pay for these was only to be derived from the tax on property, and there was little in the new state but the above-mentioned lands. Onerous taxes were levied by new laws, and if these were not paid the property was put up for sale.
>
> The petitioners, finding themselves unable to face such payments because of the rates of interest, taxes, and litigation expenses, as well as having to maintain their families, were compelled to sell, little by little, the greater part of their old possessions.
>
> Moreover, we see with deep pain that efforts are being made to induce those honorable bodies [the Land Commission and the courts] to pass laws authorizing bills of review, and other illegal proceedings, with a view to prolonging still further the litigation of our claims.[13]

The Pico Act of 1859 was passed by the California State Legislature and was approved by the voters of the proposed "Territory of Colorado." It was sent to Washington, D.C., but the secession crisis of 1860, i.e., the coming Civil War, intervened, so this proposal never came to a vote.

• 21 •

Significance of the Pacific Campaigns of the U.S.–Mexican War

By briefly summarizing the Pacific campaigns of the war, it is possible to draw six conclusions from them. They are discussed in this final chapter, as are the long-term impacts of the war on Mexico and on the United States.

Earlier in this book, the discussions of the indigenous and other peoples of Alta California, of the Mexican army in California, and of the preludes to war were all designed to set the stage for Gillespie's secret mission to California and for the results that sprang from the *de facto* American decision to bring about "regime change" (to use a modern euphemism) in Mexican California.

The *Californios* tried to get rid of Frémont once and for all when he first came down into central California from the Sierra Nevada mountains, but their half-hearted efforts failed. He soon returned to Alta California from his brief "exile" in Oregon and immediately began to play a key role in the short-lived Bear Flag Revolt and in other political and military undertakings.

The formation of the California Battalion; the naval and amphibious operations off the coasts; the *Californio* uprising; the arrival of the Army of the West and the Mormon Battalion; and the battle of San Pascual—all these constituted a cascade of events that had momentous consequences. They led, directly or indirectly, to the Treaty of Cahuenga; to Frémont's court-martial; to the Treaty of Guadalupe Hidalgo (which was largely a result of Mexican defeats elsewhere in

21 • Significance of the Pacific Campaigns

the war); and, finally, to the transition from American military rule to civilian rule in California.

Six conclusions about the California campaigns suggest themselves now:

The first and most important conclusion is that the only real prize of the war was California itself. As stated in the Introduction, the Americans had long coveted California for a number of important reasons. Possessing California would expand the United States from sea to sea, eventually making a transcontinental railroad possible. By using ports in California, American and other ships could more easily trade with Asia, especially with China. American ownership would deter any other nations, e.g., Britain or France, from thinking about planting their own colonies there. Finally, last but by no means least, it would be a lovely place to live and work in once it had been more fully developed.

The second conclusion, which may not be politically correct to voice today but which—in the interests of historical accuracy—still needs to be stated, is that it was truly an act of folly for Mexico to go to war against its much more powerful northern neighbor.

Californio forces stood no chance whatsoever against the superior numbers, technology, fire power, and discipline of American soldiers, sailors, Marines, and volunteers. Mexico itself was poor, weak, and disorganized. To mention but one proof of this obvious fact, on 9 August 1846 José Antonio Castro, the *comandante-general* of Alta California, warned Governor Pico, his superior, that he (Castro) could not possibly defend the town of Los Angeles. At best, he said, all that he could hope to do was to send into battle against the Americans no more than "one hundred men, badly armed and worse supplied."[1]

The third conclusion is that during the war the *Californios* as a whole had ambiguous and very torn loyalties. Few of them had any real allegiance to the distant, incompetent, and corrupt national government in Mexico City, but most of them did have a very strong personal attachment to their own region, their own culture (especially Roman Catholicism), and their own language. However, they soon found themselves being pulled in different directions.

On the one hand, some *Californio* landowners had married their daughters to Americans, and maintaining family solidarity counted for a very great deal in the Mexican culture. Moreover, because of the close ties some of them had forged with American traders and shipmasters, these families stood to profit financially from the advent of American rule. On the other hand, *Californios* in general were concerned about what the all-powerful and (to their eyes) quite unpredictable foreigners might conceivably do to them, their families, their friends, their religion, and their property over the long run.[2]

A fourth conclusion is that losing the war itself must have caused a good deal of psychological distress among the Mexican people as a whole. Echoes of this loss probably still survive today in their national consciousness. They lost many battles and many men. Their capital city and some of their national territory was occupied by American troops. Forced to abandon Texas and bow to the American demand that the Rio Grande would henceforth be Mexico's northern border, Mexicans also had to deal with the fact that their leaders' pursuit of folly had resulted in the surrender of more than half a million square miles of Mexican territory to the United States. As mentioned earlier, this vast area comprised all or parts of present-day California, Utah, Nevada, Arizona, New Mexico, Wyoming, and Colorado. In return, Mexico received very little from the United States, beyond an end to the fighting: namely, the Americans gave it only $15 million and agreed to take over $3.25 million in debts owed to American citizens by the Mexican government.

A fifth conclusion is that the *Califorinos*' cheerful, careless, spendthrift approach to life may have charmed their visitors but it certainly worked against the economic and therefore the military strength of their region. The Indians were forced to do all the "heavy hauling," i.e., all the exhausting, repetitive, low-level work. Their labor was in fact the wellspring from which the idyllic pastoral life of the *Californios* flowed.

Evidence of the lack of a European/American work ethic in California dates from the end of the 18th century. On 14 May 1796, for example, the Franciscan missionary Fray José Senán complained to his viceroy that the region's settlers were lazy and unproductive, reporting that they preferred to play card games rather than plow the fields. Senán attributed most of their idleness to Spain's economic policies: the high cost of goods imported from central Mexico and the low market price for the settlers' own agricultural products gave the settlers no incentive to produce more than they themselves needed to survive. That said, however, when the Mexican government came to power and relaxed the Spanish restrictions, free trade, foreign trade, and domestic production all increased. Nevertheless, under both Mexicans and *Californios*, Alta California always remained a land of still-untapped economic potential.[3]

Forty-six years later, nothing had changed. Sir George Simpson (c. 1792–1860), the energetic Canadian governor of the Hudson's Bay Company who was in effect the British viceroy for the whole of Western Canada, said after a visit to California in 1842 that the *Califorinos*

> were perhaps the least promising colonists in the world, being inferior to what the savages [the Indians] had become under the training of the priests, so that the spoliation [the secularization] of the missions tended directly to stop civilization. There were once large flocks of sheep, but now in 1842 there were scarcely any left.[4]

The American naval surgeon George Willing Clymer (1804–1884), for his part, remarked that "he never saw a Spanish Californian who was a mechanic, or who cultivated the land."[5] (In 19th century terminology, a "mechanic" was a man who practiced useful skills, e.g., simple engineering.)

Finally, rather than setting up small-scale shoe-making facilities at home to produce dress shoes, the *Californios* sold their cattle hides to New England trading ships for a song and then paid very high prices for dress shoes (made of this very same leather) which had been manufactured in Boston and then shipped back to California. In 1846 alone, for example, California exported 85,000 hides.[6]

The net result was that California failed to develop economically and, as a corollary, it remained so weak militarily that it was always ripe for conquest by foreigners. A persuasive reason for this self-inflicted poverty comes from Edwin Bryant, the former newspaper editor and *alcalde* (mayor) of San Francisco who has been quoted earlier. He wrote:

> Of natural wealth the population of California possess a superabundance, and are immensely rich; still, such have been the extortionate prices that they have been compelled to pay for the commonest artificial luxuries and wearing-apparel, that generally they are but indifferently provided with the ordinary necessities of civilized life.

The California Campaigns of the U.S.–Mexican War, 1846–1848

> For a suit of clothes, which in New York or Boston would cost seventy-five dollars, the Californian has been compelled to pay five times the sum in hides at one dollar and fifty cents [per hide]; so that a *caballero* [a gentleman], to clothe himself genteelly, has been obliged, as often as he renews his dress, to sacrifice about two hundred of the cattle of his rancho.
>
> No people, whether males or females, are more fond of display; no people have paid more dearly to gratify this vanity; and yet no civilized people I have seen are so deficient in what they most covet [luxury goods].[7]

The sixth and final conclusion is that the loss of California contributed to a lasting legacy of Mexican humiliation, distrust, and bitterness towards the United States. In addition to their hostility to what the Mexicans considered the Americans' "grab" of their territory, they were also infuriated by one of the unexpected outcomes of the Treaty of Guadalupe Hidalgo.

As noted earlier, under the terms of this treaty, the United States had promised to grant American citizenship to those Mexicans who remained in California and also promised to protect their property. Crucially, however, the United States did *not* recognize the validity of the land grants on which Mexican ranches—the mainstay of the economy—were based. Instead, the Land Law of 1851 established a Land Commission to determine the validity of the large land grants. The whole burden of proof of ownership fell on *Californio* land owners, who then faced years of extremely expensive—and, for many of them, financially ruinous—legal fees and unpaid taxes.[8]

What, then, can now be said about the long-term impacts of the California campaigns and of the other campaigns of the war, both on the United States and on Mexico? Two things stand out in the historical record: a profound forgetfulness on the American side, and a profound humiliation on the Mexican side.

The decisive American victory in the war, backed up by the rapid exploitation of California's vast mineral and agricultural wealth, paved the way for the United States to become an assertive, expansionist, transcontinental power and, eventually, a global power. That much is clear. What is equally striking, however, is how quickly and how completely the Americans put this war entirely out of their minds. As the American scholar David J. Weber explained in an interview with the PBS (the Public Broadcasting Service),

21 • Significance of the Pacific Campaigns

The U.S.–Mexican War was obliterated from the United States' national memory by the Civil War, which followed on its heels. The "great victory" began to crumble in the midst of the sectional conflict, and then Americans killing Americans, which became the great story if one wanted to think about conflict in the middle of century. The U.S.–Mexican War was then forgotten. One wonders a bit if a victory in a war that was, after all, a war of aggression to seize territory was not conveniently forgotten by Americans, because it's not one of the more honorable moments in American history.[9]

It was very easy for the Americans to forget about the U.S.–Mexican War, but impossible for the Mexicans to do so. To quote Weber again, as a result of the war

> Mexico lost the rich potential of California and its fabulous gold mines, lost the potential of the agricultural potential and the water resources that this region might have offered for what is today northern Mexico. And instead of a great pride in becoming an expansionist country like the United State developed into, Mexico developed a massive inferiority complex as a result of the war, wondering where [it] had gone wrong as a nation. How could it lose half of its national territory? The war became a scar on the national psyche.[10]

The humiliations endured by Mexico during the war were painfully apparent to its citizens during and after the war. José María Amador, the *Californio* soldier, mission administrator, rancher, and gold miner mentioned earlier in this book, was scathing in his denunciation of Governor Pío Pico and Commander General José Castro. These two men had been bitter rivals for power in Alta California before the war, and both of them fled to Mexico as soon as they faced military defeat at the hands of the Americans. In a 229-page memoir dictated in 1877 to Thomas Savage, one of Hubert Howe Bancroft's assistants, Amador said of them:

> The bad qualities of these leaders disheartened their subordinates, the troops, and the people. With a shortage of funds, only unity and patriotism could possibly have brought many people together as men of honor to defend the motherland or die in the battlefield. But nothing happened. As soon as it was found out that Frémont, with sizeable force, was coming, Castro gave orders to disband his troops. Pico did the same.
>
> Each one of them abandoned their duties under the ridiculous pretext that they were going to get help, when they knew very well that

they were not going to get it. [They certainly knew that Mexico was too weak and too poor to give them any help.] One fled by way of Sonora and the other through Baja California. It was well-known throughout California that Pico took 22,000 pesos in cash that came out of the sale of some mission assets and he never gave an account of these funds. [Pico's embezzlement occurred at a time when one Mexican peso was roughly equivalent to one American dollar, and when farmhands in California were making about $60 per month.[11]] It would be a good idea to ask him about this point.[12]

When Pico and Castro fled to Mexico, the *Californios* lost whatever remaining hopes they may have had about their ability to resist the Americans. Indeed, José María Flores, the leader of the uprising against the Americans, also ran away to Mexico. Amador reported that

the Californios who had fought along with Flores were abandoned by their leader, who also fled to Mexico. Frémont, who was coming with a battalion to reinforce Stockton, received offers of surrender. Frémont granted honorable concessions to everyone and guarantees for the Californios and this was how the campaign ended, which was the last attempt in our efforts to retain our union with Mexico.[13]

To sum up the California campaigns as a whole, it can be seen that the shadows of the *Californios* (and, of course, of their Spanish forebears) continue to greet us each day in the many place names commemorating their lives and history. The most prominent of these are probably San Francisco, Sacramento, Los Angeles, and San Diego. At the same time, however, one must not ignore the many place names commemorating the non–Hispanic participants in these campaigns, e.g., Fremont, California; Stockton, California; and Carson City, Nevada. Taken together, they all serve to remind each new generation of the great gains and great losses of the U.S.–Mexican War itself.

Chronology

1769	To counter any British or Russian thoughts of establishing their own colonies in California, and to convert the Indians, Spain establishes the first of its 21 missions.
1784	Manuel Nietos, a retired Spanish sergeant, is given one of the first and biggest land grants in Alta California.
c. 1800	California Indians provide all the labor for the Spanish missions; later, they will do the same for all the Mexican ranches and for some of the enterprises run by foreigners.
1803–1805	In these two years alone, the Russian-American Company harvests more than 17,000 sea otter pelts, most of which will be exported to China.
1810–1821	In its war of independence, Mexico throws off Spanish rule but is gravely weakened in the process.
1821	The Pacific Squadron is assigned to protect American shipping interests in the Pacific Ocean. More ships are assigned to it as war with Mexico seems increasingly likely.
1822–1846	Alta California is politically unstable: there will be 12 governors and 15 administrations between 1822 and 1846. Governor Pío Pico and army *comandante*-general José Antonio Castro are bitter rivals. In 1825, the missions are at the height of their prosperity but are secularized in 1833–1834 and lose all their lands and influence.
1834	Richard Henry Dana, Jr., joins the crew of the brig *Pilgrim* in Boston and will use his experiences in the

Chronology

	California hide trade to write an outstanding book, *Two Years Before the Mast*, published in 1840.
1834–1838	About 15,000 Indian converts lose both the protection of the missionaries and their own livestock and property.
1835	Texas, then part of Mexico, rises in revolt.
October 1837	Andrés Castillero, a Mexican army officer, goes to Alta California to prepare for the arrival of a military force there to prevent California from being conquered by the Americans, but this force is never sent.
April 1840	In his capacity as chief magistrate of the province, Castro orders the arrest of about 80 American and British nationals living in California—on the spurious charge of inciting rebellion against the Mexican government.
15 June 1840	The American sloop *St. Louis* arrives at Monterey to free the above prisoners. Castro lets them go.
5 July 1840	Having accomplished its mission, the *St. Louis* leaves Monterey.
1841	Count Eugène de Mofras, a young French diplomat, explorer, and mapmaker, is sent from Mexico City to assess the potential of California and Oregon for French business and political interests.
19 October 1842	Two American ships—the frigate *United States* and the sloop *Cyane*—arrive in Monterey, California. Mistakenly believing that war has broken out between the U.S. and Mexico, Commodore Thomas ap Jones ("ap" means "son of" in Welsh) and his forces seize Monterey. He later apologizes to Mexican officials and leaves Monterey.
1843	The Swiss adventurer John Sutter opens an impressive fort and trading post at what is now Sacramento.
1844	The American whaling fleet in the Pacific consists of 650 ships and employs 17,000 men.
1845	Thomas O. Larkin, the American Consul in Monterey, predicts that "the pear [California] is near ripe for falling" and will soon be under the control of the U.S.

Chronology

1845	The U.S. annexes Texas, probably making war with Mexico inevitable.
17 October 1845	A dispatch from Secretary of State James Buchanan to the U.S. consul in Monterey, Thomas O. Larkin, says that the U.S. will "receive as brethren" the people of Alta California "should they desire to unite their destiny with ours."
30 October 1845	U.S. Marine Corps lieutenant Archibald Gillespie meets with President Polk and is sent out on a secret mission to California.
November 1845	Manuel de la Peña y Peña, Mexican minister of foreign affairs, tries—but fails—to rally support in Mexico for a negotiated settlement rather than for war with the United States.
November 1845	Commodore John Sloat arrives at Mazatlán on the west coast of Mexico to take command of the Pacific Squadron. He has orders to seize Yerba Buena (San Francisco) and to establish a blockade of Mexican ports if war breaks out.
10 December 1845	An American expedition, led by U.S. Army captain John C. Frémont and guided by the famous scout Kit Carson, comes down from the Sierra Nevada mountains and arrives at Sutter's Fort.
1846–1849	One major result of the California campaigns is that California is ruled by a series of seven American military governors between 1846 and 1849.
1846	In his book *Life in California*, Alfred Robinson, one of the earliest American businessmen in Alta California, argues that the U.S. should annex Alta California.
April 1846	A senior British diplomat in Washington, D.C., writes that the Mexican officers are "the worst perhaps to be found in any part of the world."
25 April 1846	The Thornton Affair: a squad of American cavalrymen on patrol in a disputed border area is attacked by a Mexican cavalry unit. The U.S. will cite this incident as a fundamental reason for the war.
13 May 1846	A joint resolution by both houses of the U.S. Congress declares that a state of war exists "by an act of the

	Republic of Mexico." President Polk signs a proclamation of war.
13 May 1846	President Polk orders Brigadier General Stephen Kearny and his Army of the West to capture Santa Fe and California.
24 May 1846	Frémont orders Gillespie to stock up on war supplies from a U.S. Navy ship moored in San Francisco Bay.
25 May 1846	Governor Pío Pico informs the Mexican Ministry of Foreign Relations that war with the United States is in the offing and urgently asks for help and for money. The Ministry does not reply to him.
14 June 1846	During the 26-day-long Bear Flag Revolt, American settlers in California free themselves from Mexican rule.
15 June 1846	William B. Ide drafts a "Proclamation of the Bear Flag Revolt." It lists the grievances of the American settlers against the Mexican government and Ide's own promises for the future.
7 July 1846	Mexico declares war on the U.S.
7 July 1846	First use of the Pacific Squadron in the California campaigns: men of the USS *Savannah*, USS *Cyane*, and USS *Levant* take part in the unopposed "battle of Monterey."
9 July 1846	The USS *Portsmouth* lands 75 Marines and sailors at Yerba Buena, i.e., San Francisco. They take possession of it without firing a shot.
11 July 1846	The Royal Navy sloop *Juno* moors in San Francisco Bay; at about the same time, the British man-of-war *Collingwood* turns up outside Monterey harbor. American officials worry that these naval movements may be portents of British intervention in California.
11 July 1846	The American flag is raised at Sutter's Fort, thereby ending the Bear Flag Revolt.
12 July 1846	Orders from Secretary of the Navy George Bancroft (as augmented by his orders of 13 August 1846) direct the U.S. Navy to use the Pacific Squadron to the fullest extent feasible in the war with Mexico; i.e., the Navy is to take possession or blockade all the Mexican ports that it can.

Chronology

19 July 1846	Frémont and his men enter Monterey.
23 July 1846	The California Battalion is officially formed.
29 July 1846	The USS *Cyane* brings Frémont and about 160 of his men to San Diego. They capture the city without firing a shot.
6 August 1846	The USS frigate *Congress* captures the undefended harbor of Los Angeles.
13 August 1846	The Americans capture Los Angeles.
17 August 1846	The news that war has been declared finally reaches California. Commodore Stockton proclaims that Upper and Lower California are now part of the United States under the name of the Territory of California.
19 August 1846	Commodore Robert F. Stockton, the commanding officer of the U.S. Navy's Pacific Squadron, declares that all ports on the west coast of Mexico are now subject to an American blockade. Its purpose (and that of its two successors in 1847 and 1848) is to prevent any trade goods, food supplies, and war material from reaching Mexican forces. American sailors and Marines will provide boots-on-the-ground support by conducting numerous small-scale naval and amphibious raids.
2 September 1846	The USS *Cyane* captures two Mexican vessels at San Blas without meeting any resistance.
5 September 1846	The USS sloop-of-war *Warren* seizes the Mexican brig *Malek Adhel* at Mazatlán.
24 September 1846	Mexican captain José María Flores takes command of the *Californio* revolt against the American invaders.
25 September 1846	U.S. Army Colonel Stephen Watts Kearny sets out for California with 300 soldiers (later reduced to 100 soldiers), and is followed by the Mormon Battalion, which builds a wagon road to California.
29 September 1846	The *Californio* revolt forces the Americans to withdraw from Los Angeles.
1 October 1846	The USS *Cyane* seizes two Mexican schooners at Loreto.
7 October 1846	The *Cyane* cannonades the Mexican port of Guaymas.

Chronology

6 December 1846	Mexican lancers defeat American soldiers at the battle of San Pascual: this is the only "real" battle of the war.
1847	First known use, in print, of the phrase "the conquest of California."
2 January 1847	A clash between U.S. Marines and *Californio* lancers leads to an armistice which will end the fighting in northern California.
8 January 1847	A joint Stockton-Kearny army defeats Flores' 500-man *Californio* force at the San Gabriel River, not far from Los Angeles.
9 January 1847	These two armies meet again, this time on the plain of La Mesa, about six miles up the river. The battle is inconclusive.
10 January 1847	The Mexican residents and armed forces of Los Angeles surrender peacefully to American forces.
16 January 1847	The Treaty of Cahuenga ends the war in Alta California.
22 January 1847	The USS razee frigate *Independence* enters Monterey Bay.
3 April 1847	The USS *Portsmouth* arrives at San Lucas, where the Marine detachment lands and raises the American flag without meeting any opposition. (Similar American "flag-raisings" also occurred at San José del Cabo and at La Paz at about this time.)
30 May 1847	General Kearny sends U.S. Army lieutenant colonel Henry S. Burton and two companies of the New York Volunteers, aboard the storeship USS *Lexington*, to Baja California. Their mission is to secure the American military possession of Baja California and establish an American presence there, showing their skills and good will by undertaking various construction projects. A local American resident praises them in a letter.
3 June 1847	After the USS *Independence* leaves Baja California for San Francisco, the USS *Cyane* is the only warship remaining on the west coast of Mexico. To provide the pro–American inhabitants of La Paz with at least a fig-leaf of protection, the *Cyane* sails back and

Chronology

	forth between San José del Cabo and Mazatlán. This manoeuver effectively spells the end of the blockade: Mexican trade resumes as soon as the *Cyane* is out of sight.
27 June 1847	Prominent *Californio* residents ask the San Diego authorities to deal with Indian attacks.
21 July 1847	The storeship *Lexington* brings to La Paz two companies of New York Volunteers. They go ashore and set up a small garrison.
10 August 1847	Commodore Shubrick sends the USS *Portsmouth* and *Congress* to begin a new blockade of Mazatlán, Guaymas, and San Blas.
Mid-September 1847	When the USS *Dale* arrives at La Paz, Colonel Henry Stanton Burton orders her commander to set sail for Loreto and Mulegé to prevent supplies from being landed there and to get a pledge of neutrality from the inhabitants.
30 September 1847	To avoid a hostile reception, the *Dale* enters the port of Mulegé flying the *British* flag. U.S. Navy lieutenant Tunis Augustus Macdonough Craven, whose journal is of great historical interest, tries to go ashore himself but hostile Mexicans prevent him from doing so.
1 October 1847	The United States begins offensive operations near Mulegé. There are no casualties on either the American or the Mexican side, but since the Americans were not able to capture the town, the Mexicans count this skirmish as a victory for them.
20 October 1847	The presence of many sailors and Marines aboard the USS *Congress* forces the Mexican defenders to evacuate Guaymas.
11 November 1847	A U.S. landing force of 750 sailors and Marines of the Pacific Squadron calls on the city of Mazatlán to surrender. Since its garrison had fled the night before, the city quickly surrenders.
24 January 1848	James Marshall discovers gold at a sawmill built upstream of Sutter's Fort.
30 January 1848	Lieutenant Craven and his Marines attack and seize a Mexican garrison east of Guaymas. This fight is an

	unusually good example of the many small-scale American naval and amphibious operations in Baja California.
31 January 1848	A court-martial finds Frémont guilty of mutiny, disobedience, and conduct prejudicial to military discipline.
2 February 1848	The Treaty of Guadalupe Hidalgo officially ends the U.S.–Mexican War.
9 October 1848	The USS *Cyane* returns to Norfolk, Virginia, where she is congratulated by the secretary of the navy for her contributions to the American successes in the California campaigns.
December 1848	President Polk reports to Congress that in less than four years, almost 1,200,000 square miles of territory have been added to the U.S.
1849	By the end of this year, more than 100,000 people from all over the world will have flooded into California by land or by sea to join the Gold Rush.
1 September 1849	Military Governor Bennet Riley presides over a constitutional convention in Monterey.
1 December 1849	Peter H. Burnett is inaugurated as California's first civil governor.
9 September 1850	California becomes the 31st American state.
1851	A Land Commission is set up to determine the validity of the large land grants. The whole burden of proof falls on *Californio* landowners, some of whom will be ruined by legal fees and taxes.
1859	The Pico Act, intended by its backers to split off Southern California from Northern California, is passed by the California State Senate and is sent to Washington, D.C. However, the American Civil War intervenes and this Act is never passed; as a result, California remains undivided.

Chapter Notes

Preface

1. An informal but exceptionally well-illustrated account of *Californio* life is Jo Mora's 1947 book, *Californios*. See bibliography. Mora (1876–1947) was a writer, an artist, and a working cowboy in Mexico, Texas, and California.
2. After Willis, "U.S. Grant," p. 1.
3. After Sheppard Software, "Mexican-American War," p. 3.
4. See Katcher, *The Mexican-American War 1846–48*, pp. 2 and 37.
5. Amero, "The Mexican-American War in Baja California," p. 1., citing as good examples Brooks, *A Complete History of the Mexican War*, and Smith, *The War with Mexico* (vols. I and II). Italics added. Since Amero's own book contains many excellent contemporary quotations regarding the war in Baja California, it has been cited frequently here.
6. Haas, "War in California," p. 351, citing Robert W. Johannesen, "American's Forgotten War," *Wilson Quarterly* (Spring 1996): 96–107.
7. Cutts, *The Conquest of California and of New Mexico*, pp. 3–4.
8. Colton, *Three Years in California*, pp. 131–132.
9. After Chambers, *The Oxford Companion to American Military History*, p. 849.
10. After "Mexican-American War: Aftermath & Legacy," p. 1.
11. Quoted by Walker, *Bear Flag Rising: The Conquest of California*, pp. 155–156.
12. The nearly 50,000 documents, books, and maps he collected are the foundation of the Bancroft Library at the University of California at Berkeley. Between 1886 and 1890, Bancroft also published a seven-volume *History of California*, which is one of the standard reference sources for the early history of the state.

Introduction

1. After Nevin, *The Mexican War*, pp. 187–188.
2. Eisenhower, *So Far from God*, pp. xxii–xxiii.
3. Nevin, *The Mexican War*, p. 6.
4. Quoted by Katcher, *The Mexican-American War 1846–48*, p. 20.
5. Quoted by Katcher, *The Mexican-American War 1846–48*, p. 20.
6. This section has been drawn in large part from Castillero, "A Mexican Officer Urges Defense of Both Californias," pp. 406–412.
7. Castillero, "A Mexican Officer Urges Defense of Both Californias," pp. 409, 410, 411.
8. After Bauer, *The Mexican War 1846–1848*, p. 393.

9. Quoted by Valasco-Márquez, "Manifest Destiny: A Mexican Viewpoint on the War with the United States," p. 2.
10. After Arnold, "Too Few Ships, Too Few Guns, and Not Enough Money," endnote 5, p. 8.
11. After Chaffin, *Pathfinder*, p. 300.
12. After Harlow, *California Conquered*, p. 57.
13. Quoted by Weber, *Foreigners in Their Native Land*, citing George Tays, ed. and trans., "Pio Pico's Correspondence with the Mexican Government, 1846–1848," *California Historical Quarterly* 13, no. 2 (June 1934), pp. 117–118.
14. After PBS, "James K. Polk," p. 2.
15. After Sheppard Software, "Mexican-American War," p. 3.
16. Roosevelt, "Occupation of California," p. 1. Roosevelt explains on p. 4 of his Introduction that "in many years of collecting sketches, paintings and engravings related to the Navy of the United States, I had found virtually none which had connection with naval operations in the Pacific in 1846 and 1847. When, therefore, I had the opportunity a few years ago of acquiring the original sketch-book of Gunner William H. Meyers, U.S.N., I realized its historical value. Not only do these sketches fill a definite gap in the history of this Nation and of our sister republic of Mexico, but they also throw an interesting light on the conduct of land and naval warfare less than a hundred years ago."
17. Quoted by Janin, *Claiming the American Wilderness*, p. 59.
18. Initially, the Spanish province of Las Californias was not split into Alta California and Baja California. When it was later split, the dividing line between the two was set near Ensenada in Baja California.
19. Quoted by Janin, *Claiming the American Wilderness*, p. 66.
20. After Chaffin, *Pathfinder*, p. 269.
21. After Harlow, *California Conquered*, p. 4.
22. Ibid.
23. Mentioned by Eisenhower, *So Far from God*, p. 199, citing Hubert Bancroft, *History of California*, vol. III, p. 400. Bancroft added a footnote referencing another source. This stated that Forsyth offered $5 million "for the whole country of California."
24. Cited by Smith, *The War with Mexico*, p. 209.
25. Colton, *Three Years in California*, p. 223.
26. After Lane, "Jose Maria Amador's Rancho San Ramon," p. 1.
27. Colton, *Three Years in California*, p. 27.
28. Ibid., p. 19.
29. Yale University, "Message of President Polk, May 11, 1846," p. 2.
30. This overview is drawn in part from Hickman, "Mexican-American War 101: An Overview," pp. 1–2, and from U.S. Naval Institute, "The Mexican War, 12 May 1846," pp. 1–2.
31. After U.S. Naval Institute, "The Mexican War, 12 May 1846," pp. 1–2.
32. After Santelli, "Marines in the Mexican War," p. 55.

Chapter 1

1. The definitive source on pre-contact California Indian life is still Kroeber's book *The Indians of California*, published in 1925, but at 995 pages in length it is very unwieldy. A more manageable source is his 62-page essay "Elements of Culture in Native California," which was published in 1935. See Heizer and Whipple, *The

Chapter Notes—1

California Indians, pp. 3–65, for the text of this essay. Some of the observations below are drawn from it.

2. Indian and *Californio vaqueros* were skilled at slaughtering cattle by an exciting (for the onlookers) but very dangerous (for the riders) process known as the *nuqueo* ("nape of the neck" in Spanish). Armed only with the long knife he invariably carried, a rider would range alongside a moving, half-wild, steer and, with a quick blow with the point of the knife between the vertebrae at the nape of the neck, drop the animal dead in its tracks without any kick or struggle (Mora, *Californios*, p. 158.)

3. Quoted by Ruiz de Burton, *The Squatter and the Don*, p. 18.
4. After Delay, "Independent Indians and the U.S.–Mexican War," pp. 36, 60.
5. Heizer and Whipple, "Number and condition of California Indians today," p. 574.
6. The two primary chemicals in the poisonous plants used to take fish are saponins and rotenones. Both act on the respiratory organs of the fish but do not affect their edibility.
7. Quoted by Beebe and Senkewicz, *Testimonios*, p. 11.
8. Quoted by Beebe and Senkewicz, *Testimonios*, pp. 36–37.
9. Peonage is a form of involuntary servitude, the origins of which date to the Spanish conquest of Mexico, when the conquerors forced the poor, especially Indians, to work for Spanish planters and mine operators.
10. Quoted by Weber, *The Spanish in North America*, p. 263.
11. Quoted by Beebe and Senkewicz, *Lands of Promise and Despair*, pp. 470–471.
12. Wikipedia, "Spanish missions in California," citing Randall Milliken, *A Time of Little Choice: The Disintegration of Tribal Culture in the San Francisco Bay Area, 1769–1910* (Menlo Park: Ballena Press, 1995), pp. 172–173, 193.
13. After Hague and Langum, *Thomas O. Larkin*, p. 50.
14. This account is drawn in part from Hughes, "A Military View of San Diego," pp. 1–8.
15. Quoted by Hughes, "A Military View of San Diego," p. 5.
16. After Hughes, "A Military View of San Diego," p. 2.
17. Wikipedia, "Indigenous peoples of California," citing Barry M. Pritzker, *A Native American Encyclopedia: History, Culture, and Peoples* (Oxford: Oxford University Press, 2000), p. 113.
18. After Calisphere, "California Cultures," p. 1.
19. Lewis quoting Larkin, "California in 1846," p. 1.
20. Wikipedia, "Spanish missions in California,"citing Zephyrin Englehardt, *San Juan Capistrano Mission* (Los Angeles: Standard Printing Co., 1922), p. 348.
21. After Hughes, "The Decline of the Californios," p. 2.
22. Tennyson, "The Lotus-eaters."
23. Bancroft, *California Pastoral*, pp. 292–293.
24. Quoted by Olmsted, "Rancho Life," p. 2.
25. Quoted by Harlow, *California Conquered*, p. 333.
26. After Harlow, *California Conquered*, pp. 333–334.
27. Smith, *The War with Mexico*, p. 205.
28. Quoted by Nevin, *The Mexican War*, p. 101.
29. Sherman, *Recollections of California, 1846–1861*, p. 7.
30. There is now no agreed estimate of the number of people living in California during the years before statehood. A rough guess is that in 1846 there were about 7,000 persons of Spanish descent; 10,000 "civilized," i.e., domesticated, Indians; 700 Americans; 100 English, Irish, or Scottish people; and about 100 French, Germans,

or Italians. These figures seem to refer to the male population only ("The American Conquest of California," p. 2).

31. Weber, *Foreigners in Their Own Land*, citing Guadalupe Vallejo, "Ranch and Mission Days in Alta California," *Century Magazine* 41, no. 2 (December 1890), pp. 183, 184, 189, 191–92.

32. Colton, *Three Years in California*, p. 127.

33. Some of the following account has been drawn from PBS, "Mariano Guadalupe Vallejo."

34. After Osio, *The History of Alta California*, pp. 15–16.

35. Quoted by Beebe and Senkewicz, Introduction, *The History of Alta California*, pp. 22–23.

36. Adapted from Osio, *The History of Alta California*, pp. 89–94.

37. After Osio, *The History of Alta California*, p. 280.

38. After Osio, *The History of Alta California*, p. 344.

39. Quoted by Nevin, *The Mexican War*, p. 99.

40. Quoted by Descendants of Mexican War Veterans, "A Concise History of the U.S.–Mexican War," p. 1.

Chapter 2

1. After Smith, *The War with Mexico*, p. 206.
2. Smith, *The War with Mexico*, p. 207.
3. Fort Ross State Park, "How the Sea Otter Hunt Began," pp. 1–2. Today the sea otter population in California is around 2,000 animals, most of them living near Monterey. In addition, there are also about 168,000 sea otters in the waters off the Russian and Alaskan coasts.
4. After Bryant, *What I Saw in California*, Chapter III.
5. In some early printings of *Life in California*, Robinson also included a long ethnographic description of the Indians at Mission San Juan Capistrano, written in the 1820s by the Franciscan missionary Jerónimo Boscana.
6. Robinson, *Life in California*, pp. 231, 232.
7. After Beebe and Senkewicz, *Testimonios*, p. 91.
8. Robinson, *Life in California*, p. 150.
9. After Ocean Institute, "Pilgrim," p. 1.
10. That is to say, their own sustenance. Here Dana is referring to the Biblical miracle, described in Matt 14:17, wherein Christ feeds very large numbers of people from a minuscule amount of loves and fishes.
11. Dana, *Two Years Before the Mast*, p. 234.
12. Ibid., p. 237.
13. Comments on Sutter and Alvarado are drawn from Hurtado, "John Sutter: A Life on the American Frontier."
14. Quoted by Heizer, *Destruction of California Indians*, pp. 4–5.
15. Simkin in "John Sutter: Biography," p. 1.
16. "Life of John Augustus Sutter 1803–1880," p. 1.
17. Quoted by Simkin in "John Sutter," p. 1.
18. Today a replica of an ox-drawn emigrant wagon stands at Sutter's Fort. It is about 10 feet long, very narrow, and has no seat, no springs, and no brakes. Nevertheless, emigrants heading for California would load such a wagon with 2,000 pounds of supplies (Hayes, *Historical Atlas of California*, p. 74). Bidwell himself would go on to acquire a vast ranch in northern California; mine for gold on the Feather River;

serve as a U.S Congressman; and be described by a biographer as the "Prince of the California Pioneers" (Nunis, "Alta California's Trojan Horse," p. 315).
19. Quoted by Simkin in "John Sutter," p. 1.
20. Quoted by Simkin in "John Sutter," p. 1.
21. Quoted by Simkin in "John Sutter," p. 5.
22. Quoted by Simkin in "John Sutter," p. 1.
23. Quoted by Simkin in "John Sutter," p. 1.

Chapter 3

1. This chapter draws heavily from Bancroft, *California Pastoral*, pp. 294–301, 538–539, 549–552.
2. Adapted from Honig, "The Presidios of Alta California," pp. 5–6.
3. After Bancroft, *California Pastoral*, p. 300.
4. After Nevin, *The Mexican War*, p. 107.
5. Bancroft, *California Pastoral*, p. 304.
6. Ames and Gillespie, "Gillespie and the Conquest of California," p. 136.
7. Honig, "The Presidios of Alta California," p. 2.

Chapter 4

1. After Harlow, *California Conquered*, p. 26.
2. Castro was very much against American—and, by extension—against any other foreign control of California. Thus Dorotea Valdez's opinion was strictly subjective.
3. Quoted by Beebe and Senkewicz, *Testimonios*, p. 40.
4. After "The American Conquest of California," p. 1.
5. Quoted by Los Angeles Almanac, "Pio Pico—Last Governor of Mexican California," p. 1.
6. After California State Military Museum, "José Antonio Castro," p. 1.
7. Lewis quoting Larkin, "California in 1846," p. 9.
8. Quoted by Nevin, *The Mexican War*, p. 101. The source of this quote is not given but, judging from the context, it was almost certainly Walter Colton, the U.S. Navy chaplain who became the first American *alcalde* (mayor) of Monterey.
9. The following account is drawn from Santelli, "Marines in the Mexican War," p. 5.
10. Cited by Nevin, *The Mexican War*, p. 103. No source for this quote is given.
11. Ames and Gillespie, "Gillespie and the Conquest of California," p. 137.
12. After Santelli, "Marines in the Mexican War," p. 5.
13. The following account is drawn from Harlow, *California Conquered*, pp. 3–13.
14. Some of the information used below on the frigate *United States* comes from the article on this ship in the U.S. Navy's *Dictionary of American Naval Fighting Ships*.
15. A schooner had fore-and-aft sails on two or more of her masts. A storeship was used to store and transport supplies but could also be used to carry troops.
16. Melville, *White-Jacket*, p. 6.
17. Quoted by Harlow, *California Conquered*, p. 4.
18. Quoted by Harlow, *California Conquered*, p. 35.
19. During his travels in Alta California, on one occasion De Mofras stayed in the guestroom of a house in which 20 gallons of fine wine was stored for eventual—and very gradual—use by the local priest when celebrating Mass. The lady of the house, Señora Hartell, told an interviewer many years later that De Mofras like any good Frenchman, had sniffed out the wine and decided to sample it. He found that it was

good and drank so much of it that he was deprived of his senses. The young diplomat's drunken state made him so ill that he was forced to remain in bed for several days (Beebe and Senkewicz, *Testimonios*, p. 65).
20. Cited by Hague and Langum, *Thomas O. Larkin*, p. 34.
21. Cited by Hague and Langum, *Thomas O. Larkin*, p. 85.
22. Cited by Hague and Langum, *Thomas O. Larkin*, p. 85.
23. Quoted by Hague and Langun, *Thomas O. Larkin*, p. 127.
24. After *Jewish Encyclopedia*, p. 1.
25. Lewis quoting Larkin, "California in 1846," p. 10.
26. Some of the following points are drawn from Hague and Langum, *Thomas O. Larkin*, pp. 199, 211–212, 231, 224.
27. Quoted by Hague and Langum, *Thomas O. Larkin*, p. 227–228. Italics in original.

Chapter 5

1. This account is drawn from Simmons, "The Secret Mission of Archibald Gillespie," pp. 1–8; from Nevin, *The Mexican War*, pp. 99–100; and from "Gillespie" in the *Dictionary of American Naval Fighting Ships*. During World War II, the U.S. Navy commissioned a destroyer, *Gillespie* (DD-609), which was named after this officer.
2. Institute for Advanced Technology in the Humanities, "Gillespie, Archibald H.," p. 1. The Library of Congress does have one book devoted to Gillespie (*Messenger of Destiny: The California Adventures, 1846–1847, of Archibald H. Gillespie, U.S. Marine Corps*), written by Werner H. Marti in 1960. However, this has long been out of print, is not mentioned by the above Institute, and it does not appear to have been cited by any source known to the present authors.
3. Quoted by Nevin, *The Mexican War*, p. 99.
4. In his *California Pastoral*, the historian Bancroft has this to say about Mrs. Ord on p. 781: "Mrs. A. Ord, née de la Guerra, and whose first husband was Don Manuel Jimeno Casarin, who held several high positions in California ... dictated for me at Santa Bárbara in 1878, her *Ocurrencias de California*, a manuscript of one hundred and fifty-six pages, which is beyond doubt one of the most reliable and fascinating narratives in my collection, treating as it does not only of political affairs, about which she was fully informed, but of social life and the missions."
5. Quoted by Beebe and Senkewicz, *Testimonios*, p. 263.
6. Quoted by Hague and Langum, *Thomas O. Larkin*, p. 3.
7. Quoted by Hague and Langum, *Thomas O. Larkin*, pp. 3–4.
8. Stenburg and Gillespie, "Further Letters of Archibald H. Gillespie," p. 219.
9. Quoted by Simmons, "The Secret Mission of Archibald Gillespie," p. 7.

Chapter 6

1. After Janin and Carlson, *Trails of Historic New Mexico*, p. 81.
2. DeVoto, *The Year of Decision 1846*, p. 471.
3. Some of the following account follows McNamara, "John C. Frémont," pp. 1–2.
4. The best works on Carson are arguably those by Quaife, Utley, Sides, and Camp (see bibliography).
5. Camp, "Kit Carson in California: With Extracts from His Own Story," p. 1.
6. After Gilbert, *The Trailblazers*, p. 155.
7. Quoted by Farquhar, *History of the Sierra Nevada*, p. 58.
8. Brewerton, *Overland with Kit Carson*, p. 38.

9. Sherman, *Recollections of California, 1846–1861*, p. 22.
10. Quoted by Sides, *Blood and Thunder*, p. 490.
11. Quoted by Harlow, *California Conquered*, p. 67, citing Larkin. In this context, "guns" refers to muskets.
12. After Beck and Hasse, "Fremont and the Bear Flag Revolt," p. 3.
13. See Colton, *Three Years in California*, pp. 206–207.
14. Mora, *Californios*, p. 18.
15. Quoted by DeVoto, *The Year of Decision 1846*, p. 111.
16. The Oregon Country included all of the present-day Canadian province of British Columbia and the U.S. states of Washington, Oregon, Idaho, and small parts of Wyoming and Montana.
17. After Quaife, *Kit Carson's Autobiography*, pp. 95–96.

Chapter 7

1. When Caucasian explorers first entered the Klamath River area in the 1820s, the Klamath Indians were living in the Upper Klamath Lake area. However, later Indian uprisings and the growing value of tribal lands persuaded the U.S. Government to merge the Klamath, Modoc, and Yahooskin tribes into one "Klamath Tribe" on a single reservation in the Klamath Basin ("The Oregon History Project," p. 1).
2. Quoted by DeVoto, *The Year of Decision: 1846*, p. 200.
3. Quoted by Quaife, *Kit Carson's Autobiography*, pp. 96–97.
4. This and the following quotes in this account are drawn from Chaffin, pp. 310–311.
5. After Quaife, *Kit Carson's Autobiography*, p. 101.
6. After Quaife, *Kit Carson's Autobiography*, p. 102.
7. Quoted by Chaffin, *Pathfinder*, p. 308.
8. Quoted by Beck and Hasse, "Frémont and the Bear Flag Revolt," p. 1.
9. Quoted by Harlow, *California Conquered*, p. 85.
10. DeVoto, *The Year of Decision: 1846*, p. 198.
11. Bancroft, Chapter IV, "Causes of the Settlers' Revolt," p. 85.
12. Osio, *The History of Alta California*, p. 312, endnote 8.
13. After DeVoto, *The Year of Decision: 1846*, p. 201.

Chapter 8

1. Quoted by National Park Service, "Bear Flag Revolt, June 1846," p. 2. Some of the discussion following this quote also comes from the above source.
2. Bancroft, Chapter IV, "Causes of the Settlers' Revolt," p. 85.
3. The following quotes are taken from Bancroft's Chapter IV on the "Causes of the Settlers' Revolt," pp. 84–85.
4. Quoted by National Park Service, "Bear Flag Revolt, June 1846" p. 2.
5. Quoted by Nevin, *The Mexican War*, p. 104.
6. Bidwell, "Frémont in the Conquest of California," p. 3.
7. After Nevin, *The Mexican War*, p. 105.
8. "Proclamation of the Bear Flag Revolt," p. 1.
9. Quoted by Beebe and Senkewicz, *Testimonios*, pp. 25–29.
10. Quoted by Harlow, *California Conquered*, p. 107.
11. Quoted in "Frémont's California Battalion of Mounted Riflemen," p. 1.
12. After National Park Service, "Bear Flag Revolt, June 1846," p. 2.

13. After California State Military Museum, "Captain John Charles Fremont and the Bear Flag Revolt," pp. 2–3.
14. Nevin, *The Mexican War*, p. 105. Italics added.

Chapter 9

1. This statement has often been misquoted—due to an incorrect translation—and has her saying that "the conquest of California *did not bother the Californians, least of all the women.*" (After Gutiérrez and Orsi, *Contested Eden*, pp. 331–332. Italics added.) The correct translation is the one used in the body of this text.
2. This quotation is compiled from two marginally different translations, but in both cases the meaning is the same. The first translation is from *Testimonios*, by Beebe and Senkewicz, p. 264. The second is from Weber, *Foreigners in Their Native Land*, p. 127, citing Angustias de la Guerra Ord, *Occurrences in Hispanic California*, trans. and ed. Francis Price and William H. Ellison (Washington, D.C., 1956, p. 59.) Reprinted by permission of the Academy of American Franciscan History.
3. Quoted by Harlow, *California Conquered*, p. 123.
4. After Harlow, *California Conquered*, p. 123.
5. Yerba Buena was well-established as a small but viable port. In 1837, William Richardson, initially a London-born cabin boy who had jumped ship there, had risen to become the captain of the port. His maritime report for 1837 gives a clear idea of trade at that time: He found that 25 ships had entered the port: 10 from the United States, 5 from Mexico; 5 from the United Kingdom, 2 from Russia, 2 from Ecuador and 1 from Hawaii. California exports included hides, cow horns, suet (an inferior form of beef tallow), lard, dried meat, potatoes, flour, wool, otter pelts, deerskins, calabashes, live cattle, sheep, wheat, seeds, maize, oats, and beans. The total declared value of goods exported from San Francisco Bay in 1837 was $75,711 (after Maldetto, "William Richardson and Yerba Buena Origins," p. 4).
6. From Bryant, *What I Saw in California*, Chapter III.
7. Quoted in "Frémont's California Battalion of Mounted Riflemen," p. 1.
8. Quoted in "Frémont's California Battalion of Mounted Riflemen," pp. 1–2. Unlike the later short-barreled Winchester and other centerfire carbines of the cowboy era, their muskets and rifles were too long to be carried conveniently in leather scabbards strapped to the saddles of their horses.
9. Burdett, *Life of Kit Carson*, pp. 303–304.
10. The American inventor Samuel Colt first patented his famous revolver in 1836. U.S. Army officers who tested it in 1840 reported that it shot "with accuracy and force." It was the first practical revolver and the first practical repeating firearm. When empty, its five-shot cylinder could be replaced with a loaded five-shot cylinder without too much delay. Known as the Colt Patterson revolver, surviving examples which are in good condition now command very high prices from gun collectors.
11. Long-bladed, heavy-duty, fighting knives were equally well-adapted to stabbing or slashing. In the days before the Colt revolver became widely available, a Bowie knife with a long blade was the most reliable last-ditch weapon a man could carry.
12. Quoted in "Frémont's California Battalion of Mounted Riflemen," p. 1.

Chapter 10

1. Harlow, *California Conquered*, pp. 138–139.
2. After Bauer, *Surfboats and Horse Marines*, p. 162.
3. Twenty-three pounds was not the weight of the rifle itself, but an indication

of the caliber of the rifle. For example, one pound of lead could be melted down to make 25 balls for a .58 caliber rifle. Thus a mountain man might refer to such a weapon as a "25-pound" rifle. The rifle itself would weigh, on the average, about 10½ pounds.

4. Wise, *Los Gringos*, pp. 50–53.

5. For example, in his letter of 26 August 1846 to the Secretary of the Navy (quoted by Denger, "Los Angeles in the War with Mexico," p. 4), Stockton bragged: "Thus in less than a month after I assumed command of the United States forces in California, we have chased the Mexican Army more than three hundred miles along the coast; pursued them thirty miles in the interior of their own country, routed and dispersed them; secured the territory for the United States; ended the war, restored peace and harmony among the people; and put a civil government into successful operation."

6. Du Pont would later write that "the *Cyane* is all I could wish for—a fine sea vessel and of large size, with a beautiful cabin." When sailing her around Cape Horn on his way to Boston, he remarked that "the *Cyane* rounded the Cape easily; we came round the west coast of the Cape with awful speed before the northwest gales, scudding before the seas that make a man's hair stand on end, but this ship is the finest I ever saw for the most dangerous operations. We did not suffer from the cold" (Center for Living History, p. 6).

7. Quoted by Nevin, *The Mexican War*, p. 108.

8. Bryant, *What I Saw in California*, pp. 1–3, 6–7.

9. Quoted by Amero, "The Mexican-American War in Baja California," p. 1. Much of the information on Baja California that follows in this chapter is drawn from this same article.

Chapter 11

1. Knox, *Naval Sketches of the War in California*, pp. 24–25.
2. Quoted by Cutts, *The Conquest of California and New Mexico*, p. 246.
3. After Santelli, "Marines in the Mexican War," p. 55.
4. After Santelli, "Marines in the Mexican War," pp. 3–4.
5. After Knox, *Naval Sketches of the War in California*, pp. 39–40.
6. After Cutts, *The Conquest of California and New Mexico*, pp. 105–110.
7. After Chaffin, *Pathfinder*, p. 340.
8. After Bauer, *Surfboats and Horse Marines*, p. 158.
9. After Harlow, *California Conquered*, p. 154.
10. The following information on the capture of the brig *Malek Adhel* comes from Bauer, *Surfboats and Horse Marines*, p. 172.
11. Colton, *Three Years in California*, p. 151.
12. After Harlow, *California Conquered*, p. 249.
13. Quoted by Cutts, *The Conquest of California and New Mexico*, p. 264.

Chapter 12

1. Quoted by Amero, "The Mexican-American War in Baja California," citing *The Journal of Lieutenant Tunis Augustus Macdonough Craven, USN, United States Sloop of War Dale* (San Francisco: Ward Richie Press, 1973), pp. 65–68. In the endnotes, this source is hereafter cited simply as "Craven."

2. Quoted by Amero, "The Mexican-American War in Baja California," p. 2, citing "Memorandum of Captain Henry W. Halleck Concerning the Expeditions in Lower

California, 1846–1848," in turn citing *The Mexican-American War in Baja California*, Doyce B. Nunis, Jr., ed., pp. 102–103.
   3. Quoted by Amero, "The Mexican-American War in Baja California," citing Craven, *Journal*, p. 80.
   4. Quoted by Knox, *Naval Sketches of the War in California*, pp. 35–36.
   5. Quoted by Amero, "The Mexican-American War in Baja California," citing William P. Ryan, *Personal Adventures in Upper and Lower California, 1848–1849*, Vol. 1 (London: William Shobert Publisher, 1850), pp. 138–139.
   6. Quoted by Ruiz de Burton, *The Squatter and the Don*, p. 11, citing Bancroft's *California Pastoral*.
   7. Quoted by Amero, "The Mexican-American War in Baja California," p. 5, citing Buffum, p. 144.

Chapter 13

   1. Sternberg and Gillespie, "Further Letters of Archibald H. Gillespie," p. 224.
   2. After Harlow, *California Conquered*, p. 161.
   3. Quoted by Bauer, *Surfboats and Horse Marines*, p. 174.
   4. This account follows Nevin, *The Mexican War*, pp. 111, 116–117; and Harlow, *California Conquered*, pp. 165–167.
   5. Quoted by Simmons, "The Secret Mission of Archibald Gillespie," p. 5.
   6. After Santelli, "Marines in the Mexican War," p. 16.
   7. After Santelli, "Marines in the Mexican War," p. 18, quoting Downey, *The Cruise of the Portsmouth, 1845–1847: A Sailor's View of the Naval Conquest of California* (New Haven: Yale University Press, 1959). No page number given.
   8. Quoted by Cutts, *The Conquest of California and New Mexico*, pp. 157–159.

Chapter 14

   1. The above comments are drawn in part from California Pioneer Heritage, "Kearny's Army of the West," pp. 1–3.
   2. Quoted by Hague, *Road to California*, p. 217.
   3. Quoted by Cutts, *The Conquest of California and New Mexico*, p. 181.
   4. Quoted by Coy, "The Battle of San Pascual," p. 6.
   5. *Vaqueros* wore rough buckskin shoes with a leather sole and a low heel, often with pieces of heavy leather sewed on at the heels to help support heavy spurs. If he was not wearing moccasins, which he sometimes did, Carson was probably wearing such shoes, rather than high-heeled cowboy boots, which are very ill-suited for walking over rough country. Beale, for his part, was probably wearing low-heeled military shoes (After Mora, *Californios*, pp. 17, 100).
   6. Quoted by Quaife, *Kit Carson's Autobiography*, pp. 116–117. Because Carson was illiterate, he dictated the story of his life as far as the year 1858 to his friend Colonel DeWitt Clinton Peters, a U.S. Army doctor.
   7. Quoted by Simmons, "The Secret Mission of Archibald Gillespie," p. 5.
   8. Some of the following comments on the Mormon Battalion are drawn from Hague, *Road to California*, pp. 241–290.
   9. After Hague, *Road to California*, pp. 241–242.
   10. Quoted by Hague, *Road to California*, pp. 255–256.
   11. Quoted by Hague, *Road to California*, p. 265.
   12. Quoted by Hague, *Road to California*, p. 286.

13. After Hague, *Road to California*, p. 290.
14. Quoted by Cutts, *The Conquest of California and New Mexico*, p. 264.

Chapter 15

1. Quoted by Simmons, "The Secret Mission of Archibald Gillespie," p. 6.
2. Although use of the waterproof percussion cap significantly reduced the problem of damp gunpowder, rainwater could still run down the bore of the rifle, especially when it was carried muzzle-up by means of a sling; leak through the wadding over the bullet itself; and wet the gunpowder. The ultimate solution was the adoption of the self-contained metallic cartridge, e.g., the .44 Henry cartridge. This waterproof cartridge was designed in 1860 and was used with great success in the Henry Repeating Rifle of the American Civil War era. Virtually all modern firearms today use self-contained metallic cartridges.
3. Quoted by Griswold del Castillo, "The U.S. Mexican War in San Diego, 1846–1847," p. 5.
4. Quoted by Griswold del Castillo, "The U.S. Mexican War in San Diego, 1846–1847," p. 5.
5. Quoted by Quaife, *Kit Carson's Autobiography*, pp. 111–112.
6. Quoted by Harlow, *California Conquered*, p. 187.

Chapter 16

1. Frémont, "Full Defence...," p. 9.
2. Quoted by Nevin, *The Mexican War*, p. 118. No original source given.
3. Some of the following comments are drawn from the "Treaty of Cahuenga," p. 1, and from Denger, "The Treaty of Campo de Cahuenga," pp. 1–5.
4. After Denger, "The Treaty of Campo de Cahuenga," pp. 2–5.
5. After Princeton's "Treaty of Cahuenga," p. 1.

Chapter 17

1. After Harlow, *California Conquered*, p. 303.
2. In his wonderful book *Roughing It* (1872), Twain said of his silver mining experiences in Nevada: "I would have been more or less than human if I had not gone mad like the rest. Cartloads of solid silver bricks, as large as pigs of lead, were arriving from the mills every day, and such sights as that have given substance to the wild talk about me. I succumbed and grew as frenzied as the craziest" (p. 152).
3. This quote is attributed to Twain's character Mulberry Sellers, who appears in *The American Claimant* (1892).
4. These examples come from Harlow, *The Forty-Niners*, pp. 82–86.
5. After Colton, *Three Years in California*, p. 202.
6. Quoted by Johnson, *The Forty-Niners*, pp. 22–23.
7. Quoted by Johnson, *The Forty-Niners*, p. 23.
8. After Johnson, *The Forty-Niners*, p. 26.
9. Quoted by Johnson, *The Forty-Niners*, p. 27.
10. Quoted by Johnson, *The Forty-Niners*, p. 28.
11. Quoted by Johnson, *The Forty-Niners*, p. 17.
12. After Johnson, *The Forty-Niners*, p. 32.
13. Buffum, *Present at the Beginning of the Gold Rush*, p. 2.
14. Ibid., p. 5.

15. After Johnson, *The Forty-Niners*, p. 35.
16. Quoted by Johnson, *The Forty-Niners* , p. 38.
17. Quoted by Johnson, *The Forty-Niners*, p. 33.
18. The following account closely follows Griswold del Castillo, *The Treaty of Guadalupe Hidalgo*, pp. 67–68.
19. After Harlow, *California Conquered*, p. 281.
20. After Harlow, *California Conquered*, p. 319.
21. Some of the following comments on Riley follow Harlow, *California Conquered*, pp. 323–325.
22. After Harlow, *California Conquered*, pp. 330–331.

Chapter 18

1. This account is drawn in part from Eisenhower, *So Far from God*, pp. 230–231; and from DeVoto, *The Year of Decision: 1846*, pp. 472–473.
2. After Anne F. Hyde, Introduction, p. xix, in *Frémont's First Impressions*.
3. Frémont, "Defense," pp. 57–58.

Chapter 19

1. Griswold del Castillo, "War's End: Treaty of Guadalupe-Hidalgo," p. 1.
2. Quoted by Amero, "The Mexican-American War in Baja California," p. 3, citing Proclamation, November 4, 1847. House Executive Document 1, Serial 537 (Washington, D.C., 1848), pp. 1084–1085.
3. Quoted by Amero, "The Mexican-American War in Baja California," citing *A Compilation of Messages and Papers of the Presidents*, Vol. V (New York, 1897–1911), pp. 2388–2392.
4. Quoted by Amero, *The Mexican-American War in Baja California*, p. 4.
5. Quoted by Amero, *The Mexican-American War in Baja California*, p. 4.
6. Yale Law School, "Treaty of Guadalupe Hidalgo," p. 2.
7. Ibid.
8. After Griswold del Castillo, "War's End," p. 2.
9. Private communication of 6 May 2014 from Richard Griswold del Castillo.
10. Cited by Velasco-Márquez, "A Mexican Viewpoint on the War with the United States," quoting a July 8, 1864, letter from Virginia Randolph Trist.

Chapter 20

1. On becoming governor of California, Kearny issued at Monterey on 1 March 1847 a very gracious "binding-up-wounds" Proclamation to the People of California. Its concluding section reads in part: "For many years California has suffered great domestic convulsions; from civil wars, like poisoned fountains, have flowed calamity and pestilence over this beautiful region. These fountains are now dried up; the stars and stripes now float over California ... Americans and Californians! from henceforth one people. Let us then indulge in one hope; let that be for the peace and tranquility of our country. Let us unite like brothers, and mutually strive for the mutual improvement and advancement of this our beautiful country, which within a short period cannot fail to be not only beautiful but also prosperous and happy" (quoted by Cutts, *The Conquest of California*, pp. 210–211).
2. Some of these comments on Riley's role in the transition to constitutional government are drawn from Harlow, *California Conquered*, pp. 325–353.

3. These comments are drawn from "Biographical Notes: Joaquin Murrieta," p. 1; "Man vs Myth," pp. 1–2; and the California State Military Museum's article on "California State Rangers," pp. 1–5.
4. Quoted in "Man vs Myth," p. 1.
5. Quoted by Harlow, *California Conquered*, p. 327.
6. Quoted by Denger, "California's Constitutional Convention of 1849," p. 1. Much of the following information in this section is drawn from pp. 2–3 of this same source.
7. Quoted by Denger, "California's Constitutional Convention of 1849," p. 1.
8. Quoted by Denger, "California's Constitutional Convention of 1849," p. 2.
9. Quoted by Denger, "California's Constitutional Convention of 1849," p. 3.
10. Quoted by Harlow, *California Conquered*, p. 352.
11. After Harlow, *California Conquered*, pp. 352–353.
12. After Library of Congress, "Compromise of 1850," p. 1.
13. These quotations are taken from Digital History ID 567, "The Public Land Commission," pp. 1–3.

Chapter 21

1. Quoted by Nevin, *The Mexican War*, p. 108.
2. Adapted from Griswold del Castillo, "The U.S.–Mexican War in San Diego, 1846–1847: Loyalty and Resistance," p. 1.
3. After Hackel, "Land, Labor, and Production," p. 111.
4. After Bancroft, *California Pastoral*, p. 452.
5. After Bancroft, *California Pastoral*, p. 437.
6. After Bauer, *The Mexican War*, p. 15, note 24, citing Thomas O. Larkin, "Description of California Prior to the Year 1846."
7. Bryant, *What I Saw in California*, p. 1.
8. Some of these comments are drawn from the Introduction in Ruiz de Burton's *The Squatter and the Don*, p. 19.
9. Weber, "The Aftermath of War: Many Truths Constitute the Past," p. 2.
10. Ibid., pp. 1–2.
11. After Lebergott, "Wage Trends, 1800–1890," p. 252.
12. Quoted by Mora-Torres, *Californio Voices*, pp. 187–188.
13. Quoted by Mora-Torres, *Californio Voices*, p. 191.

Bibliography

"The American Conquest of California." http://elane.stanford.edu/wilson/html/chap2/chap2sect5.html. Accessed 4 January 2014.
Ames, George Walcott, Jr., and Archibald H. Gillespie. "Gillespie and the Conquest of California. From Letters Dated February 11, 1846, to July 8, 1848, to the Secretary of the Navy." *California Historical Society Quarterly* 17, no. 2 (June 1938), pp. 123–140. http://www.jstor.org/stable/25160772. Accessed 19 June 2014.
Amero, Richard W. "The Mexican-American War in Baja California." http://www.sandiegohistory.org/journal/84winter/war.htm. Accessed 31 January 2014.
Arnold, Linda. "Two Few Ships, Two Few Guns, and Not Enough Money: The Mexican Navy, 1846–1848." *The Northern Mariner/Le Marin du nord* IX, no. 2 (April 1999), pp. 1–10.
Bancroft Hubert Howe. *California Pastoral, 1769–1848*. San Francisco: History Company, 1888.
_____. *History of California*. Chapter IV. Causes of the Settlers' Revolt. http://www.bearflagmuseum.org.BancroftIntroTOC.html. Accessed 21 June 2014.
_____. *History of California*. Chapter XXIX. Lower California, 1800–1848. http://archive.org/details/northmexicans02bancrich. Accessed 4 September 2013.
Barraza, Angélica G. "Voices of Californianas: Spanish-Mexican Women of San Diego, Alta California, 1870." San Diego History Center. http://www.sandiegohistory.org/women/californianas.htm. Accessed 13 March 2014.
Bauer, K. Jack. *The Mexican War 1846–1848*. Lincoln: University of Nebraska Press, 1974.
_____. *Surfboats and Horse Marines: U.S. Naval Operations in the Mexican War, 1846–48*. Annapolis: United States Naval Institute, 1969.
Beck, Warren A., and Ynez B. Hasse. "Frémont and the Bear Flag Revolt." http://www.militarymuseum.org/BFR.html. Accessed 25 August 2013.
Beebe, Rose Marie, and Robert M. Senkewicz, eds. *Lands of Promise and Despair: Chronicles of Early California, 1535–1846*. Santa Clara: Santa Clara University and Heyday Books, 2001.
_____, and _____. *Testimonios: Early California Through the Eyes of Women, 1815–1848*. Berkeley: Heyday Books and the Bancroft Library, University of California, 2006.
Bidwell, John. "Frémont in the Conquest of California." http://www.sfmuseum.net.hist6/fremont.html. Accessed 14 February 2014.
"Biographical Notes: Joaquin Murrieta." http://www.inn-california.com/articles/biographic/murrietabionotes.html. Accessed 10 June 2014.
Bozie, William J., Jr. "A Chronology of the U.S.–Mexican War, 1845–1848: Battles,

Bibliography

Skirmishes & Other Important Events." http:www.dmwv.org/mexwar/chron1845-6.htm. Accessed 21 September 2013.

Brewerton, George Douglas. *Overland with Kit Carson: A Narrative of the Old Spanish Trail in '48*. Intro. Marc Simmons. Lincoln: University of Nebraska Press, 1993.

Bryant, Edwin. *What I Saw in California*. http://www.authorama.com/what-i-saw-in-california-3html and www.authorama.com/what-i-saw-in-california-9.html. Accessed 21 March 2014.

Buffum, Edward Gould. "Present at the Beginning of the Gold Rush: Journalist Edward Gould Buffum Pans Gold in California in 1848." http://historymatters.gmu.edu/d/6513. Accessed 3 June 2014.

Burdett, Charles. *Life of Kit Carson: The Great Western Hunter and Guide*. Philadelphia: John E. Potter, 1869.

California Pioneer Heritage Foundation. "A Unit of Kearny's Army of the West." http://californiapioneer.org/for-history-buffs/mormon-battalion/15-a-unit-of-kearny percentE2 percent... Accessed 27 April 2014.

California State Military Museum. "The Battle of Monterey." http://www/militarymuseum.org/Monterey1.html. Accessed 22 June 2014.

_____. "California State Rangers." http:www.militarymuseum.org/CaliforniaStateRangers.html. Accessed 10 June 2014.

_____. "Captain John Charles Fremont and the Bear Flag Revolt." http://www.military/museum.org/fremont.html. Accessed 16 February 2014.

Calisphere. "California Cultures—Hispanic Americans: Spanish Colonization and Californios (1769–1800s)." http://www.calisphere.universityofcalifornia.edu/calcultures/ethnic_groups/subtopic3a.html. Accessed 8 September 2013.

Camp, Charles L. "Kit Carson in California: With Extracts from His Own Story." *California Historical Society Quarterly* 1, no. 2 (October 1922), pp. 111–151. University of California Press in association with the California Historical Society. http://jstor.org/stable/25613577. Accessed 30 June 2014.

Castillero, Andrés. "A Mexican Officer Urges Defense of Both Californias." In Rose Marie Beebe and Robert M. Senkewicz, eds., *Lands of Promise and Despair*. Santa Clara: Santa Clara University and Heyday Books, 2001, pp. 406–412.

"Castro, José Antonio, Comandante-General and Acting Governor of California." http:www.militarymuseum.org/castro.html. Accessed 29 November 2013.

Center for Living History. Home page with information about the *Cyane* project. http://www.cyane.org. Accessed 30 March 2014.

Chaffin, Tom. *Pathfinder: John Charles Fremont and the Course of American Empire*. New York: Hill and Wang, 2002.

Chambers, John W., ed. *The Oxford Companion to American Military History*. Oxford: Oxford University Press, 1999.

Colton, the Rev. Walter. *Three Years in California*. New York: Barnes, 1850. (Reprinted by the Scholarly Publishing Office of the University of Michigan; no date given for reprint.)

Coronel, Antonio. "1840s: Life and Customs in Mexican California." In Rose Marie Beebe and Robert M. Senkewicz, eds., *Lands of Promise and Despair: Chronicles of Early California, 1535–1846*. Santa Clara: Santa Clara University and Heyday Books, 2001, pp. 446–452.

Coy, Owen. C. "The Battle of San Pasqual: A report of the California Historical Survey Commission with Special Reference to its Location." Sacramento: California State Printing Office, 1921.

Craven, Lieutenant Tunis Augustus Macdonough. *A Naval Campaign in the Californias—1846–1849. The Journal of Lieutenant Tunis Augustus Macdonough Craven,*

Bibliography

U.S.N. United States Sloop of War, Dale. Ed. John Haskell Kemble. San Francisco: Book Club of California, 1973.
Cutts, James Madison. *The Conquest of California and New Mexico, by the Forces of the United States, in the Years 1846 & 1847.* Philadelphia: Carey & Hart, 1848.
Dana, Richard Henry, Jr. *The Seaman's Friend, Containing a Treatise on Practical Seamanship.* Mineola: Dover, 1997.
_____. *Two Years Before the Mast: A Personal Narrative of Life at Sea.* Ed. and intro. Thomas Philbrick. New York: Penguin, 1986.
"Defense of Lieut.Col. J.C. Fremont before the military court martial, Washington, January, 1848." (Bancroft Library, full text.) https://archive.org/stream/defence oflieutco00frrich/defenseoflieutco00frrich_djvu.txt. Accessed 2 May 2014.
Delay, Brian. "Independent Indians and the U.S. Mexican War." *American Historical Review,* February 2007.
Denger, Mark J. "Early California: California's Constitutional Convention of 1849." http:www.militarymuseum.org/Constitution/html. Accessed 10 May 2014.
_____. "The Mexican War and California: Los Angeles and the War with Mexico." http://www.militarymuseum.org/MexWarLA.hrml. Accessed 7 September 2013.
_____. "The Mexican War and California: The Treaty of Campo de Cahuenga." http://www.militarymuseum.org/Cahuenga.html. Accessed 1 September 2013.
Descendants of Mexican War Veterans. "A Concise History of the U.S.–Mexican War." htm://www.dmwv.org/mexwar/history/calcon.htm. Accessed 31 August 2013.
DeVoto, Bernard. *The Year of Decision: 1846.* New York: Truman Talley, 2000.
Dictionary of American Naval Fighting Ships. "Gillespie." http://www.history.navy. mil/DANFS/g5/gillespie.htm. Accessed 12 March 2014.
_____. *United States.* www.history.navy.mil/dansf/ul/united_states.htm. Accessed 28 May 2014.
Digital History. "The Public Land Commission: Digital History ID 567." http://www.digitalhistory.uh.edu/disp_textbook_print.cfm?smtid=3&psid=567. Accessed 9 May 2014.
Eisenhower, John S.D. *So Far from God: The U.S. War with Mexico, 1846–1848.* Norman: University of Oklahoma Press, 2000.
Embajada de México en Estados Unidos, Secretaría de Relaciones Exteriores. "Mexico after Independence." http://embamex.sre.gob.mx/eua/index.php/en/meetmex/508-mexican-history?start=4. Accessed 22 February 2014.
Farquhar, Francis P. *History of the Sierra Nevada.* Berkeley: University of California Press, 2007.
Faulk, Odie B. *Destiny Road: The Gila Trail and the Opening of the Southwest.* New York: Oxford University Press, 1973.
Fort Ross State Park. "How the Sea Otter Hunt Began." http://www.fortrossstatepark.org/seaotter.htm. Accessed 10 November 2013.
Frémont, John C. *Frémont's First Impressions: The Original Report of His Exploring Expeditions of 1842–1844.* Intro. Anne F. Hyde. Lincoln: University of Nebraska Press, 2012.
"Frémont's California Battalion of Mounted Riflemen." http://www.longcamp.com/batt.html. Accessed 7 September 2013.
Garavaglia, Louis A., and Charles G. Worman. *Firearms of the American West, 1803–1865.* Niwot: University Press of Colorado, 1998.
Gilbert, Bill. *The Trailblazers.* Alexandria: Time-Life Books, 1973.
Griswold Del Castillo, Richard. " A Short Overview of California Indian History." http://www.nahc.ca.gov/califindian.html. Accessed 16 September 2013.
_____. "The U.S.–Mexican War in San Diego, 1846–1847: Loyalty and Resistance."

The Journal of San Diego History 49, no. 1 (Winter 2003). http://www.sandiego history.org/journal/v49–1/war.htm. Accessed 4 October 2013.

———. *War's End: The Treaty of Guadalupe Hidalgo: A Legacy of Conflict*. Norman: University of Oklahoma Press, 1990.

Gutiérrez, Ramón, and Richard J. Orsi, eds. *Contested Eden: California Before the Gold Rush*. Berkeley: University of California Press, 1998.

Haas, Lizbeth. "War in California, 1846–1848." In Ramón A. Gutiérrez and Richard J. Orsi, eds., *Contested Eden: California Before the Gold Rush*. Berkeley: University of California Press, 1998, pp. 331–355.

Hackel, Steven W. "Labor, and Production: The Colonial Economy of Spanish and Mexican California." In Ramón A. Gutiérrez and Richard J. Orsi, eds., *Contested Eden: California Before the Gold Rush*. Berkeley: University of California Press, 1998, pp. 111–146.

Hague, Harlan. *Road to California: The Search for a Southern Overland Route, 1540–1848*. Lincoln: Authors Choice Press, 2001.

Hague, Harlan, and David J. Langum. *Thomas O. Larkin: A Life of Patriotism and Profit*. Norman: University of Oklahoma Press, 1990.

Harlow, Neal. *California Conquered: The Annexation of a Mexican Province, 1846–1848*. Berkeley: University of California Press, 1989.

Hayes, Derek. *Historical Atlas of California*. Berkeley: University of California Press, 2007.

Heizer, Robert F. and M.A. Whipple. *The California Indians: A Source Book*, 2d ed. Berkeley: University of California Press, 1971.

———, ed. *The Destruction of California Indians*. Lincoln: University of Nebraska Press, 1993.

Hickman, Kennedy. "Mexican American War—Aftermath of the Mexican American War." http://militaryhistory.about.com/od/mexicanamericanwar/a/MexicanEnd.htm. Accessed 1 October 2013.

———. "Mexican-American War 101: An Overview." http://militaryhistory.about.com/od/mexicanamericanwar/p/Mexican101.htm. Accessed 1 October 2013.

Honig, Sasha. "The Presidios of Alta California." http://www.militarymuseum.org/Presidios.html. Accessed 19 May 2014.

Hosley, William. *Colt: The Making of an American Legend*. Amherst: University of Massachusetts Press, 1996.

Hughes, Charles. "The Decline of the Californios." http://www.sandiegohistory.org/journal/75summer/decline.htm. Accessed 26 February 2014.

———, ed. "A Military View of San Diego in 1847: Four Letters from Colonel Jonathan D. Stevenson to Governor Richard B. Mason." http://www.sandiegohistory.org/journal/74summer/letters.htm. Accessed 26 February 2014.

Hurtado, Albert L. *John Sutter: A Life on the North American Frontier*. Norman: University of Oklahoma Press, 2006.

Janin, Hunt. *Claiming the American Wilderness: International Rivalry in the Trans-Mississippi West, 1528–1803*. Jefferson, NC: McFarland, 2006.

———. *Fort Bridger, Wyoming: Trading Post for Indians, Mountain Men and Westward Migrants*. Jefferson, NC: McFarland, 2001.

———, and Ursula Carlson. *Trails of Historic New Mexico: Routes Used by Indians, Spanish and American Travelers through 1886*. Jefferson, NC: McFarland, 2010.

Jewish Encyclopedia. http://www.jewishencyclopedia.com/articles/9729-leidesdorff-william. Accessed 24 May 2014.

Johnson, William Weber. *The Forty-Niners*. New York: Time-Life Books, 1976.

Katcher, Philip. *The Mexican-American War 1846–48*. Oxford: Osprey, 2004.

Bibliography

Kelsey, Harry. *Discovering Cabrillo*. Altadena: Liber Apertus Press, 2004.
Knox, Capt. Dudely W. *Naval Sketches of the War in California*. New York: Random House, 1939.
Kroeber, A.L. *Handbook of the Indians of California*. New York: Dover, 1976.
Lane, Beverly. "Jose Maria Amador's Rancho San Ramon." Museum of the San Ramon Valley. http:www.museumsrv.org/srvn_vh_RanchoAmador.html. Accessed 4 December 2014.
Larkin, Thomas O. "California in 1846 and its resources as then known. A Report to the U.S. Government." Reprinted from "The Pacific Monthly," December 1863, in Oscar Lewis, *California in 1846*. San Francisco: Grabhorn Press, 1934.
Lebergott, Stanley. "Wage Trends, 1800–1900." *Trends in the American Economy in the Nineteenth Century*. Princeton: Princeton University Press, 1960, pp. 449–500. www.nber.org/chapters/c2486. Accessed 6 December 2014.
Library of Congress. "Compromise of 1850." http://www.loc.gov/rr/program/bib/our doc/Compromise1850.html. Accessed 11 May 2014.
"Life of John Augustus Sutter 1803–1880." http://score.rims.k12.ca/us/activity/sutters fort/pages/sutter.html. Accessed 29 November 2013.
Los Angeles Almanac. "Pio Pico—Last Governor of Mexican California." http://www.laalmanac.com/history/hi05s.htm. Accessed 18 December 2013.
Lowman, Hubert A. *The Old Spanish Missions of California*. Arroyo Grande: Hubert A. Lowman, 1989.
Lugo, José del Carmen. "1840s: Life on a California Rancho." In Rose Marie Beebe and Robert M. Senkewicz, eds., *Lands of Promise and Despair: Chronicles of Early California, 1535–1846*. Santa Clara and Berkeley: Santa Clara University and Heyday Books, 2001, pp. 434–445.
Maldetto, K. "William Richardson and Yerba Buena Origins." http:foundsf.org/index.php?title=WILLIAM_RICHARDSON_AND_YERBA_BUENA_O... Accessed 8 May 2014.
"Man vs. Myth: Joaquin Murrieta." http://www.laits.utexas.edu/jaime/cwp4/JMG/man.html. Accessed 10 June 2014.
McNamara, Robert. "John C. Frémont, Explored the West and Made Manifest Destiny Practical." http://history1800s.about.com/od/americamoveswestward/a/John-C-Fremont-biography.htm. Accessed 7 December 2013.
Melville, Herman. *White-Jacket*. Oxford: Oxford University Press, 1992.
"Mexican-American War: Aftermath & Legacy." http://militaryhistory.about.com/mexicanamericanwar/a/MexicanEnd.htm. Accessed 10 June 2014.
Minster, Christopher. "Timeline of the Mexican-American War." http:latinamerican-historyabout.com/od/Mexican-AmericanWar/a/Timeline-Of-The-Mexi... Accessed 21 September 2013.
MissionTour. "Military Governors." http://missiontour.org/related/militarygov.htm. Accessed 10 May 2014.
Monroy, Douglas. "The Creation and Re-creation of *Californio* Society." In Ramón A. Gutiérrez and Richard J. Orso, eds., *Contested Eden: California Before the Gold Rush*. Berkeley: University of California Press, 1998, pp. 173–195.
Mora, Jo. *Californios: The Saga of the Hard-riding Vaqueros, America's First Cowboys*. Ketcham: Dover Hill, 1994.
Mora-Tores, Gregorio, trans. and ed. *Californio Voices: The Oral Memoirs of José María Amador and Lorenzo Asisara*. Denton: University of North Texas Press, 2005.
National Park Service. "Bear Flag Revolt, June 1846." http://www.nps.gov/goga/history culture/bear-flag-revolt.htm. Accessed 14 February 2014.

Bibliography

Naval History Heritage Command. "Dictionary of American Naval Fighting Ships: Cyane." http://www.history.navy.mil/danfs/c16/cyane-ii.htm. Accessed 30 March 2014.
Nevin, David. *The Mexican War*. Alexandria: Time-Life Books, 1978.
_____. *The Soldiers*. Alexandria: Time-Life Books, 1974.
Nordhoff, Walter. *The Journey of the Flame*. Berkeley: Heyday, 2003.
Nunis, Doyce B., Jr. "California's Trojan Horse: Foreign Immigration." In Ramón A. Gutiérrez and Richard J. Orsi, eds., *Contested Eden: California Before the Gold Rush*. Berkeley: University of California Press, 1998, pp. 299–330.
Ocean Institute. "Pilgrim." www.ocean-institute.org. Accessed 24 January 2014.
Olmsted, Nancy J. "Rancho Life, 1833–1846." http://foundsf.org/index.php?title=Rancho_Life,_1833–1846. Accessed 23 September 2014.
"The Oregon History Project." http://www.ohs.org/education/oregonistory/historical_records/dspDocument.cfm?doc_ID... Accessed 21 June 2014.
Osio, Antonia María. *The History of Alta California: A Memoir of Mexican California*. Trans., ed., and annotated Rose Marie Beebe and Robert M. Senkewicz. Madison: University of Wisconsin Press, 1996.
PBS. "James K. Polk (1845–1849)." http://www.pbs.org/kera/usmexicanwar/prelude/jp_james_k_polk_p2.html. Accessed 23 January 2014.
_____. "New Perspectives on the West: Mariano Guadalupe Vallejo (1808–1890)." http://www.pbs.org/weta/thewest/peoples/s_z/vallejlo.htm. Accessed 24 November 2013.
_____. "President Mariano Paredes y Arrillaga." http://www.pbs.org/kera/usmexicanwar/biographies/mariano_paredes_y_arrillaga.html. Accessed 5 April 2014.
Peterson, Walt. "Baja California: a short visit to one of the most interesting places on earth." http://www.baja-web.com/history/main-his.html. Accessed 2 April 2014.
Plummer, Lee. "The Vallejo Family: A Military History of Early California." http://www.militarymuseum.org/Vallejo.html. Accessed 29 December 2013.
"Proclamation of the Bear Flag Revolt." http://www.huntington.org/education/goldrush/advent/hm4116tran.html. Accessed 20 October 2014.
Quaife, Milo Milton, ed. *Kit Carson's Autobiography*. Lincoln: University of Nebraska Press, 1935.
Redmon, Michael. "Alfred Robinson." http://www.independent.com/news/2010/oct11/alfred-robinson/. Accessed 29 November 2013.
Regan, Geoffrey. "The Battle of San Pascual." http://www.militarymuseum.org/SanPasqual.html. Accessed 1 May 2014.
Risk, James. "The Pacific Theater of Naval Warfare in the Mexican-American War." http://www.militarymuseum.org/NavyMexWar.html. Accessed 18 February 2014.
Robinson, Alfred. *Life in California during a residence of several years in that territory, comprising a description of the country and the missionary establishments, with incidents, observations, etc.; with an appendix bringing forward the narrative from 1846, to the occupation of the country by the United States*. San Francisco: William Doxey, 1891. Nabu Public Domain Reprints.
Roosevelt, Franklin Delano. "Occupation of California" (Roosevelt's Introduction to the book *Naval Sketches of the War in California*, by Capt. Dudley W. Knox, USN). http://www.aztecclub.com/meyers/meyers01.html. Accessed 24 June 2014.
Ruiz de Burton, María Amparo. *The Squatter and the Don*. Rosaura Sánchez and Beatrice Pita, eds. Houston: Arte Público Press, 1997.
Russell, Carl P. *Guns on the Early Frontiers: A History of Firearms from Colonial Times*

Bibliography

Through the Years of the Western Fur Trade. Lincoln: University of Nebraska Press, 1957.
Santelli, Gabrielle M. Neufeld. "Marines in the Mexican War." Occasional Paper. Ed. Charles R. Smith. Washington, D.C: History and Museums Division, Headquarters, U.S. Marine Corps, 1991.
Sheppard Software. "Mexican-American War." http: www.shephardsoftware.com/Mexicoweb/factfille/Unique-facts-Mexico.htm. Accessed 16 September 2013.
Sherman, General William T. *Recollections of California, 1846–1861.* http://memory.loc.gov/cgi-bin/query/r?ammem/calbk@field(DOCID+@lit(calbk085div2). Accessed 9 April 2014.
Sides, Hampton. *Blood and Thunder: The Epic Story of Kit Carson and the Conquest of the American West.* New York: Anchor, 2007.
Simkin, John. "John Sutter." http://www.spartacus.schoolnet.co.uk/USAsutter.htm. Accessed 29 November 2013.
Simmons, Brigadier General Edwin H. "The Secret Mission of Archibald Gillespie." https://www.mca-marines.org/gazette/secret-mission-archibald-gillespie. Accessed 26 September 2013.
Singletary, Otis A. *The Mexican War.* Chicago: University of Chicago Press, 1960.
Smith, Justin Harvey. *The War with Mexico,* 2 vols. New York: Macmillian, 1919.
Stenberg, Richard R., and Archibald H. Gillespie. "Further Letters of Archibald H. Gillespie: October 20, 1845, to January 16, 1846, to the Secretary of the Navy." *California Historical Society Quarterly* 18, no. 3 (September 1939), pp. 217–228. http://www.jstor.org/stable/25160822. Accessed 19 June 2014.
Tanner, Ogden. *The Ranchers.* Alexandria: Time-Life Books, 1977.
Tennyson, Alfred Lord. "The Lotus-eaters." http://www.poetryfoundation.org/poem/174631. Accessed 28 May 2014.
"Treaty of Cahuenga." http://www.princeton.edu~achaney/tmve/wolo100k/docs/Treaty_of_Cahuenga.html. Accessed 24 December 2013.
Trinkle, William J. "A Brief History of the Bear Flag." http://www.bearflagmuseum.org/History.html. Accessed 14 February 2014.
U.S. Naval Institute. "The Mexican War, 12 May 1846." http://www.navalhistory.org/2011/05/12/the-mexican-war-12-may-1846. Accessed 1 October 2013.
Utley, Robert M. *A Life Wild and Perilous: Mountain Men and the Paths to the Pacific.* New York: Holt, 1997.
Valasco-Márquez, Jesús. "Manifest Destiny: A Mexican Viewpoint of the War with the United States." http://www.pbs.org/kera/usmexicanwar/prelude/md_a_mexican_viewpoint.html. Accessed 9 May 2014.
Walker, Dale L. *Bear Flag Rising: The Conquest of California.* New York: Forge Books, 1999.
Weber, David J. "The Aftermath of War—Many Truths Constitute the Past: The Legacy of the U.S.–Mexican War. A Conversation with David J. Weber, Southern Methodist University." http://pbs.org/kera/usmexicanwar/aftermath/many_truths.html. Accessed 28 August 2013.
_____. *The Spanish Frontier in North America.* New Haven: Yale University Press, 1992.
_____, ed. *Foreigners in Their Native Land: Historical Roots of the Mexican Americans.* Albuquerque: University of New Mexico Press, 1973.
Wikipedia. "Indigenous peoples of California." http://en.wikipedia.org/w/index.php?title=Indigenous_people_of-California&printable=... Accessed 11 October 2013.
_____. "Spanish missions in California." http://en.wikipedia.org/w/index.php?title=Spanish_missions_in_California&printable=yes. Accessed 11 November 2013.

Bibliography

Willis, John C. "U.S. Grant," 'Causes of the Mexican War.'" http: www.sewanee/edu/faculty/willis/Civil_War/documents/Grant/html. Accessed 12 September 2013.

Wise, Henry Augustus. *Los Gringos: An Inside View of Mexico and California, with Wanderings in Peru, Chili, and Polynesia.* http://www.gutenberg.org/files/32178-h32178-h.htm. Accessed 23 March 2014.

Woodworth, Steven E. *Manifest Destinies: America's Westward Expansion and the Road to the Civil War.* New York: Random House, 2011.

Yale Law Library. The Avalon Project. "Treaty of Guadalupe-Hidalgo: February 2, 1848." http://avalon.law.yale.edu/19th_century/guadhida.asp. Accessed 8 April 2014.

Yale University. "Message of President Polk, May 11, 1846." http:www.yale.edu/law/lawweb/avalon/presiden/messages/Polk01.htm. Accessed 30 September 2013.

Index

Acapulco 17, 71, 114, 116, 126
Adams, John Quincy 19
Adams-Onis Treaty of 1821 77
alcalde (mayor) 4, 20, 21, 43, 102, 108, 132, 167, 177, 193
Alta (Upper) California 1, 70, 110, 114, 165, 185, 198
Alvarado, Juan B. 30, 52, 53, 68, 192
American Civil War 2, 4, 40, 66, 82, 155, 173, 179, 188, 199
American military governors in California 130, 156, 157, 158, 159, 164, 167, 170, 171, 183, 188
American River 55, 153, 155
Amero, Richard W. 3, 189, 197, 198, 200
Argüello, Luis 42
Arguello, Santiago E. 33, 42
Arizona 1, 2, 19, 143, 176
Arkansas River 19, 77, 81
Armstrong, James 68
Army of the West 23, 79, 139, 141, 142, 143, 174, 184, 198

Baja (Lower) California 1, 11, 12, 16, 17, 18, 35, 48, 111, 112, 117, 118, 119, 123, 124, 127, 130, 149, 163, 164, 165, 180, 186, 188, 189, 190, 197, 198, 200
Bancroft, George 60, 74, 75, 113, 114, 132, 184
Bancroft, Hubert Howe 6, 37, 59, 60, 73, 89, 91, 129, 170, 179, 189, 190, 191, 193, 194, 195, 198, 201
Bautista de Anza, Juan 18
Beale, Edward F. 141, 142, 198
Bear Flag Revolt 5, 45, 70, 79, 90, 91, 93, 94, 95, 96, 97, 99, 101, 102, 103, 168, 174, 184, 195, 196

Benicia, California 71
Benton, Thomas H. 78, 79, 86, 88, 89, 141
Biddle, James 119, 121
Bidwell, John 54, 55, 94, 192, 195
Bigler, Henry 153, 154
Bliss, Robert L. 143
Boston 48, 49, 50, 51, 66, 74, 177, 178, 181, 197
Brewerton, George Douglas 81, 194
Bryant, Edwin 102, 108, 177, 192, 196, 197, 201
Bryant, Sturgis and Company 48
Buchanan, James 70, 72, 75, 183
Buenaventura River 80
Buffum, Edward Gould 130, 155, 156, 198, 199
Burnett, Peter H. 171, 188

Cabo San Lucas (Cape San Lucas) 12
Cabrillo, Juan Rodriguez 16
California banknotes 43
California Battalion (i.e., California Volunteer Militia; U.S. Mounted Rifles) 73, 105, 107, 108, 109, 115, 117, 119, 151, 160, 174, 185, 195, 196
California Constitutional Convention of 1849 71, 170, 188, 201
California Indians 25, 26, 27, 28, 30, 31, 32, 33, 41, 42, 46, 97, 181, 191, 192
California State Rangers 169, 201
California Trail 54
Las Californias 1, 16, 36, 190
Californios 1, 5, 21, 32, 33, 34, 37, 38, 39, 40, 42, 46, 47, 49, 51, 60, 62, 63, 75, 77, 79, 81, 83, 85, 90, 91, 92, 94, 96, 98, 99, 100, 106, 107, 113, 115, 132, 133, 134, 135, 141, 145, 146, 147,

211

Index

148, 149, 150, 157, 167, 170, 171, 172, 173, 174, 175, 176, 177, 180, 189, 191, 195, 198
Camp, Charles L. 79
Canada 67, 177
Canyon de Chelly 82
Carrillo, José Antonio 150
Carson, Kit 77, 79, 80, 81, 82, 83, 86, 87, 88, 103, 108, 139, 140, 141, 142, 145, 146, 148, 162, 183, 194, 195, 196, 198, 199
Castillero, Andrés 11, 12, 182, 189
Castro, José 60, 62, 63, 91, 92, 93, 100, 179
Castro, Manuel 83, 90
casualties in U.S.–Mexican War 5, 29, 44, 123, 126, 149, 187
Cermeño, Sebastián Rodrigo 17
César, Julio 31
Chatard, Frederick 126
Che-muc-tah 141
Coloma, California 55, 152, 153
Colorado 1, 2, 19, 77, 79, 82, 165, 172, 173, 176
Colton, Walter 4, 20, 21, 38, 39, 41, 82, 117, 189, 190, 192, 193, 195, 197, 199
Cook, Philip St. George 143
Craven, Tunis Augustus Macdonough 122, 123, 126, 127, 187, 197, 198
Cutts, James Madison 4, 189, 197, 198, 199, 200

Dana, Richard Henry, Jr. 50, 51, 52, 181, 192, 204
Dana Point, California 51
de la Peña y Peña, Manuel 13, 183
de la Torre, Joaquín 93
de Neve, Felipe 57
de Pedrorena, Miguel 33
de Portolá, Gaspar 18
de Ulloa, Francisco 16
DeVoto, Bernard 78, 89, 194, 195, 200, 204
Díaz, Porfirio 15
Downey, Joseph T. 136, 198
Drake, Sir Francis 17
Duflot de Mofras, Eugène 67
DuPont, Samuel F. 108, 115, 120

East India Squadron 111
Eisenhower, John S.D. 9, 189, 190, 200

Emerson, Ralph Waldo 86
Emory, William H. 149
Estanislao (Indian chief) 42, 43, 45

Felipe III, King of Spain 17
Filomena, Isadora 29
Flores, José María 132, 134, 149, 150, 180, 185, 186
Folsom, Joseph L. 155
Forrest, French 65
Fort Ross 45, 48, 192
Frémont, John Charles 73, 77, 78, 79, 80, 81, 82, 83, 84, 85, 86, 87, 88, 89, 90, 91, 92, 93, 96, 97, 98, 102, 103, 104, 105, 107, 108, 110, 115, 117, 132, 137, 140, 141, 149, 150, 151, 159, 160, 161, 162, 167, 174, 179, 180, 183, 184, 185, 188, 194, 195, 196, 199, 200

Garcia, Manuel (Three Fingered Jack) 168
Gavilán Peak (Fremont Peak) 83
Gillespie, Archibald 60, 64, 73, 74, 75, 76, 85, 89, 90, 91, 96, 97, 107, 108, 132, 133, 134, 135, 136, 137, 145, 146, 147, 148, 150, 160, 174, 183, 184, 193, 194, 198, 199
Gold Rush 20, 32, 41, 52, 56, 71, 79, 152, 153, 155, 157, 158, 168, 170, 188, 199
Grant, Ulysses S. 2
Guaymas, Mexico 12, 114, 117, 122, 123, 127, 185, 189
Guerra, Angustias de la 74, 99, 194, 196

Hall, Joseph B. 115
Halleck, Henry W. 124, 164, 197
Hammond, Thomas C. 146
Harlow, Neal 3, 105, 190, 191, 193, 195, 196, 197, 198, 199, 200, 201
Hastings, Lansford 55
Hastings Cutoff 55
Heywood, Charles 125, 126, 127, 128
hide and tallow trade 48
Hittell, Theodore Henry 73
Hock Farm 54
Honig, Sasha 61, 193
Horse Marines 4, 136, 196, 197, 198

Ide, William B. 70, 95, 184

212

Index

Jicarilla Apaches 82
Johnson, Abraham R. 140, 146, 147
Jones, Thomas ap Catesby 65, 67, 68, 69, 70, 157, 182

Kearny, Stephen W. 23, 79, 112, 117, 118, 119, 139, 140, 141, 142, 145, 146, 148, 149, 150, 151, 159, 160, 161, 167, 184, 185, 186, 198, 200
Klamath Indians 87, 195
Klamath Lake and Upper Klamath Lake 84, 85, 86, 195
Knox, Dudley W. 15, 112, 197, 198
Kroeber, Alfred L. 25, 190

La Paz, Baja California 12, 111, 117, 118, 119, 120, 121, 122, 123, 125, 126, 128, 129, 130, 131, 132, 164, 186, 187
Larkin, Thomas O. 34, 38, 63, 69, 70, 71, 72, 74, 75, 82, 83, 85, 89, 96, 133, 182, 183, 191, 193, 194, 195, 201
La Vallette, Elie A.F. 123
Ledyard, John 47, 48
Leese, Rosalía 95, 96
Leidesdorff, William 70
Lewis, Montgomery 124, 125, 191, 193, 194
López de Santa Anna, Antonio 13, 15
Loreto, Baja California 117, 122, 129, 187
Lummis, Charles Fletcher 35

Manifest Destiny 2, 78, 86, 92, 163, 189
Maria de Echeandia, José 35
Marine Guards 65, 74
Marrón, Juan María 33
Marshall, James W. 55, 56, 97, 153, 154, 156, 187
Mason, Richard Barnes 130, 156, 160, 164, 167
Mazatlán, Mexico 12, 68, 113, 114, 115, 116, 120, 122, 125, 126, 163, 183, 185, 187
McKinstry, George 53
Melville, Herman 65, 66, 193
Merritt, Ezekiel 93
Mervine, William 76, 85, 99, 101, 135, 136
Miranda, Francisco Palacios 119, 125
Mission Indians 32, 57

missionaries 18, 25, 29, 32, 34, 35, 36, 182
missions 11, 18, 25, 31, 32, 34, 35, 36, 39, 41, 42, 53, 57, 95, 124, 177, 181, 191, 194
Missroon, John 119
Miwok Indians 17
Monroe, James 19
Monterey 4, 17, 18, 19, 20, 21, 30, 34, 35, 38, 39, 41, 42, 44, 48, 51, 57, 58, 62, 63, 64, 65, 68, 69, 70, 71, 74, 75, 81, 83, 85, 93, 96, 99, 100, 101, 102, 103, 104, 105, 107, 114, 115, 117, 118, 131, 137, 155, 156, 158, 160, 170, 182, 183, 184, 185, 186, 188, 192, 193, 200
Montgomery, John B. 85, 90, 101, 114, 120, 160, 192
Mormon Battalion 119, 139, 141, 142, 143, 144, 151, 153, 154, 174, 185, 198
Mulegé, Baja California 122, 123, 187
Murrieta, Joaquin 168, 169, 201

Naglee, Henry M. 128, 129, 130
Nevin, David 10, 97, 189, 191, 192, 193, 194, 195, 196, 197, 198, 199, 201
New Mexico 2, 4, 10, 19, 23, 79, 80, 81, 82, 139, 140, 164, 176, 189, 194, 197, 198, 199
New York Volunteers 118, 119, 120, 121, 128, 130, 155, 186, 187
Nietos, Manuel 36, 181
Nordhoff, Walter 18
Nueces River 22
Nueva Helvetia (New Switzerland) 53

Ordóñez de Montalvo, Garcia Rodriguez 16
Oregon-California Trail 54
Osio, Antonio María 42, 43, 192, 195

Pacific Squadron 3, 6, 23, 65, 67, 69, 76, 104, 105, 111, 112, 113, 114, 115, 118, 119, 125, 139, 151, 157, 163, 181, 183, 184, 185, 187
Palomáres, José P. 147
Paredes, Mariano 13
Pico, Andrés 145, 146, 147, 150, 151
Pico, Antonio María 172, 173
Pico, Pío 5, 14, 32, 60, 62, 63, 92, 175, 179, 180, 181, 184, 190, 193
Pico Act of 1859 172, 173, 188

213

Index

Pineda, Manuel 123, 124, 125, 126, 128, 129
Poinsett, Joel R. 19
Polk, James K. 14, 15, 22, 23, 70, 73, 74, 75, 130, 140, 142, 156, 156, 159, 160, 161, 164, 167, 183, 184, 188, 190
presidio (frontier military garrison) 19, 43, 44, 45, 52, 57, 58, 59, 61, 193
pueblo (town or small city) 60, 63, 82, 114

Radford, William 116
Rancho Los Nietos 36
Rancho Pescadero 172
Rancho Petaluma 45
Rancho San Bernardino 141
Ridge, John Rollin ("Yellow Bird") 169
Riley, Bennet 158, 167, 170, 171, 172, 188, 200
Rio Grande River 22, 143, 176
Robinson, Alfred 48, 49, 50, 183, 192
Roosevelt, Franklin Delano 15, 190
Royce, Josiah 54
Ruiz de Burton, Maria del Amparo 129, 191, 198, 201
Russian-American Company 48, 181
Ryan, William R. 128, 129, 198

Sacramento 52, 53, 55, 76, 97, 105, 120, 160, 169, 180, 182
Sacramento River 25, 34, 52, 53, 72
Sacramento Valley 25, 34, 36, 47, 53, 54
San Blas, Mexico 12, 18, 71, 115, 116, 122, 126, 185, 187
San Francisco (Yerba Buena) 17, 43, 44, 45, 49, 50, 51, 52, 57, 58, 62, 70, 71, 72, 75, 76, 94, 102, 108, 114, 117, 120, 155, 157, 169, 177, 180, 183, 184, 186, 197
San Francisco Bay 18, 32, 45, 47, 54, 58, 64, 85, 90, 92, 97, 101, 116, 134, 135, 143, 158, 184, 196
San Jacinto, battle of 15, 32
San Joaquin Valley 64
San José del Cabo, Baja California 119, 120, 124, 125, 126, 127, 128, 130, 131, 186, 187
San Pascual (Pasqual), battle of 5, 145, 146, 147, 148, 174, 186, 198
sea otter trade 27, 48, 181, 192
Selfridge, Thomas 122, 123

Las Sergas de Esplandián 16
Serra, Junipero 18
Shamans 30, 31
Shannon, Wilson 13
Sherman, William T. 40, 81, 130, 155, 191, 195
Shubrick, William Branford 118, 121, 122, 124, 125, 126, 128, 160, 163, 164, 187
Silva, Mariano 100, 101
slavery 2, 165, 167, 170, 172
Sloat, John Drake 100, 101, 103, 107, 108, 113, 114, 115, 167, 183
Smith, Justin Harvey 39, 47, 189, 190, 191, 192
Smith, Percifor 157, 167
Solano, Francisco (Suisun Chief) 29, 30, 45
soldiers 5, 18, 19, 23, 29, 42, 43, 44, 53, 58, 59, 60, 61, 82, 97, 112, 119, 125, 129, 132, 137, 145, 158, 175, 185, 186
Sonoma, California 30, 45, 46, 90, 93, 94, 95, 96, 100
Stearns, Abel 2
Stockton, Robert Field 105, 106, 107, 108, 110, 111, 115, 116, 118, 132, 134, 135, 136, 142, 149, 150, 159, 160, 161, 167, 180, 185, 186, 197
Sutter, Johann Augustus 52, 53, 54, 55, 56, 97, 107, 153, 154, 155, 182, 192, 193
Sutter's Fort 77, 85, 86, 90, 92, 94, 99, 102, 120, 183, 184, 187

Talbot, Theodore 132, 137
Taylor, Bayard 171
Taylor, Zachary 22, 23
Texas 2, 10, 11, 13, 15, 19, 20, 22, 23, 49, 68, 105, 176, 182, 183, 189
Thornton, Seth 22
Thornton Affair 22, 183
Tichenor, L.S. 54
Todd, William L. 44
Todos Santos, Baja California 118, 124, 128
Treaties of Velasco 22
Treaty of Cahuenga 76, 118, 149, 150, 151, 174, 186, 199
Treaty of Guadalupe Hidalgo 24, 130, 151, 152, 163, 164, 165, 166, 172, 174, 178, 188, 200

214

Index

Treaty of Paris 1763 67
tribelet 26, 27, 29
Trist, Nicholas 166
Tuchman, Barbara 12
Twain, Mark 152, 199
Tyler, John 13, 70

U.S. Congress 13, 14, 22, 62, 80, 156, 157, 164, 170, 172, 173, 183, 188
U.S. Marines 4, 5, 23, 65, 68, 101, 111, 112, 113, 114, 117, 119, 123, 124, 125, 126, 127, 130, 132, 135, 136, 158, 175, 184, 185, 186, 187, 190, 193, 196, 197, 198
U.S. Navy 3, 4, 6, 20, 60, 64, 65, 67, 74, 78, 90, 93, 96, 99, 105, 109, 111, 112, 113, 117, 118, 119, 122, 123, 124, 126, 131, 132, 139, 157, 184, 185, 187, 188, 190, 193, 194, 197

Valdez, Dorotea 30, 62, 193
Vallejo, Mariano Guadalupe 26, 29, 40, 41, 42, 44, 45, 46, 62, 70, 92, 93, 94, 96, 154, 192
Vallejo, Salvador 26
Valparaiso, Chile 67
vaqueros (cowboys) 37, 38, 146, 191, 198
Veracruz, Mexico 23, 100, 139, 165
Vizcaíno, Sebastián 17, 57

Walpole, Frederick 103
Wise, Henry Augustus 106, 197

Yaqui Indians 126, 127, 129

Zorro 170

www.ingramcontent.com/pod-product-compliance
Ingram Content Group UK Ltd.
Pitfield, Milton Keynes, MK11 3LW, UK
UKHW041957140426
5217IPUK00015B/847